DISCOVERING
COMMON
MISSION

LUTHERANS AND EPISCOPALIANS
TOGETHER

edited by

ROBERT BOAK SLOCUM
and DON S. ARMENTROUT

 CHURCH

Church Publishing Incorporated, New York

Library of Congress Cataloging-in-Publication Data

Discovering common mission : Lutherans and Episcopalians together / edited
by Robert Boak Slocum and Don S. Armentrout.
      p. cm.
      Includes bibliographical references (p.) and index.
        ISBN 13: 978-0-89869-393-5 (pbk.)
        1. Evangelical Lutheran Church in America—Relations—Episcopal
      Church—History. 2. Episcopal Church—Relations—Evangelical
      Lutheran Church in America—History. 3. Anglican Communion—
      Relations—Lutheran Church—History. 4. Lutheran
      Church—Relations—Anglican Communion—History. 5. Christian
      union—United States—History. Church—Unity. 6. Episcopacy and
      Christian union. I. Slocum, Robert Boak, 1952- II. Armentrout, Donald S.

BX5928.5.E95 D57 2003   280'.042—dc21

2003048975

Church Publishing Incorporated
445 Fifth Avenue
New York NY 10016

www.churchpublishing.org

5 4 3 2 1

CONTENTS

PREFACE

After years of discussions and some resistance, the Evangelical Lutheran Church in America and the Episcopal Church have begun a relationship of full communion, based on the document "Called to Common Mission." This opens possibilities in terms of mutual support, cooperation in the work of mission, and interchangeability in deploying clergy. At a deeper level of who we are, what we know, and how we live in faith, we have much to learn from each other and much to offer. This ecumenical relationship is a step in response to Jesus' prayer that we may all "be one." In itself, this ongoing relationship represents a significant moment in the history of American Christianity as our churches representing the reformed and catholic traditions enter into full communion. But, as the saying goes, "the devil's in the details." It is our hope that the grace is to be found in the details as well. This book contains a variety of essays and other documents that address in detail the hopes, the steps of progress, and the frustrations of discovering common mission. We believe that it is necessary to face squarely both the possibilities and challenges for this relationship of our churches to thrive. It is our prayer that the common mission of Lutherans and Episcopalians will go forward, and that the materials collected here will prove helpful.

Robert Boak Slocum   Don S. Armentrout

DEDICATION AND ACKNOWLEDGMENTS

We dedicate this book to all participants in the ecumenical dialogues and conversations that have culminated in the full communion of the Evangelical Lutheran Church in America and the Episcopal Church, as based in the document "Called to Common Mission."

We wish to thank Ms. Shawn Horton, Administrative/ Faculty Secretary of the School of Theology, the University of the South, Sewanee, Tennessee, and Mrs. Samantha Johnson, Secretary of the Church of the Holy Communion, Lake Geneva, Wisconsin, for their patient and careful assistance in the preparation of this book. We also wish to thank Frank Tedeschi and the editorial staff of Church Publishing Incorporated for their encouragement and technical assistance for the completion of this project.

Robert Boak Slocum   Don S. Armentrout

1

THE ECCLESIOLOGY OF *CALLED TO COMMON MISSION**

J. ROBERT WRIGHT

This essay seeks to offer an ecclesiological analysis and evaluation, from an Anglican viewpoint, of the agreement establishing "full communion" between the Evangelical Lutheran Church in America (ELCA) and the Episcopal (Anglican) Church in the U.S.A. (ECUSA), for which I was a principal drafter from the Episcopalian side. Full communion was to begin if and when the same text was passed by both churches, and that happened on July 8, 2000, by decisive vote of the Episcopal Church at its General Convention meeting in Denver, Colorado, following an earlier and positive vote by the Churchwide Assembly of the ELCA. Liturgically, the agreement was first celebrated jointly by both churches with their presiding bishops in what many would understand to be a concelebration of the Eucharist at Washington National Cathedral on January 6, 2001.

---

* Earlier versions of some portions of this essay previously appeared in *International Kirchliche Zeitschrift* (July-September 2001) and in *The Anglican* 30:4 (October, 2001).

Ecclesiologically, this agreement establishes a shared ministry in the historic episcopate for the sake of common mission in proclaiming and serving the gospel on the basis of the agreed document entitled "*Called to Common Mission: A Lutheran Proposal for Revision of the Concordat of Agreement*" (CCM).

In the words of Episcopalian Presiding Bishop Frank Griswold, "This agreement is a very significant sign to the ecumenical community that our two churches can live in communion with one another for the sake of a greater unity in the service of a common mission. Besides allowing an interchange of ordained ministers, this agreement gives us the confidence to go forward together in a sharing of our resources and traditions for the sake of a greater good in evangelism, witness, and service." In the words of the Lutheran Presiding Bishop at that time, H. George Anderson, the adoption of this agreement by both churches "shows the world a new way to be one in Christ. Helping the world to believe must always be our priority as we work out our new life together. Our faithful witness to the Gospel will be strengthened as we 'recognize in each other the essentials of the one catholic and apostolic faith' (CCM para. 4)."

The acceptance of *Called to Common Mission* represents for the Episcopal Church at least two firsts in church history. It is the first time in the history of the Episcopal Church that any major ecumenical proposal with another church in this country—in this case coming from over thirty years of official and unofficial dialogue and piles of papers and seemingly endless debates and discussions—has actually gotten so far as to be affirmed and ratified by our General Convention. This itself is virtually unprecedented. And CCM also represents, secondly, the first time that two churches have reached across to each other from two sides of the Reformation divide, one church that has retained the historic episcopate and another church that did not but is open to it, now agreeing on the basis of their official documents and positions, and ready to walk side by side in full communion with each other. Sacramentally, the entry of the ELCA into the historic episcopate took place with the installation of the new ELCA Presiding Bishop Mark Hanson in Rockefeller Chapel at the University of Chicago on October 6, 2001. Such events are now becoming part of a worldwide pattern within Anglicanism and Lutheranism in many countries, commended and reinforced by dialogues and similar agreements in many places. The ultimate purpose of full communion, which does not itself constitute a merger, is the visible unity in mission which Christ wills for all his people.

Ecclesiologically, the CCM document builds upon the interim eucharistic sharing that the two churches had already reached and officially voted in 1982, which was further strengthened in the 1988 dialogue volume *Implications of the Gospel*. Following the two churches' agreement on the gospel itself, the original full-communion document, "Concordat of Agreement," received the nearly unanimous vote of the Episcopal Church's General Convention in 1997 but was narrowly defeated by the ELCA later the same summer. After the defeat of the Concordat of Agreement, the ELCA resolved to try again, producing its own proposal, but in consultation with Episcopalian representatives, and the final result is the document *Called to Common Mission* that has passed the ELCA by nearly seventy percent and the Episcopal Church by a very substantial majority of perhaps ninety percent or better. It was from the side of the ELCA that the suggestion came to rename the Concordat of Agreement as *Called to Common Mission*, thus challenging the Episcopal Church to share in mission.

Let us turn now to a brief examination of the contents of this agreement. It is not a "merger" but rather a relationship of "full communion," which is defined as "a relation between distinct churches in which each recognizes the other as a catholic and apostolic church holding the essentials of the Christian faith." As the text agrees, "Full communion includes the establishment locally and nationally of recognized organs of regular consultation and communication.... Diversity is preserved, but this diversity is not static. Neither church seeks to remake the other in its own image, but each is open to the gifts of the other as it seeks to be faithful to Christ and his mission. They are together committed to a visible unity in the church's mission to proclaim the Word and administer the Sacraments."

From this beginning, the text then describes our agreement in the doctrine of the faith, which is based upon the foundation documents of the two churches, including first the Bible, then the Book of Common Prayer (BCP) and the Augsburg Confession, as well as, at a lesser level, the agreements that have come out of the various official dialogues. The document includes an agreement on ministry, that of all the baptized and also that of the ordained, the latter being the classical area where Anglicans and Lutherans have had their differences. "We agree that the one ordained ministry will be shared between the two churches in a common pattern for the sake of common mission," the document affirms. By contrast, the Porvoo Agreement between the British and Irish Anglican Churches and the Nordic and Baltic Lutheran Churches establishes a "closer" degree of communion, but does not use the term "full communion," and the Meissen Agreement between the Church of England and the Evangelical Churches in Germany does not resolve the remaining difference over episcopal succession.

In CCM, there is less verbal description about the common mission to which the two churches believe they are now called, primarily because such mission is an open field and the document's major purpose was to clear off the remaining differences over ordained ministry that were restraining mission from happening in common. Having agreed earlier about the gospel and its implications, which was a major Lutheran concern, and the Episcopal Church by the text of the CCM now recognizing in the Augsburg Confession the essentials of the one catholic and apostolic faith (which was also a Lutheran condition or demand), and by the agreement in CCM on the essentials of ordained ministry (a major Episcopalian concern), the two churches now see the way clear for a sharing and enhancement that can lead to the continuation and extension of Christ's mission in the world. Ecclesiologically, the overall pattern for planning that is now intended can be described as interaction of Lutheran and Episcopal structures of leadership at all levels, there being no longer any theological excuse not to do this planning together for the sake of the common goal. Interaction, of course, is not the same thing as integration, because the two churches retain their own existences.

This shared leadership and interaction may include, for example, sacramental sharing and common celebration of the Eucharist, participation of bishops in the laying-on-of-hands at the ordination/installation of new bishops, interchangeability of clergy upon invitation, regular representation of the other church at each church's diocesan conventions or synodical assemblies, the symbolic presence and actual participation of bishops and others from time to time at major events in the life of the other church, representation of the other church in each church's structures of mission, sharing of resources and programs and staff, periodic joint meetings of the Episcopal House of Bishops and the Lutheran Conference of Bishops as well as of other churchwide officers, regular consultations on the basis of common issues or overlapping regions, elimination of duplicated facilities, closer sharing of ecumenical dialogues, intentional prayer for each other at all levels, common planning for evangelization, clustering in sparsely populated areas, increased sharing of education at all levels (seminaries, retreats, instructional materials, parish programs), sharing of chaplaincies in military, medical and prison ministries, common facing of ethical and social issues, and joint approaches to multi-cultural and multi-ethnic situations in urban areas. Of course most of these things have been done before, but now in full communion there is a practical impulse as well as an ecclesiological incentive for them to happen. All this is more easily possible now that both churches have formally stated that they agree on the essentials of the Christian faith. The document also provides for a joint commission to monitor all this and to assist in its implementation, and that commission has already been established.

These provisions, in turn, are energized by the agreement on ministry, because the two churches have now reached a level of trust and confidence sufficient to make their ordained pastors and priests interchangeable in full communion. Within this future pattern, three particular ministries are named. The first is the historic episcopate, which is obviously a traditional Anglican concern although it is understandably a less urgent matter to the Lutherans, who in America have not previously known it or, in some cases, have even feared it in its British and Roman and Swedish Lutheran manifestations. Nonetheless, in their willingness to accept it, the Lutherans here agree to enter and receive this catholic credential of the ministry of bishops already held by three-quarters of the world's Christians, including millions of Lutherans in other parts of the world, and which Anglicans affirm in the fourth point of the Chicago-Lambeth Quadrilateral (the text of which is now included within the Episcopal Church's 1979 Book of Common Prayer, 878). It is described in the CCM as "an evangelical, historic succession," the word "evangelical" being added at Lutheran insistence. The use of "evangelical" in this way is an assurance that the historic episcopal succession, like everything in the church, stands under the word of God and must always serve the gospel. The Anglican claim has long been, as Archbishop Michael Ramsey remarked many years ago in his book *The Gospel and the Catholic Church*, that the historic episcopate is, and must be, founded upon the gospel itself. It was the complaint of so many at the time of the Reformation that their bishops were *not* serving the gospel that led the reformers to lay aside the episcopacy back then. Bishops, as the Augsburg Confession insists, must be "evangelical" in the sense that they must always serve the gospel and teach its doctrine. Could any Anglican disagree?

Let the following caution about episcopacy be added at this point. The intricate details of episcopacy in the practice of the churches that have it are hard enough for Episcopalians (i.e., American Anglicans) to understand, let alone for Lutherans who have no first-hand experience of it! The background can begin with the fact that already in the nineteenth century Anglicans were seeing the "historic episcopate" not only as a link with the church of the early ages but also as one of the apostolic signs of a spiritual and universal Christian church surpassing boundaries of particular peoples and nations and denominations. The term "historic episcopate" was popularized by William Reed Huntington in late-nineteenth-century America in his book *The Church-Idea*, and then as the fourth point of the Chicago-Lambeth Quadrilateral of 1886-88 (in addition to scriptures, creeds, and sacraments, all four being points upon which it insists that the future unity of the church must be based); and the term and concept of "historic episcopate" has gained widening ecumenical acceptance ever since then. Present-day developments in the world, sometimes described as "globalization," suggest that his insight was prophetic, and that the connectedness of bishops in all places and all ages is a powerful contemporary witness that the church proclaims the gospel unto all peoples to the end of time.

In Lutheran terms, on the other hand, the historic episcopate can be seen, and by many Lutherans *is* seen, as an effective means for implementing Article 7 of the Augsburg Confession (1530) with other churches on a basis that extends beyond those Lutherans who subscribe to it. Once there is an agreement on gospel and sacraments between a Lutheran church and a non-Lutheran one, as Article 7 of the Augsburg Confession hopes for, the time-honored means of linking them is the historic episcopate. This view is predicated upon an understanding, now quite common among Lutherans in America although not yet embraced by a minority of them, that classical and confessional Lutheranism, rather than considering itself a new church representing the earliest type and form of protestantism, actually claims to be a reform movement within the church catholic for the sake of the gospel, and that its Augsburg Confession should be considered a proposal for such reform. This seems to be the dominant and prevailing, but not the only, ecclesiology among American Lutherans today.

It is thus against this background that the CCM sees the historic episcopate as a succession of bishops and their teaching that traces back to the ancient church, pointing to the centrality of Christ and the doctrine of the apostles, at the same time that such bishops also serve as leaders of the church into the future, overseeing the mission of the

church today and responsible for their successors in ministerial office. While the historic episcopate is defined thus in
CCM, the concept of apostolic succession is broadened in
CCM (on the basis of recent theological studies and agreements among many churches, as well as the understandings
that preceded in the Niagara Report) to include not only the
historic episcopate but also "the churches' use of the apostolic scriptures, the confession of the ancient creeds, and
the celebration of the sacraments instituted by our Lord."
That is, apostolicity is understood, ecclesiologically, as
comprising all four points of the Quadrilateral and not just
episcopacy alone. The ministry of *episkope*, therefore, is
agreed in CCM to be "one of the ways, in the context of
ordained ministries and of the whole people of God, in
which the apostolic succession of the church is visibly
expressed and personally symbolized in fidelity to the
gospel through the ages." The terms "ordination" and
"installation," as legitimate translations of the same original
Greek, are used interchangeably in the CCM document for
the rite by which one becomes a bishop by prayer for the
gift of the Holy Spirit accompanied by the laying-on of
hands of other bishops, and the Episcopal Church agrees to
understand all future Lutheran bishops so "installed" in the
historic episcopate as having been "ordained" to that ministry.

There are various ways specified in the CCM that a person's tenure of the office of bishop may terminate, as is true
in the Episcopal Church; and a bishop's lifelong tenure of
the order of bishop is neither specified nor denied, as is also
the case with the Episcopal Church. The concept of indelibility of holy order is implied, from an Anglican viewpoint,
in the provision of sacramental intentionality, as the ELCA
in the CCM "agrees that all its bishops chosen after both
churches pass this Concordat will be installed for pastoral
service of the gospel with this church's intention to enter

the ministry of the historic episcopate." Anglicans would understand such an intention of a church to enter the ministry of the historic episcopate, thus, as an acceptance in principle of the sacramental understanding that goes with it and is generally held by the churches that already stand within it; and it is on this same basis that the Episcopal Church understands and generally assumes the concept of "indelibility," a term that it also does not use in its official documents. But neither does CCM say that diocesan bishops in the Episcopal Church, or synodical bishops in the ELCA, cease to be "bishops" upon their retirement or removal from office. Episcopalians, especially bishops in the Episcopal Church, did not press this point in the discussions, or demand that some explicit written statement of lifelong indelibility be inserted into the CCM text, probably because the Episcopal Church has no official document that defines such lifelong status. Lutherans, on the other hand, seemed also content with the document's silence on this point, simply because the vast majority of them would say, for what they think are "evangelical" reasons, that they do cease to be "bishops" upon the end of their term of office, although an Episcopalian might hope that reflecting over the course of time they might eventually decide that they do not want to remain the one church in the historic episcopate that stands in left field on this question. On the side of "lifelong" interpretation, though, it can be added that the CCM text (para. 18) does agree that any "subsequent" installation of a bishop chosen after full communion has begun, such as a synodical bishop who is later elected to serve in another synod, will *not* include an additional laying-on-of-hands.

The detailed provisions as to how all this will happen over time are also spelled out, including acceptance of canon 4 of the First Ecumenical Council (Nicaea I, AD 325) so that at each ordination/installation of a new bishop "at least three bishops already sharing in the sign of the episcopal succession will be invited to participate." At least one of the bishops participating in the laying-on-of-hands at each such event will be from the other church, in order to give visible expression to the full communion that is shared. These provisions were carefully observed at the installation of the new Lutheran presiding bishop Mark Hanson. In all these ways, therefore, the concerns of the fourth point of the Quadrilateral are met. It is also noteworthy that in CCM the Episcopal Church has agreed, at Lutheran insistence, that structures for review of the ministry of bishops will be established for the sake of "evaluation, adaptation, improvement, and continual reform in the service of the gospel."

Although the Quadrilateral does not speak of three distinct orders, the Episcopal Church, in keeping with catholic Christianity of which it is a part, maintains all three, as the Preface to its Ordinal makes clear (BCP, 510). Thus it has been accustomed to see priesthood and diaconate as comprised within the historic episcopate, and so the CCM also includes agreements on the latter two ordained ministries as well. On the basis of the voted intention of the ELCA to enter the historic episcopate, in effect a pledge of the episcopal ministry that both churches will share for the future, the Episcopal Church in CCM has voted to acknowledge the full authenticity of those already ordained as pastors within the ELCA. This point is a major aspect of the ecclesiology in the theological writings of the Roman Catholic Raymond E. Brown and the Eastern Orthodox John D. Zizioulas.

Let me offer a bit more detail of the way in which the writings of Brown and Zizioulas did influence at least the Episcopalian membership of the drafting committee. In his book *Priest and Bishop: Biblical Reflections*, Raymond

Brown raised the question of whether the Roman Catholic Church, if it eventually comes to agreement with another church on every essential point of the Christian faith except the historic episcopate, would require the re-ordination of every pastor of that other church in a retrospective linear succession stretching back into past history, and he concluded in the negative: that what would be more important is what the churches agree will happen for the future. And from the writings of Zizioulas, let me paraphrase briefly his argument in Chapter 5 of *Being as Communion*: On the question of episcopal succession (not doctrinal succession), in the biblical and early patristic sources that survive we can distinguish two basic approaches to the notion of the church's continuity with the apostles. On the one hand, the apostles are conceived as persons entrusted with a mission to fulfill. They are sent in a process of linear movement, from God to Christ to the apostles and their successors. We may call this approach "historical." But on the other hand, the apostles are also conceived as persons with an eschatological function, not so much as those who follow Christ but as those who surround him at the end of time. This is an image that confronts history already now with a presence and vision from beyond history, a proleptic approach that presupposes the end that was really there from the beginning and is realized already now in the celebration of the eucharist and the proclamation of the gospel.

The former approach, the historical one, is most clearly expressed in patristic writing in the First Epistle of Clement (God sends Christ, Christ sends the apostles), whereas the latter approach, the eschatological one, is found primarily in another source of this same early period, the letters of St. Ignatius of Antioch, especially those to the Magnesians and Trallians. In these letters of Ignatius we find the apostles united as a college and surrounding Christ in his kingdom, in a continuity expressed finally not by linear succession but by the church's vision of the kingdom at the end of time as it gathers to partake of the eternal life of God offered to the world at the eucharistic banquet-table.

And whereas the former approach (the historical) implies only a continuity of survival in linear time, a transmission of authority from past to present that creates a retrospective linear continuity but not an eschatological one, the latter approach (the eschatological) implies a vision of the future, an anticipation of the end that is already being realized in the here and now, a continuity that transforms the present into the future that is already seen and pledged even now. Thus we may say that the Holy Spirit, in this latter approach, is active in transforming a linear historicity into an eschatological presence, as it were, a living memory of the future that is based more upon promise than upon pedigree.

The CCM was therefore able to make its ecclesiological breakthrough by reasoning, at least on the Episcopalian side, from the work of Brown and Zizioulas that questions of episcopacy and validity of ordination can better be resolved if there is a solemn pledge for the future from both sides, rather than by conducting an historical investigation into the pedigrees of the past. If agreement for the future can be reached, condemnation of the past is unnecessary. The authenticity of past Lutheran ministries could therefore be acknowledged "up front" by American Anglicans, at the same time that both churches could agree about episcopacy and ordination for the future. Such dispensation from strict conformity to a canonical norm is historically within the authority of a properly constituted synod, such as the General Convention of the Episcopal Church, when it is agreed to be for the positive common good. In the Roman Catholic tradition the principle is known as *ecclesia supplet*, and in the Eastern Orthodox tradition the principle is known as *oikonomia*. Probably not all Lutherans would reach this same ecclesiological understanding of the CCM agreement, and only its text itself is authoritative, but I am presenting here the way that many Episcopalians will read it.

In CCM the foregoing dispensation, for the sake of interchangeability of Lutheran pastors with Episcopal priests until such time as all Lutheran clergy are ordained by bishops in the historic succession, is accomplished by the momentous act of temporarily suspending (only in the case of pastors previously ordained in the ELCA or its predecessor bodies) the seventeenth-century restriction in the Preface to the Ordination Rites that no person be allowed to function in the historic ministerial orders within this church unless he or she has received the laying-on-of-hands by bishops in the historic succession. This suspension in CCM is based on the enormous theological convergences discovered over the decades of dialogue and is adopted precisely in order to secure the future implementation of the Preface's intention, namely the preservation and sharing of the historic episcopate. The word "temporary" here does not mean that, after an unspecified period of time, the suspension would cease for those Lutheran clergy whose interchangeability had previously been accepted, after which point they themselves would now have to be ordained in the Episcopal Church because the CCM's "temporary" clause had expired. What the document does mean is that eventually its own temporary suspension will terminate once all future Lutheran clergy have been ordained by their own bishops standing in the apostolic succession of the historic episcopate. After that point, no more suspension will be necessary. Under the terms of the CCM, that point will eventually come, as the ELCA agrees that a bishop shall regularly preside and participate in the laying-on-of-hands at the ordination of all clergy, there being no "planned exceptions" acknowledged by the Episcopal Church. As we shall see below, the meaning of this provision has subsequently engendered controversy.

Present ELCA pastors who were not ordained in the ELCA or its predecessor bodies, and pastors not ordained by a bishop in historic succession who transfer into the ELCA from other traditions in the future, are not interchangeable after the beginning of January 2001, under the CCM's provisions. Nor does interchangeability recognize any lay celebration of the Eucharist whatsoever, which still happens occasionally within the ELCA in isolated situations. The language of suspension in CCM is understood to imply continued acceptance of the normative character of ordination in or by episcopal succession, and the suspension is for the unity and mission of the church and its common good. Separate resolutions of implementation have also been passed by both churches.

As regards the diaconate, in CCM "both churches acknowledge that the diaconate, including its place within the threefold ministerial office and its relationship with all other ministries, is in need of continuing exploration, renewal, and reform, which they pledge themselves to undertake in consultation with one another." Under the CCM, ordained deacons in the Episcopal Church are recognized by the ELCA as "fully authentic ministers in their respective order." Although the CCM does not require the ELCA to "ordain" any of its deacons, deaconesses, or diaconal ministers, it does provide for the sharing of some diaconal functions of such persons with ordained deacons in the Episcopal Church. In the ELCA, diaconal ministers and deaconesses are "consecrated" through prayer for the Holy Spirit and with the laying-on-of-hands, but they are officially not understood as being "ordained." Of course the

Episcopal Church would wish that this situation were slightly different, but it is also true that most of the Lutheran churches with whom the Anglican churches of Britain and Ireland have already signed the Porvoo Statement do not "ordain" deacons (the exception being Sweden); and the fourth point of the Chicago-Lambeth Quadrilateral does not expect agreement on an ordained diaconate for the sake of full communion.

If these are the agreements about ordained ministry that had to be settled in CCM and which make it in some ways a very technical document, we may also note that in it the Episcopal Church "acknowledges and seeks to receive the gifts of the Lutheran tradition, which has consistently emphasized the primacy of the Word." These gifts are of a quite different sort from the historic episcopate and the ordering of ministry, and they have to do with the consistent Lutheran concerns for the primacy of the gospel, the centrality of Jesus Christ in holy scripture, and a tradition of theological integrity that is quite distinct from generic Protestantism, as well as in their focuses upon preaching, evangelism, church growth, Christian education, mission both domestic and foreign, and lay ministry. In all these ways Anglicans have so much to learn from them!

Let me cite an example by way of personal testimony concerning my own renewed appreciation for the doctrine of justification by grace through faith that I gained over the course of some twenty years of dialogues and meetings with the Lutherans. Previously, as a typical American Anglican/ Episcopalian, I had tended to think of justification by faith as some musty old formula that may have done good service back in the sixteenth century, a formula that we still retain in number 11 of our 39 Articles (BCP, 870) but which has long since ceased to be of much vital or practical importance. But eventually I came to conclude that I was wrong.

I came to conclude that justification, that principle or criterion that most characterizes the Lutheran theological insight and about which the Lutherans have recently reached an agreement with the Roman Catholic Church, has a contemporary significance or relevance much needing to be heard in our day. At least in America in the Episcopal Church, many of us are tempted to think that we are justified not so much by faith as by material success, or by political correctness, or by charismatic experience, or by pious acts, or by good deeds of a humanitarian nature. All these ways and still others are competing in the public square against the basic truth of the gospel, that it is by faith alone, by grace through faith, that we are set right with God. All these competitors are cheap and inadequate substitutes; but the Lutherans have continued to stand for the real thing, and now they offer it to us in full communion. This is one of the many insights or gifts that Lutherans bring to us (although, as I shall suggest at the end of this essay, many Anglicans would fear that an over-emphasis upon it can diminish the importance of ecclesiology).

CCM is also an ecclesiological statement with the potential of enormous ecumenical ramifications. It says to Protestant churches that they need not fear the historic episcopate and the true catholic tradition as something hostile to women or as an abstract concept devised to condemn their past histories, and at the same time it is a call to the Orthodox and Roman churches to look to future possibilities with their own scholars like Brown and Zizioulas, as well as to grant equal status to women and to open the historic ordained ministry to the other half of the human race. CCM is in this as in so many ways a sign of hope and reconciliation to a world that cries out for the churches to show the way in unity.

Thus the ecclesiology of CCM remains intact, and subsequent unilateral developments in one church, unless agreed by the other, cannot change the written agreement even though they may dampen its spirit. All this was, indeed, the promise of CCM until the ELCA decided to alter its ecclesiology unilaterally. On Saturday, August 11, 2001, it was reported in *The New York Times* and elsewhere, in a story written by the Associated Press, that the Lutheran Churchwide Assembly in Indianapolis was debating "whether to rewrite a unity pact with the Episcopal Church that only went into effect in January." Lutheran "denominational leaders," the story continued, were "proposing a constitutional change to let pastors rather than bishops ordain new clergy 'in unusual circumstances' to meet conscientious objections of clergy candidates." Presiding Bishop Frank Griswold, the story went on, had "warned Lutheran leaders in March that the proposed change...could be seen as 'a unilateral alteration of the mutual commitment that both our churches have solemnly made.'" Then the words of Lutheran Presiding Bishop H. George Anderson at the Assembly itself were quoted, to the effect that he was "not comfortable about making unilateral changes, especially when Episcopal leaders have expressed dismay." But, the story continued, "he said the change was necessary for unity within his denomination."

This is what the world was told was about to happen, and the next day it did. Once again with accuracy, *The New York Times* in a story written by the Associated Press reported that the Lutheran Assembly had "approved a rewrite of an ecumenical pact with the Episcopal Church that went into effect in January. It would allow clergy on grounds of conscience to be ordained by pastors rather than bishops." And Presiding Bishop Griswold was also quoted again, in the same story, as responding that the Lutherans' decision "appears to be a unilateral alteration of the mutual commitment that both of our churches have solemnly made."

Other details, public for all to see, were soon to emerge. According to Episcopal News Service, the new Lutheran bylaw allows that "for pastoral reasons in unusual circumstances, a synodical bishop may provide for the ordination by another pastor of the ELCA of an approved candidate," but also says that "prior to authorization of such an ordination, the bishop of the synod of the candidate's first call shall consult with the presiding bishop as this church's chief ecumenical officer and seek the advice of the Synod Council." Presiding Bishop Anderson in his opening address at the Assembly strongly urged its adoption, pleading that this was necessary to preserve the unity of the ELCA and clearly wishing to leave his church "united" as he retired from its leadership. He explained afterwards that originally he "had great doubts about the bylaw," but in the end he had changed his mind and come to believe that it would "serve as unity for our church." No Lutheran bishop or member of their Church Council spoke publicly against it. In spite of such massive pressure from above, however, nearly a third of the Lutheran Assembly resisted and the final vote in favor of the bylaw was only 683 to 330, the motion thus passing by a mere eight votes more than the 675 needed for the required majority.

Ecclesiologically, it was clear to most knowledgeable observers that this provision to allow non-episcopal ordination "in unusual circumstances" was the exact reversal of the decision of the previous Churchwide Assembly that there would be "no planned exceptions" to episcopal ordination. There the ELCA had voted its intention as a church "to enter the ministry of the historic episcopate" and voted its "provision that a bishop shall regularly preside and participate in the laying-on-of-hands at the ordination of all clergy" (CCM paras. 18, 20), the rationale for adding the word "regularly" to paragraph 20 of the original CCM text being that this word "does not imply the possibility of planned exceptions but allows for pastoral discretion in emergencies" (flood, snowstorm, or sudden death of the bishop were proposed as examples; see Minutes of the 1999 Churchwide Assembly, Section IV, page 10.4). This slogan phrase, "no planned exceptions," had in fact persuaded many hesitant Episcopalians to vote for the CCM.

But now in August of 2001 it was clear to many that the minority who had opposed the CCM had finally caused enough commotion and fear that they might secede if their demand for exceptions was not met, and the Lutheran leadership had decided that this group had to be placated in order to keep them. A motion to delay the whole matter until the next Churchwide Assembly of 2003 so that a truly bilateral amendment to the text of *Called to Common Mission* could be developed in conjunction with the Episcopal Church failed. Later a motion that bishops also could be installed outside the historic succession was overwhelmingly rejected, by vote of 786-194, although some predicted that it was the camel's nose already peering under the tent. One additional vote, which gave encouragement to some, was a resolution offered by the Chair of the Lutheran Conference of Bishops affirming that church's "abiding dedication to live fully" into its full communion relationship with the Episcopal Church. This passed by a vote of 870 to 105, although many were amazed that 105 voting members of the ELCA Churchwide Assembly (just over 10 percent) did not want their church to live fully into the bilateral commitments it had previously voted.

The ecclesiological reasons why the Episcopal Church, and the whole of worldwide catholic Christianity, oppose this bylaw are well known, and they are predicated not upon how frequently it is used but upon its very existence, the very reason why the Lutheran minority so avidly fought for it. The reasons in opposition to the bylaw had already been outlined earlier by Presiding Bishop Griswold in his public letter to Presiding Bishop Anderson dated March 20, 2001, which said, in part: "This proposal for the ELCA seems to create two classes of clergy, it ensures that the argument over CCM will continue, it allows for denial of that which was previously agreed, it threatens the role of bishop as focus of unity in service to Word and Sacrament, and it could jeopardize future hopes of the ELCA for closer relations and full communion with the majority of other churches that already perform ordinations in the historic catholic tradition and thus do not acknowledge ordinations by pastors." The last point was underscored by Bishop Christopher Epting, the Ecumenical Officer of the Episcopal Church, in his address to the Assembly: "It seems to us dangerous ecumenically to start changing the terms of full communion agreements once they have been voted and implementation begun. Ecumenical partners across the board begin wondering if these agreements are trustworthy or not!"

In the light of this unilateral action by the ELCA, therefore, some in the Episcopal Church are now calling for termination of the relationship, others are suggesting that the full communion is no longer full but only partial or impaired, and some in other churches are now questioning whether the ELCA is a reliable or credible ecumenical partner whose word can be trusted, while within the ELCA itself certain interest groups are now asserting that "unusual circumstances" can also be used to invalidate other rules and solemn decisions. Whatever peace and superficial unity the ELCA leadership may have achieved for the short term, certainly a wet blanket had been cast over its relations with others and a bucket of cold water poured on "common mission" just as it was getting started.

Yes, a dampening of enthusiasm, but was this unilateral action a sufficient cause for the Episcopal Church to suspend or terminate the entire agreement? Given the fact that the Episcopal Church itself does not have a perfect track record of abiding by its own decisions, given that the ecclesiology of the written agreement still stands, and given that the Episcopal Church had already immunized itself against such an attempt at unilateral alteration by its "Mind of the House" resolution (passed by its bishops on April 3, 2000, and later by its General Convention) which provided that no Lutheran pastor subsequently ordained not by a bishop would be eligible for interchangeability even if he or she sought it, the only question remaining was whether the bylaw's very existence now constitutes a defect of ecclesiology embraced by the ELCA at the very moment that it has moved to enter the historic episcopacy itself. To put the matter bluntly, would any catholic church in its right mind, claiming to stand in the historic episcopacy as the ELCA now does, proceed to declare that bishops are not necessary in all cases for the conferral of holy orders? To churches in the catholic tradition historical precedents are important, and one such precedent does actually come to mind, namely the various instances in the late Middle Ages when the Roman Catholic Church, by direct decree of the papacy, gave permissions for Holy Orders to be conferred by persons who were not bishops.[1]

Would the ELCA in virtue of its new bylaw now want itself to be associated with what most students today would label as one of the most extreme irregularities of the late medieval papacy? Are Lutheran bishops now being given powers by the ELCA Churchwide Assembly analogous to those claimed by certain late medieval popes on this point? Of course I am sure this was far from the intention of the minority who pressed their point and finally won on the bylaw question, but the parallel now exists in history and its implications will bear further exploration. After all, many who see the very existence of the Lutheran bylaw as a new defect in Lutheran ecclesiology may be less eager to condemn it outright when they realize that, however undesirable, it was a practice also followed at times by the late medieval papacy! (There does exist such uncritical admiration of the Roman Church within the ELCA, as I have discovered, just as among some Episcopalians). Episcopalians, likewise, may be less eager to condemn the bylaw if they can be persuaded that the Lutherans have adopted it for serious theological reasons and not just pragmatically, for fear of schism. I have come to have many friends within the Lutheran minority who opposed the CCM, but I am not sure that their resons were being endorsed by the majority who voted for the bylaw.

There are two sides to every question, and beyond the astounding parallel to some medieval popes not widely admired today, I do believe there are other factors that also merit reflection as the Episcopal Church considers whether to claim that it has been offended and to offer some major retaliation, or merely to dismiss this action as an insignificant defect embraced for political reasons and understandable within the context of the more Protestant ecclesiological context that excessive emphasis upon the teaching about justification has inevitably engendered. In addition to exploring the theological rationale for the Lutheran bylaw in light of the actions of some late medieval popes, I think there are other related facts that the two churches need to consider and evaluate bilaterally: 1) The Episcopal Church continues to seek full communion with the Roman Catholic Church in spite of the actions of the late medieval popes. In fact, this continues even in spite of the present pope's opposition to the ordination of women as well as the Roman Church's official opposition to married clergy, just as the

Roman Church continues to seek full communion with Anglicans in spite of their positions to the contrary. 2) The typical Anglican defense of episcopal ordination is that the bishop is the regulator or overseer of ordination within a diocese or synod, and the ELCA bylaw preserves that principle. 3) The fourth paragraph of the Chicago-Lambeth Quadrilateral, on ministry, names only the historic episcopate, which the Lutherans have now voted to reaffirm, and does not include a list of the things a bishop can or must do. 4) The CCM (para. 13) allows that the ELCA is free to explore its own particular interpretation of an episcopal succession that is both evangelical and historic, in consultation with its partner church, and this it is beginning to do. And 5) The CCM (para. 14) provides that for the Episcopal Church full communion will not be fully realized until the time when there is a shared ministry of all bishops in the historic episcopate. The ELCA Assembly by 89.2% did affirm its church's "abiding dedication to live fully" into its full communion relationship with us, and that time may still be some way in the future.

Clearly there has been some emotional impairment and hindrance to common mission in both churches as a result of the ELCA's action, but whether there will be any formally binding and longer-lasting impairment remains for time to tell. The debates of the Episcopal Church's 2003 General Convention in Minneapolis will certainly be some indication. I conclude with this question: If Lutherans and Episcopalians were starting their ecumenical dialogue afresh, would the existence of this tiny bylaw by itself be grounds not to proceed at all? Without endorsing what the ELCA has done, can we still hope to live in full communion and common mission with them and they with us? Should part of our living into full communion now be some sort of conference, of theologians and historians and others from both churches, to consider such questions, to probe and articulate the ecclesiology we now share?

NOTES

[1] A seminal discussion of this evidence, especially as it appears in fifteenth-century historical records of such popes as Boniface IX, Martin V, and Innocent VIII, was published in English by Lawrence N. Crumb, "Presbyteral Ordination of the See of Rome," in *Church Quarterly Review* 164 (January-March, 1963), 19-31. Crumb states, "The legalistic and administrative outlook of the late Middle Ages, combining for a while with an emphasis on the priesthood as the highest order, produced a polity which has been dubbed 'papal Presbyterianism.' Perhaps one of the best arguments for the sacramental view of the episcopate is found in the irregularities which the administrative emphasis not only made possible but actually approved" (29). For the continuation of this discussion even into modern times, and the Anglican opposition to it, see E. L. Mascall, *The Recovery of Unity: A Theological Approach* (London: Longmans, Green and Co., 1958), 210-13. Mascall finds that "Roman theologians are agreed that without a papal delegation a presbyter cannot confer major orders. In arguing for the validity of the ordinations in the cases just referred to they are not maintaining the essential validity of ordination by presbyters, but the power of the pope to overrule by his administrative authority the sacramental structure of the Church; they are arguing not for presbyterianism but for popery" (213). For an apparent Lutheran defense of the exercise of such authority by the papacy, in the context of twentieth-century Lutheran dialogue with the Roman Church, see Arthur Carl Piepkorn, "A Lutheran View of the Validity of Lutheran Orders," in *Lutherans and Catholics*

in Dialogue IV: Eucharist and Ministry, ed. Paul C. Empie and T. Austin Murphy (Washington, D.C.: United States Catholic Conference, 1970). The literature on this question, in English and other languages, is more extensive than one might think, but it is scattered in obscure places.

2

CALLED TO COMMON MISSION AND THE EPISCOPATE*

MARTIN E. MARTY

A *personal framework:* I have been asked to present a Lutheran view of the historic episcopate (henceforth: "episcopate"). I am fully aware that members of the Evangelical Lutheran Church in America were of two minds concerning the Concordat of Agreement at the Churchwide Assembly in 1997 and may be of several minds, not concerning the goal of communion with the Episcopal Church, but about that church's practice related to the episcopate and how that relates to the Evangelical Lutheran Church in America. Concentrating on the subject of bishops, episcopacy, and the episcopate necessarily distracts from other features in the revised Concordat of Agreement, especially the witness to the gospel and the drive for mission. In order to help put this in perspective I choose this personal introduction.

---

* This paper was presented to the Churchwide Assembly of The Evangelical Lutheran Church of America in August 1999.

A teacher once taught me about a certain kind of subject: "Take this very, very, very seriously—but not *too* seriously." So it should be, in my view, with the episcopate. You cannot realize "full communion" with the Episcopal Church without also receiving the episcopate. It is important to remind ourselves of that. During the months of our drafting "A Lutheran Proposal for a Revision of the Concordat of Agreement," we never found any Episcopal colleague on the drafting committee or in the church's leadership who could envision such communion being advanced without our dealing with the episcopate. Nor could they cite any Episcopalian who could. We further found no Episcopal participant in any ecumenical discussion, indeed no Episcopal theologian of this century, who pictured full communion without the episcopate.

We have to be clear: any Lutherans, however creative and imaginative or visionary they may be, who say that they propose and desire full communion with Episcopalians but without the episcopate are wasting time, breath, and ink. If they insist on rejecting our reception of the episcopate, they are in effect asking us to end all efforts at "Agreement" and to go our separate ways, probably permanently.

Given instead this opportunity to offer to the world and the world-church this new national sign of unity between, on one hand the most widespread and, on the other, the largest of the bodies defined during the sixteenth-century Reformation, we have undertaken acts of imagination and we have asked for the kind of vision and courage that God can provide, along with a new zest for our common mission.

Never in our discussions was the episcopate presented in a fierce, rigid, dogmatic *"Frisz Vogel, oder stirb!"* ["Eat, bird, or die!"] spirit. Instead it was presented as a self-defining element in the Anglican Communion and potential gift to churches that would enter communion with any of its national bodies. To ask the Episcopal Church to surrender the episcopate would be to ask it to break with the worldwide Anglican Communion and with four centuries of its common life. To ask this would also be equivalent to asking Lutherans to define their life together apart from insistence on common witness in faith, as this appears in the Concordat of Agreement.

For those reasons, we learned to take the episcopate "very, very, very seriously." But then we remind ourselves not to take it "*too* seriously." The movement of faith and hope within *Called to Common Mission* has to do with mission, with unity in the gospel, with response to Christ's commands, promise, and prayers concerning the manifesting of unity. The episcopate receives so much attention this year because it is (a) somewhat unfamiliar to most of us; (b) offensive if presented as something Lutherans would have to accept in their own body as being of the essence of Christ's Church; (c) the feature that evoked most comment in 1997; (d) the one element that has practical implications, is regarded as a novelty, and hence something that merits scrutiny.

I am also mindful that to some ELCA members what follows may look like paraphrases of an old song and a movie title: "Just a Spoonful of Sugar Helps the Episcopate Go Down" or "How I Stopped Worrying and Loved the Episcopate," as if it were a bitter medicine or a bomb. I am equally aware that another wing of ELCA congregants will read this and reach for other old songs to explain what is going on. Those who have long advocated our reception of the episcopate would sing "At Last" or hear me waking up and singing "I'm Beginning to See the Light." They think of life with the episcopate as having been abandoned for practical reasons in Reformation times. Most of us instead indicate that we are ready to be convinced on this subject, if such a move can advance Christian mission, can be a sign of response to the gift of unity, and will not contradict what Lutherans do regard as of the essence of the church ministry marked by "word and sacrament."

Now for the personal witness: before being called to this drafting task, I cannot remember ever having written or spoken a word favoring the episcopate for Lutherans. Like so many, I could always "take it or leave it," live with it or without it. I can recall having reported, four decades ago when covering the ecumenical circuit, how frustrated Lutheran ecumenical leaders were whenever this or that spokesperson for Anglicanism gave the impression that the episcopate was indeed not only of the *esse,* the very being of the church, but that all other Christians should join him in such definition and acknowledgment, if there was to be any common realization of signs of Christian unity.

Were we talking "merger," which we are not, instead of proposing a well spelled-out "communion" between two bodies that would remain "autonomous," we would have to deal with more implications of the episcopate. We took great pains these months to be assured and to have the document clearly and precisely say that Episcopalians do *not* expect Lutherans to start accepting the episcopate as a matter of faith as something essential to our understanding of the ministry of word and sacrament. Many Episcopalians take pains to say that they do not accept and enjoy it on such terms, that it is not an article of faith among them. They well know that they cannot expect us, in the year 2000 or some such time, to wake up some morning and say, "Now we believe . . ." in it. We can, however, wake up then and rejoice in full communion and common mission, while welcoming potential gifts that can come with the episcopate.

I hope that the sixteen months of prayerful study ahead of us will be marked by an eagerness on the part of all, no matter what our preconceptions, to foster discussion in ways that will lead to renewal and resolve, not divisiveness, within the Evangelical Lutheran Church in America. I hope that they will be ones in which to experience a spirit among us that indicates our ability to listen to each other; a spirit of openness, a readiness to hear arguments respectfully and empathically expressed; a note of repentance where necessary, and a readiness to change. Having stolen a word from "our" Dietrich Bonhoeffer above ("Eat, bird . . . ") let me borrow from "their" Richard Hooker: "All change is inconveniencing, including change from worse to better." Church life in the future without episcopacy, in my view, would not be "worse," but, I would argue, that "better" would be "common mission," "agreement," and "a sign of unity," that is represented and experienced in a "full communion" whose terms and reality include some features of the historic episcopate and reception of the episcopate itself.˙

DEFINING THE TERM EPISCOPATE

To discipline our talk about the episcopate, we will begin by reference to *Called to Common Mission*. Twelve times this document refers to the term *episcopate* prefaced by the adjective *historic* and *twice* to bishops "in historic succession." The dictionary merely describes the

---

* *After four months of torture for an historian, which means that in drafting we were allowed no footnotes, I cannot resist one here. (Watch for a few footnote-like parentheses as well in the text that follows!) During a dictionary survey of terms associated with "Episcopal," Episcopacy," and "Episcopate,"* I found two extreme words between which we make our way: *Episcopicide*, "the crime of murdering a bishop," and *Episcopolatry*, "'Worship' of Bishops." I would rather think, somewhere between these extremes, that bishops are or can be gifts of God for "oversight" in a church that makes its way between extremes of anarchy and authoritarianism.

episcopate, apart from the adjective, first as "the position, term, or office of a bishop"; second, irrelevantly here, as a jurisdiction, a diocese; and third, as "bishops considered as a group," as in "episcopacy." None of these ordinary dictionary usages covers what is at issue in the Concordat discussions. One has to turn to church dictionaries for definitions of the "episcopate" when connected with the adjective or with an explanatory phrase about "succession." The writer in the *Corpus Dictionary of Western Churches* (Washington: Corpus, 1970) is helpful as he or she points to two churchly usages of "historic episcopate." First,

> understood strictly it describes the office of bishop as derived from the Apostles through an unbroken series of ordinations. The idea of the historic episcopate has always been central in the Anglican and Episcopal Churches; the specific phrase has been prominent; esp. in ecumenical discussions, since the Chicago-Lambeth Quadrilateral (1888). The fourth point of the Quadrilateral declared as essential to Christian unity: "The Historic Episcopate, locally adapted in the methods of its administration to the varying needs of the nations and peoples called of God into the unity of His Church."

Then:

> taken in a wider sense, the historic episcopate means episcopacy as a historically accepted institution or function in the Church. This broader sense of the historic episcopate leaves aside the question of a valid succession of ordinations, and whether the office of bishop is a human or divine institution. In the first sense, the historic episcopate is one aspect of apostolic succession as understood by the Roman Catholic, Eastern, and Old Catholic Churches and by those in the Anglican Communion. In the broader sense, the Constitution of the Church of South India (1941) accepted the historic episcopate, but without declaring any theory of its meaning.

During our months of drafting, we pressed Episcopal partners and their colleagues in history, theology, and ecclesiology and did not find many of them ready to point us to references to the episcopate that would find Anglicans "declaring any theory of its meaning" or agreeing on one. Some Episcopalians, it is true, have seen the episcopate to belong to the essence *(esse)* of the church. But you will hear others say, as Lutherans do, that bishops belong to the *bene esse*, the "well being," or the *plene esse*, which means that it is part of the "fullness of being" of the church. Some will wink and observe others acting as if bishops are of the *male esse*, the bad essence of the church. The point is Episcopalians are as varied and vague about defining this subject as Lutherans are about defining exactly what ordination means. They hear us being vague about how "succession" has occurred among us when pastors (in New Testament language, "presbyters"), through laying-on-of-hands and prayer, have "ordained" others.

A TYPICAL CONTEMPORARY ANGLICAN EXPRESSION ON THIS SUBJECT

During this period of study I was impressed by a booklet, *Apostolicity and Succession,* a "House of Bishops Occasional Paper" that was introduced by the Archbishop of Canterbury and commended to the whole church. What it says would presumably parallel what the Episcopal Church in the United States also holds. Not once does it use the language of the episcopate as being part of the *esse* of the church. It treats "so-called apostolic succession" as "so-called," precisely because "this expression is easier to use than to define" and because it is seldom used in an unambiguous way. No clear theory or doctrine appears on these pages (3).

The booklet quotes the Pullach Report, of Anglican-Lutheran International Conversations: "In confessing the apostolic faith as a community, all baptized and believing Christians are the apostolic church and stand in the succession of apostolic faith" (7). There is no claim by Anglicans that apostolic succession in the episcopate is specified and mandated in the New Testament but only that "the ministry of oversight emerged from the New Testament times" (17).

The booklet also quotes with apparent favor some lines from a Lutheran-Roman Catholic dialogue of 1981:

> [These historical, especially sixteenth-century] considerations provide the basis for a Lutheran evaluation of the historic succession as a sign of such unity. The Lutheran conviction is that acceptance of communion with the episcopal office in historic succession is meaningful not as an isolated act, but only as it contributes to the unity of the church in faith and witness to the universality of the gospel of reconciliation [26]. That moment of Lutheran evaluation is now here, and we on the committee who agree with *Called to Common Mission* readily identified with the sense of that paragraph and its concluding Lutheran witness.

RECEPTION OF THE EPISCOPATE WITHOUT A PARTICULAR THEORY

What *Called to Common Mission* makes clear is that Lutherans, in respect to the episcopate, do not have to adopt "any theory of its meaning" in order to have full communion with the Episcopal Church. They can put their own interpretation on the subject, as most Anglicans do. It is not likely that many of them would find a way to square the notion of its being of the essence *(esse)* of the church with the Augsburg Confession's statement that it is sufficient to agree concerning the teaching of the gospel and the administration of the sacraments to express unity in the church. No single specific pattern of church order was clearly stipulated in the New Testament. No special forms of it—including those expressions familiar to us—are commanded or defined in any detail. Yet we enjoy ministry including that of ordained clergy.

Were we talking merger, which we emphatically are not, we would have to reckon with the Episcopal Church's consistent word that reception of the historic episcopacy would be "essential" for such an expression of the full unity of the church.

Do Episcopalians believe that some sort of magic gets passed on through the "unbroken series" of ordination by the laying-on-of-hands? No. They don't even believe that they can prove there *is* an unbroken series, and their historians—and the Archbishop of Canterbury at the 1996 meeting of all the bishops of the Episcopal Church and the Evangelical Lutheran Church in America—typically said they can prove that from time to time it *has* been "broken," if we are thinking of a tactile transmission through laying-on-of-hands. While the leadership knows that in some folklore and still on popular levels, some Anglicans hold to what others dismiss as a "pipeline view of apostolic succession," most of their theologians dismiss such a notion. They see each ordination of a pastor as a new, specific and creative event in the general line of succession.

I have considered typical what an Episcopal bishop, Arthur Vogel, wrote while commenting on the original Concordat. "There is no need to claim that present-day bishops stand in direct unbroken succession to the Twelve; it is sufficient to acknowledge that the role of bishops in the church today mirrors the role of the Twelve in Jesus' day" (James E. Griffiss and Daniel F. Martensen, eds., *A Commentary on "Concordat of Agreement"* [Minneapolis: Augsburg Fortress, 1994], 50).

What Episcopalians take seriously is that the ministry of bishops "in succession" and "in the historic episcopate" represents one sign of unity in their communion and, they hope, some day again a sign of unity of most Christians. The ministry of bishops is also intended to serve as a ministry of "oversight," which is what "episcopacy" means, in the proclamation of the gospel and the whole ministry of a church.

Putting to work the historic episcopate and the practice of the laying-on-of-hands would become part of the practice of the Evangelical Lutheran Church in America if both bodies adopt the *Concordat of Agreement*.

Where ELCA members do not feel at ease with such a move, one could say about it in minimalist terms that the only differences they would or need ever see are, first, the presence of an Episcopal bishop (or more, if they'd want) at the installation (not ordination) of the presiding bishop of the Evangelical Lutheran Church in America and synodical bishops in the years ahead. The second would have a Lutheran bishop present with the laying-on-of-hands and prayer at ordinations of pastors (as these bishops now are, or as they now authorize someone to represent them). For clergy, supposing they would be at a bishop's installation, plus their own ordination if they are new candidates, there would go two or three hours of their life—installation of bishops and ordination of pastors tend to be long services—that would not look very little different from the services we now know.

The rite as envisioned recalls something that most of the Christian church has done since the Council of Nicea in 325, where the presence of three bishops was and is a sign of concern that more than the local is involved in oversight within the church.

One would hope that among those who have not hitherto welcomed it, emotions attendant to this potential change, with which they might at first be uneasy, will be countered by the experience of the blessings of full communion and common mission. One would further hope that as yet unforeseen blessings would also result from the reception among ELCA members of this version of the episcopate.

LUTHERANS ELSEWHERE ENJOYING THE EPISCOPATE

To argue that Lutherans cannot be in communion with churches that have the historic episcopate or that the episcopate is incompatible with Lutheranism would be to make a judgment that some Lutheran churches on all continents who have kept or have renewed it are non-Lutheran or bad Lutherans. *Called to Common Mission* in fact envisions installations at which the historic episcopate is to be recognized by the involvement of other Lutheran bishops in that episcopate. They can and, one hopes for the sake of demonstrating the catholicity of Lutheranism, they would call on Lutheran bishops from the Lutheran Salvadoran Synod of El Salvador or the Church of Sweden; the Evangelical Lutheran Church in Malaysia and Singapore or the Finnish Evangelical Lutheran Church; the Evangelical Lutheran Church in Zimbabwe or Lutheran churches from Baltic nations; from the Evangelical Lutheran Zulu Church or the Tamil Evangelical Lutheran Church from India—or numbers of others.

It is significant that students of world Lutheranism have difficulty determining who has, and makes a point of, the historic episcopate, and who does not. These Lutheran churches around the world which are in the episcopate tend to be in motion, sometimes in mergers, often being renewed and redefining themselves, and thus not standing still to be catalogued. Their motion is always marked by the Lutheran Confessions' identification of ministry with word and sacrament, something that would not change among us upon celebration of a Concordat of Agreement and the beginnings of life together in full communion.

BACK TO BASICS: WHAT ARE BISHOPS IN THE EPISCOPAL CHURCH?

While most Lutherans have begun to become acquainted with Episcopal bishops and priests during the time since 1982 of our *Interim Eucharistic Agreement* and the beginnings of experiment in joint mission and ministry, a Lutheran view of the episcopate should include observations concerning bishops as conceived and in action—as described and experienced by Episcopalians. What are bishops?

First, they belong to the *laos,* the "whole people of God," and are part of "a royal priesthood" who exercise "the ministry of the baptized" exactly as Lutheran laity, pastors, and bishops together now do. They do not surrender this status or vocation upon being elected as bishops. In an important statement by the Anglican Communion in 1981 it was said that "in Christ's one holy, Catholic and Apostolic Church, every member has, in virtue of his or her own baptism, his or her special vocation and ministry." It is in that context that "the episcopate has a particular responsibility" with several specific tasks (quoted in Daniel F. Martensen, ed., *Concordat of Agreement: Supporting Essays* [Minneapolis: Augsburg Fortress, 1991], 63).

Second, bishops are priests, in Anglican terms, which means they belong to the clergy just as Lutheran pastors do. They do not stop being priests or, as we read of their job description, pastors, when elected bishop.

Third, they are elected by the people, not appointed by the Archbishop of Canterbury or any superior analogous to the pope in Roman Catholicism.

Fourth, they acquire a couple of duties that Lutheran bishops do not have and are not likely to adopt. They do all the confirming, for example.

Fifth, they are in what our document calls "life service," but what this means practically is carefully stated and regulated in the constitution and canons of the Episcopal Church. Bishops are not any more free to set up shop and spell out duties for themselves than are Lutheran pastors post-retirement.

If we wish to be basic, we should look carefully at the lived life of the church for any and all its members. An Episcopalian each week at worship opens the Book of Common Prayer, ordinarily in its 1979 version, and can read a catechism on the ministry:

> Question: Who are the ministers of the Church?
>
> Answer: The ministers of the Church are lay persons, bishops, priests, and deacons.
>
> Question: What is the ministry of the laity?
>
> Answer: The ministry of lay persons is to represent Christ and his Church; to bear witness to him wherever they may be; and, according to the gifts given them, to carry on Christ's work of reconciliation in the world; and to take their place in the life, worship, and governance of the Church.
>
> Question: What is the ministry of a bishop?
>
> Answer: The ministry of a bishop is to represent Christ and his Church, particularly as apostle, chief priest, and pastor of a diocese; to guard the faith, unity, and discipline of the whole Church; to proclaim the Word of God to act in Christ's name for the reconciliation of the world and the building up of the Church; and to ordain others to continue Christ's ministry.

> Question: What is the ministry of a priest or presbyter?
>
> Answer: The ministry of a priest is to represent Christ and his Church, particularly as pastor to the people; to share with the bishop in the overseeing of the Church; to proclaim the Gospel; to administer the sacraments; and to bless and declare pardon in the name of God (BCP, 855-56).

The catechism then goes on to define the ministry of the deacon, but that definition is irrelevant here because the Concordat does not commit Lutherans to ordaining deacons as they continue to serve in our diaconal ministry.

The rest of what is basic appears in the rite of "The Ordination of a Bishop," also in the Book of Common Prayer. The bishop-elect is described: "the clergy and people . . . have chosen" this person to be bishop. He or she solemnly declares belief that the Holy Scriptures are the Word of God and that he or she will "engage to conform to the doctrine, discipline, and worship of the Episcopal Church" (BCP, 513). The people have to declare that it is their will that the person be ordained a bishop. In "The Examination" there is a question whether the bishop "will encourage and support all baptized people in their gifts and ministries" (BCP, 518). One has to go beyond the Thirty-nine Articles, the Book of Common Prayer, and its catechism for any reference to apostolic succession or the historic episcopate, except for the Chicago-Lambeth Quadrilateral in the Historical Documents section at the back of the Prayer Book (877-878).

Since I am to give a Lutheran view of episcopacy and the episcopate, I can only say that all the rest of what is spelled out in the commitment of a bishop ought to make Lutheran and other evangelical hearts sing. The bishop is "to be one with the apostles in proclaiming Christ's resurrection and interpreting the Gospel"; testifying, guarding the faith and unity and discipline of the Church; celebrating and providing for the administration of the sacraments; ordaining; "to be in all things a faithful pastor and wholesome example for the entire flock of Christ" (BCP, 517). New bishops are to adopt a heritage and express a joy. They are to pray and to study, that they "may have the mind of Christ." They are to enlighten the minds and stir up the conscience of their people; to share in the government of the whole church with "all others who minister in the Church"; to "show compassion to the poor and strangers, and defend those who have no helper," and, as expressed in a prayer, to lead a "pure, and gentle, and holy life" (BCP, 521).

Some Lutherans wish that the Episcopal Church *did* have an agreed-upon theory about the historic episcopate, a defined historical justification of its versions of apostolic succession, or some doctrinal or dogmatic statement. Anglican theologian John H. Rodgers, Jr., put it well:

> Anglicans have no theory of the episcopate that is required of all Anglicans. We have in fact never really agreed on a particular theology of the episcopate. We are, however, agreed on the fact and value of the historic episcopate, as expressive of the oneness of the gospel and the unity of the church in time and space, as well as an office that has unique potential for serving the gospel in the preaching and teaching of the church . . . .To be sure, we have the treasure in earthen vessels. The episcopate in historic succession is an earthen vessel that we feel has the blessing of the Lord upon it. We seek to commend it to you (Martensen, 67).

THE ISSUE OF "EARTHEN VESSELS" IN THE EPISCOPATE

When Episcopalians ask for theories, historical justification, and doctrinal definition of our Lutheran ordering of the pastoral ministry in the context of church governance, they find us speaking about it much as they do about their ministries, including the episcopate. Yet we too see this ministry of pastors as a gift to be enjoyed, despite its earthen-vessel character.

In 1997 some Evangelical Lutheran Church in America members made reference to horror stories about earthen vessels, in some cases of "the unworthiness of the Ministers" in the episcopate. The "Articles of Religion" adopted in the United States in 1801 and in the Book of Common Prayer deal with such exceptions, in classic Christian (including Lutheran) ways:

> **XXVI. Of the Unworthiness of the Ministers, which hinders not the effect of the Sacraments.**
>
> Although in the visible Church the evil be ever mingled with the good, and sometimes the evil have chief authority in the Ministration of the Word and Sacraments, yet forasmuch as they do not the same in their own name, but in Christ's, and do minister by his commission and authority, we may use their Ministry, both in hearing the Word of God, and in receiving the Sacraments. Neither is the effect of Christ's ordinance taken away by their wickedness, nor the grace of God's gifts diminished from such as by faith, and rightly, do receive the Sacraments ministered unto them; which be effectual, because of Christ's institution and promise, although they be ministered by evil men.

Enough said? No:

> Nevertheless, it appertaineth to the discipline of the Church, that inquiry be made of evil Ministers, and that they be accused by those that have knowledge of their offences; and finally, being found guilty, by just judgment be deposed (See BCP, 873).

Detailing a Lutheran view of how Episcopal bishops in the episcopate share in the government of their church is not necessary or important here, since, as *Called to Common Mission* makes clear, while the two churches would and, one hopes, will become interdependent, they remain "autonomous" and "neither church seeks to remake the other in its own image, but each is open to the gifts of the other as it seeks to be faithful to Christ and his mission."

Further: "Our ordained ministries will still be regulated by the constitutional framework of each church" (paragraph 8). "Each remains free to explore and further develop its own understanding of the nature and function of the ministry of bishops in historic succession." And, in case there is any doubt: "By thus freely accepting the historic episcopate for the sake of the unity of the church, the Evangelical Lutheran Church in America does not thereby affirm that the historic episcopate is necessary or essential for the unity of the church" (paragraph 16).

Lutherans critical of the Episcopal Church sometimes speak negatively about its hierarchical character, since there are three orders of ministry. Or they surmise that bishops in succession might limit the laity. Hierarchy is as hierarchy does. Bishops and the episcopate can be as readily viewed as part of the *economy* of the church as it can be seen in *hierarchy*. There are good hierarchies and bad ones. This Lutheran as a journalist can gladly (or sadly!) point out that the most un- or anti-hierarchical, the most fiercely congregational bodies in American Protestantism are today in action and fact the most authoritarian. Their leaders can and do take unilateral actions of great moment. Further, this Lutheran as historian is ready upon request to point to hundreds of examples of the lay ministry, the priesthood of all believers and the ministry of the baptized being realized in the Anglican churches through the centuries. These are examples that have world-historical significance. They are not easily matched elsewhere and cannot fairly be overlooked, dismissed, or demeaned. The laity are encouraged, not stifled. But, back to bishops, the important words:

> The Episcopal Church remains free to maintain its
> conviction that sharing in the historic episcopate,
> while not necessary to the being of a church, is essen-
> tial to full communion; the Evangelical Lutheran
> Church in America remains free to maintain that the
> historic episcopate is not necessary for full commu-
> nion (paragraph 11).

Some reacted negatively at the Churchwide Assembly
in 1997 to phrases which might have suggested that the
Episcopal Church "in the historic episcopate" demeaned
ministries such as those in the Evangelical Lutheran
Church in America because it did not at present continue
in that historic episcopate. To that concern the important
lines in *Called to Common Mission* are:

> The Episcopal Church by this Concordat recognizes
> that the ministers ordained in the Evangelical Lutheran
> Church in America or its predecessor bodies *are and
> have been fully authentic* [italics mine, paragraph 13].

or that:

> The Episcopal Church endorses the Lutheran affirma-
> tion that the historic catholic episcopate under the
> Word of God must always serve the gospel, and that
> the ultimate authority under which bishops preach
> and teach is the gospel itself (paragraph 15).

That Lutheran affirmation implies reference to the two
lines of the Augsburg Confession that troubled some
Lutherans as they appraised the Concordat of Agreement
and the possible reception of the historic episcopate.
Agreement in word and sacrament is sufficient for the true
unity of the church, according to that confession. How do
we address this?

Lutherans already help assure this faithfulness of ministry with their own current version of apostolic succession, which includes the laying-on-of-hands, generation
after generation, century after century, by pastors who

have previously received this gift through acts that also go back to the apostles. They, we, make all kinds of provisions for "oversight," *episkope.* Yes, word and sacrament *are* the divinely instituted instruments of grace behind and through ordained ministry. But these are not limiting and confining words in respect to what Lutheran churches such as the Evangelical Lutheran Church in America might freely adopt. They can receive the practice of oversight associated with bishops in the historic succession without adopting any belief that compromises word and sacrament.

ATTENTION TO A "SIGN" BUT NOT A GUARANTEE

During these months of studying the episcopate and its relation to apostolic succession, I often had the experience that through reception of the episcopate, clearly as a "sign though not a guarantee," we were also receiving in new ways the gift of the early Christian church. Like the modern church, not least of all within the Episcopal Church in the Anglican Communion and the Evangelical Lutheran Church in America as part of world Lutheranism, we are dealing with suffering churches. We are bewildered by our global repositioning, our location in the midst of secularity and pluralism, the challenges of relativism and muffled witness. We are together challenged and together we welcome all the company and the gifts and signs that we can receive and impart.

I cannot close without spending a moment on the second of two four-letter words that kept coming up in our drafting and studying. (The first, of course, was *esse.*) I refer to *sign.* The historic episcopate and apostolic succession were additional "signs," not "marks," not "guarantees." The word is short and simple, but it merits notice. Let me quote from Anglican philosopher S. W. Sykes. Keep our topic in mind as you read:

One of the most helpful definitions was offered by the American philosopher C. S. Pierce: "A sign," he said, ". . . is something that stands to somebody for something in some respect or another." Very many things fall within that definition: a word in language, uttered or written; a sound like a sigh or a groan; a gesture or other body language; a physical state, like blushing or a high temperature; any action that might signify an attitude—all these come directly from human beings. But many more examples of signs are found within nature or in physical objects: smoke may be a sign of fire; a sound from a machine may indicate that it is functioning; an object can be designated as a symbol for a political or religious group, or in dreams can be interpreted to represent an event, an attitude, or a person (quoted in Ephraim Radner and R. R. Reno, *Inhabiting Unity: Theological Perspectives on the Proposed Lutheran-Episcopal Concordat* [Grand Rapids, Mich.: Eerdmans, 1995], 22).

Then Sykes sensibly makes his point on our subject by quoting Lutheran theologian George Lindbeck:

What the Reformers objected to was the idea that succession constitutes a guarantee or criterion of apostolic faithfulness, but once one thinks in terms of the sign value of continuity in office, this difficulty vanishes. Signs and symbols express and strengthen the reality they signify, but the sign can be present without the reality, and the reality without the sign (as, for example, is illustrated by the relation of the flag and patriotism). Thus it is apostolicity in faith and life that makes the episcopal sign fruitful, but not the other way around, and this ought not to be turned into an excuse for neglecting the sign (25).

The early church gave later centuries three gifts to which we might associate the word *apostolic*. It took centuries of life "without a theory" to form what we might call *"the apostolic canon"* to help assure the integrity of the gospel everywhere. A second gift is *"the apostolic creed,"* the Apostles' Creed, and with it doctrines we consider and call apostolic. Third was oversight in the form of *"the apostolic episcopate."* The apostles did not literally have a direct hand in formulating the first two of these, any more than we think—or at least than we need to believe—that they did in keeping unbroken a chain of oversight that became the apostolic episcopate.

Three-fourths of today's Christians remain in that version of succession, and the Lutherans of the sixteenth century give evidence that they would have kept it but for historical accidents that forced them to improvise. The choices many of them made—to turn the princes into bishops—were unfortunate. We have been improvising ever since and have lived with a variety of modes of ordering the church. Receiving the historic episcopate can mean resuming the appreciation of a gift of oversight in a form that has ancient roots, finds global expression, and is responsibly hedged by safeguards on the part of Lutherans. We believe that the Evangelical Lutheran Church in America is capable of bringing forth new promises through it, as we are *Called to Common Mission.*

3

THE HISTORIC EPISCOPATE IN THE CONTEXT OF APOSTOLIC SUCCESSION*

MARK DYER

INTRODUCTION

I am sincerely pleased and humbled to have been called out of the bull-pen to pitch what I pray will be the last final innings of the Lutheran-Episcopal pilgrimage to full communion. I have been asked to consider the theological reality of the historic episcopate and its implications for full communion.

First I must say that it is theologically impossible to consider the historic episcopate apart from the more fundamental theological reality of apostolic succession, for the historic episcopate is only one element in the Spirit-filled succession of orthodox apostolic faith from one generation to another.

---

* This paper was originally presented to the House of Bishops of the Episcopal Church meeting at the Kanuga Conference Center, Hendersonville, North Carolina, March 9, 1996.

This paper will primarily concern itself with apostolic succession. I will first recall the definition of apostolic succession given to us from the agreed statement of Lutheran-Episcopal Dialogue II (LED II). We will then consider how some of the house churches of the sub-apostolic period formed their lives in order to survive, to grow and preserve the gospel witness after the departure of the apostolic persons. How did they provide for the apostolic succession of the gospel? Then we will see how the church in the post-apostolic period provided for the living of faithful gospel life in a period of persecution and heresy. These four elements became definitive as the way to insure orthodox apostolic succession. Finally we will consider what all of this has to say about the historic episcopate and our God-given and Holy Spirit-directed quest for full communion among our churches in Christ Jesus.

APOSTOLIC SUCCESSION

LED II in its agreed statement (p. 32) defined apostolicity as "the Church's continuity with Christ and the apostles in its movement through history." Apostolic succession is a "dynamic diverse reality" embracing faithfulness to apostolic teaching, participation in baptism, prayer, and the eucharist, "sharing in the Church's common life of mutual edification and caring, served by an ecclesiastically called and recognized pastoral ministry of word and sacrament," and continuing involvement in the apostolic mission of the church by proclaiming the gospel through word and deed. Apostolic succession is not to be understood only in terms of the historic episcopate.

Apostolic succession has to do with two realities. First, it is the church's continuity with Christ and the apostles in its movement through history and second it is how that continuity is achieved from one generation to another.

THE SUB-APOSTOLIC PERIOD

The reality of succession became a major concern of the emerging New Testament communities. It was the reality of survival. What was the church to do to preserve the apostolic tradition of the gospel after the apostolic person or guide had departed this life? The sub-apostolic period is the last one-third of the first century. That was the period when most of the New Testament would be formed, and the sacraments of baptism and eucharist would become central to the life of the Christian community. Apostolic succession took various forms during this period. Of the possible six or seven ecclesiologies present during this period we will consider three.[1]

First, the Pauline legacy as described in the pastoral epistles (1 and 2 Timothy and Titus) tells of communities that established continuing stability upon the firm ministry of the presbyter-bishops. The ministry of the presbyter-bishop would be to have "a firm grasp of the word that is trustworthy in accordance with the teaching, so that he (the presbyter-bishop) may be able to preach with sound doctrine and to refute those who contradict it" (Titus 1:9). The presbyter-bishop who is responsible for preserving the apostolic tradition is to be beyond the slightest moral reproach. He is to be loving, holy, sober, and kind as a husband, father, teacher and administrator. Sound doctrine will be guaranteed through a succession of presbyter-bishops whose ministry would, in essence, embody the magisterium for the community. In the pastoral epistles we see the highly structured office of presbyter-bishop responsible for teaching and administration. Both he and his family must adhere to a very clear and moral life. This structure, established to insure apostolic tradition, strictly divided the community into the *ecclesia docens* (the teachers) and the *ecclesia discens* (the learners).

Let's turn now to the ecclesial-christology of Colossians and Ephesians. Rather than responding to ever-present doctrinal danger by emphasis on apostolic doctrine preserved by a succession of apostolic teachers, the authors of Colossians and Ephesians speak of the church as the Body of Christ. Jesus Christ "is the image of the invisible God, the first born of all creation . . . all things have been created through him and for him . . . . He is the head of the body, the church . . . . For in him all the fullness of God was pleased to dwell, and through him God was pleased to reconcile to himself all things whether on earth or in heaven, by making peace through the blood of his cross" (Col. 1:15-20). God the Father "chose us in Christ before the foundation of the world to be holy and blameless before him in love. He destined us for adoption as his children through Jesus Christ" (Eph. 1:4-5). This ecclesiology speaks of the church not the churches.

This Body of Christ ecclesiology personalizes the church and encourages love for the church. The author of Colossians attributes these words to the apostle Paul, "I am now rejoicing in my sufferings for your sake, and in my flesh I am completing what is lacking in Christ's afflictions for the sake of his body, that is, the church" (Col. 1:24). As Jesus Christ gave himself up for the church, St. Paul rejoices that he can give himself up for the church. Now that the apostle has gone to heaven, others will give themselves up for the church, the body of Christ. Hence we see a succession of love for Christ and for the church, which will insure doctrinal continuity. True lovers of the church do not embrace heresy. As long as the baptized have faith in Jesus Christ, love the church as his body and live the holy life, the church will continue; for Christ "is the image of the invisible God." Christ "in whom the fullness of God was pleased to dwell" is "the head of the church and we are the

Body" (Col. 1:15, 18, 19). It is important to note that in Colossians-Ephesians there is little mention of the church as an institution.

Another ecclesial community with its own distinctive church order and theological ecclesial vision is the community of the beloved disciple. Johannine ecclesiology has its firm roots and life in a very high *logos* christology. Jesus is the Word of God, the Father's Son from before creation. He is the source of divine life for all who come to him. All are called to come and believe in Jesus as a vine that gives life to its living branches. Jesus is the only source of light, life and eternal salvation.

Through faith in Jesus, one is born again and given new life in baptism. This new life is nourished and sustained by "the bread that came down from heaven" and "the one who eats this bread will live forever" (John 6:58). Dignity is conferred on the baptized because they are loved with the same love with which the Father loves Jesus; because Jesus has laid down his life for them; because they are chosen as God's friends to whom all has been made known; in Jesus all have seen the Father; because they have the gift of prayer in order to go forth and bear fruit as disciples; because the Paraclete is continually with the body of believers, teaching them everything and reminding them of all Jesus said and did.

The essence of Johannine ecclesiology is a deeply personal faith relationship with Jesus, and loving one another as Jesus loves in the presence and power of the Holy Spirit. This community of the beloved disciple included Samaritan and Gentile converts as well as Palestinian and Hellenist Jewish Christians. It has no traces of ecclesiastical position or status. All have seen the Father because all have faith and love Jesus.

It is interesting to note the ministry of women in the community of the beloved disciple. The Samaritan woman is the first faithful evangelista. Martha becomes the bearer of apostolic faith, "You are the Christ, the Son of God." Mary Magdalene is the first to encounter the risen Jesus. This Mary, during the Middle Ages, was called *apostola apostolorum.*

The question for the community of the beloved disciple is not whether the church will survive the death of its apostolic leaders, but whether the love of and for Jesus will be sustained by faithful Christians. The continuing faith and love of Jesus by his disciples and the continuing presence of the Paraclete will be the intrinsic character of the church through the ages. All the church needs to do is to be faithful. There is no hint at episcopal historic succession in the Johannine community.

I cite three examples of ecclesiology that emerged during the sub-apostolic period, the time when most of the New Testament writings were being formed, for two reasons: First, the concern during this period is for survival and the faithful succession of the gospel of Jesus Christ; and yet in only one instance is there a hint at the succession of an historic episcopate in the presbyter-bishops of the pastoral epistles. Second, there is sufficient evidence that in the major urban centers such as Antioch and Ephesus there probably were four or five different Christian house churches, each with a differently focused ecclesiology of succession living in *koinonia,* full communion with one another. Apparently these different ecclesial elements of gospel succession of the churches did not constitute an obstacle to full communion in the last one-third of the first century.

THE RISE OF BASIC ECCLESIAL ELEMENTS OF APOSTOLIC SUCCESSION

With the onslaught of one heresy after another—e.g., gnosticism, the rigorist puritan Montanism, heresies concerning baptism, the doctrine of Christ and the Holy Trinity—it became necessary for the church to establish orthodox apostolic succession. Four elements emerged as instruments of apostolic succession of the gospel: the sacraments, baptism and eucharist; the creeds; the threefold ministry of deacon, presbyter and bishop in historic succession; and the canon, or holy scripture. The Christian community firmly believed that it had the authority of Christ and the guidance of the Holy Spirit to develop these basic ecclesial elements of apostolic succession.

The earliest of the elements of apostolic succession were the sacraments of baptism and the holy eucharist. The letters of Paul (e.g., Romans 6:4) speak of baptism as the beginning of new life in Christ and entrance into the community of the faithful. "Therefore we have been buried with him by baptism into death, so that, just as Christ was raised from the dead by the glory of the Father, so too we might walk in newness of life" (Romans 6:4). The risen Christ in the Gospel of Matthew sends his disciples out to baptize all peoples with the promise that he will always be with them. By the second and third centuries a very rich and highly developed catechesis was part of the life of those preparing to be baptized.

Paul would write to the Corinthians about the tradition of eucharist. I "received from the Lord what I have handed on to you, that the Lord Jesus on the night he was betrayed took a loaf of bread, and when he had given thanks, he broke it and said, 'this is my body that is for you. Do this in remembrance of me.' In the same way he took the cup also, after supper, saying, 'this cup is the new covenant in my blood. Do this as often as you drink it, in remembrance of me.' For as often as you eat this bread and drink the cup, you proclaim the Lord's death until he comes" (1 Corinthians 11:23-26). Before the time of Justin Martyr (mid-second century), the eucharist took the basic shape we recognize today.

The catechesis and celebration of the liturgy of baptism; the reading of sacred scripture, the teaching, the prayers and holy communion at eucharist, were the place where primary theology was presented and experienced. This insured apostolic succession of orthodox doctrine in word and sacrament among and by the whole people of God. Doxology, right praise of the Holy Trinity, is the primary element of apostolic succession.

The second element of apostolic succession was, for the most part, conceived and born in the life of the liturgies of baptism and eucharist. Primary theology presented and experienced in sacramental worship of the Holy Trinity gave birth to the earliest creeds. The primitive creeds formed in the baptismal liturgies soon became part of eucharistic liturgies. The great creeds of the Orthodox Councils of the Church at Nicea, Chalcedon, and Constantinople would also find a place in the liturgical life of the Church.

Baptism, eucharist and creed are the primary place of the orthodox succession of apostolic life of the gospel for the people of God.

Within a few years after the apostolic period, St. Ignatius was writing to churches in Syria and Asia that clearly had developed the threefold ministry of deacon, presbyter and bishop. The growing churches of those early centuries soon saw the personal, collegial and communal office of the bishop as a central element in orthodox apostolic life. The historical succession of bishops became a significant element in the orderly and orthodox transmission of the gospel and the mission of the church. "The historic episcopate declares to us that the gospel is not only an idea or a proposition, or a proclamation, but the animating force of a living community communicated over and over again from one person to another. The bishop, in this succession, is thus a living image of the unity of the faithful in and with God, a unity yet to be consummated but already at work in us across the barriers of time and space."[2]

The historic episcopate became central to the apostolic ministry of promoting, safeguarding, and serving the life of the gospel in the church. Bishops in apostolic, historical succession are the symbols and personal focus of the life and mission of the gospel of Jesus Christ as they pray and worship, preach and teach, and serve the people of God. Bishops exercise their historic apostolic ministry *personally* in being *accountable* to and faithful to the God who has called the person to this ministry, *collegially* by being accountable to and faithful to brothers and sisters in the same ministry, and *communally* by being accountable to the whole church and in the service of the gospel for the world.

The fourth element of apostolic succession is the first in primacy and last in temporal formation. The church, led by the Holy Spirit of God, found it necessary to speak to itself and others concerning those writings which would be included, and those writings which would not be included, as part of its canonical life. By the mid-second century Christians were beginning to develop a scriptural canon around the writings of Paul (2 Peter 3:15-16). The canon of the four gospels was regularized by the late second century. From the fourth century on there was pretty much agreement on the New Testament canonical writings.

The sacraments of baptism and eucharist; the creeds; the ordained ministry of bishops in historic succession, presbyters, and deacons; and the canon of holy scripture are the four Spirit-inspired and God-given gifts to the church for the sake of the gospel of Jesus Christ. These are the basic elements of apostolic succession. Faithful and holy living within the context of these elements will insure the transmission of orthodox apostolic faith. However, in the hands of the unfaithful Christian, no one of these, nor all of them together, is the guarantee of true doctrine.

CONCLUSION

There might even have been a time when one of the elements of apostolic succession—let us say, the historic episcopate—was held by those who were unfaithful to the gospel and who, furthermore, were active obstacles to the reformation of the church and the office of bishop. Should a faithful Christian community then blindly follow blind guides? Or should the faithful set about a reformation of life that would guarantee the orthodox succession of the gospel of Jesus Christ in word and sacrament; in creed; and the apostolic ministry of ordained pastors, even if this meant a break in historic succession?

Let us say that there is a reformation community that has done just that. There is a reformation community that took the risk to break historic episcopal succession for the sake of the succession of the gospel of Jesus Christ. Let us go on to recognize the fact that since the time of the Reformation and for more than four hundred years this Reformation church has lived in friendship and peace with us Anglicans and even recently we have recognized that in each of our communions the gospel of Jesus Christ is preached and taught in word and sacrament.

Now for the sake of the gospel, the Evangelical Lutheran Church in America on the basis of the Concordat of Agreement with Episcopalians is ready to agree that all its bishops will be understood as ordained, like other pastors, for life service of the gospel in the pastoral ministry of the historic episcopate. Lutherans will further agree to revise the ELCA's rite of the Installation of Bishop to reflect this understanding. The Lutheran Church also agrees to make constitutional and liturgical provision that only bishops shall ordain clergy.

Why will Lutherans give all this holy and prayerful consideration? It is for the same reason we will give it holy and prayerful consideration. Because on the night before he died, Jesus prayed that his sisters and brothers might be one as he and the Father are one. Jesus lived out that intercessory prayer by dying on the cross of forgiveness and reconciliation.

So what do we need to do? We are being asked to endorse the Lutheran affirmation that the historic catholic episcopate under the word of God must always serve the gospel, and that the ultimate authority under which bishops preach is the gospel itself (Concordat 6). Also we are being asked to begin the process for enacting a temporary suspension in the case only, of the seventeenth-century restriction that "no persons are allowed to exercise the offices of bishop, priest or deacon in the church unless they are so ordained, or have already received such ordination with the laying on of hands by bishops who are themselves duly qualified to confer Holy Orders." The purpose of this temporary suspension is to permit the full interchangeability and reciprocity of all Lutheran pastors and Episcopal priests or presbyters without further ordination or supplemental ordination whatsoever (Concordat 5).

We should do this, I believe, in the light of the agreement that the threefold ministry of bishops, presbyters and deacons in historic succession will be the future pattern of the one ordained ministry of word and sacrament in both churches. Full communion will deepen our common fidelity to the gospel; strengthen our life in the doctrine of the gospel; and enrich the historic episcopate; all for the mission of God, Father, Son, and Holy Spirit.

NOTES

[1] For this section I am in debt to the excellent work of Fr. Raymond E. Brown in *The Church the Apostles Left Behind* (New York: Paulist Press, 1984).

[2] William Countryman, "The Gospel and the Institutions of the Church with Particular Reference to the Historic Episcopate," *Anglican Theological Review* 66:4 (1984): 402-415.

4

CALLED TO COMMON MISSION

Is It Worth the Tribulation?

JON S. ENSLIN

The approval of full communion between the Evangelical Lutheran Church in America and the Episcopal Church was manifestly difficult. While the Episcopal Church approved the Concordat of Agreement with apparent ease at its 1997 General Convention, some grumbling over the canonical decisions suspending the Preface to the Ordinal of 1662 for ELCA clergy remains. There are members of the ECUSA eager to find reasons to rescind their historic agreement.

The Evangelical Lutheran Church in America had much more difficulty. The ELCA failed to approve the Concordat of Agreement at its 1997 Assembly by just a few votes short of the required two-thirds majority. After much anguish, that same Assembly decided to try again at their next assembly two years later by a vote of 995 to 15. They also asked that the document be rewritten in language more common to Lutherans and that materials be prepared for further study, helping Lutherans understand the Episcopal Church more clearly. Two years later *Called to Common Mission* was approved by a vote of 716 to 317, a full 27 votes more than the required two-thirds. The 2000 General Convention of the Episcopal Church accepted *Called to Common Mission* as the basis for full communion.

Resistance within a portion of the ELCA continues, primarily because of the acceptance of bishops being installed into the "historic episcopate." For some traditions within the ELCA, especially those who came to this country to avoid persecution from Lutheran bishops within the historic episcopate in their native land, this was a bitter pill and a violation of evangelical freedom. Some within the ELCA still hope to find ways to abrogate this agreement. As a way of dealing with continued theological objections, as well as some misunderstandings, the 2001 Assembly of the ELCA passed a very limited "exceptions" clause. This allowed a first-call person in the ELCA to be ordained by someone who is not a bishop within the historic episcopate, but only in rare, carefully defined circumstances, and only as authorized by the bishop. (As of this writing, 378 first-call candidates have been ordained, or soon will be, since the "exceptions clause" was passed. Two candidates have requested ordination according to the exceptions. One has been "exceptionally" ordained.)

For the ELCA the exceptions clause is an evangelical adaptation of the historic episcopacy, something specifically allowed in CCM. It is an administration of the historic episcopacy "locally adapted." Unfortunately, this practice has raised concerns among some members of the ECUSA that the ELCA is trying to find ways of avoiding a central part of the agreement, something essential to the ECUSA's self-understanding. Some within the ECUSA are asking that the agreement be reconsidered.

Rather than being an instrument of unity and community, it would appear on the surface that CCM is more divisive than unifying, a source of tribulation rather than *koinonia*. Has all of this ecumenical activity helped bring Christians closer together or has it created tensions that will drive them further apart? Will the results be worth the risk?

While tension may dominate discussion and strident voices may capture the ear, much suggests that CCM has already begun to accomplish precisely what it promised.

RECOGNITION OF ESSENTIAL ONENESS

While full communion falls short of organic unity, it nonetheless is an amazing expression of what the Christian communions hold in common. There is:

- Agreement in doctrine, enough so any remaining disagreements are no longer considered church-dividing.
- Mutual sacramental understanding and recognition.
- Exchangeability of members, enabling transfers of laity between communions.
- A willingness to invite members of the other church into the most significant rituals of the host church.
- Recognition of the validity of one another's ministries, something Christian communions have found problematic.
- Interchangeability of clergy, often a source of difficulty and division between communions.
- A commitment to be accountable to one another, both in decisions about relationships with other churches and in missional planning.
- Mutual planning, working and serving together, pooling resources and gifts.

In a world where Christians have frequently seen each other as rivals, even enemies, these are no small matters.

They break the momentum of divisiveness and begin to establish a sense of concord. We no longer are isolated in our thoughts or in our missional activity. We see our connection to others, even though we are not fully united.

At its very core this is a theological issue. When is the division of the Body of Christ justifiable?

> There is one body and one Spirit, just as you were called to the one hope of your calling, one Lord, one faith, one baptism, one God and Father of all, who is above all and through all and in all (Ephesians 4:4-5).

Lutherans have always believed that the unity of the Church is a gift of God's grace. Too often we have presumed to "sin in order that grace may abound." It is our division that must be justified, not our working toward unity.

I once traveled to India where I visited the headquarters of the Church of North India. Graciously received by the General Secretary, I asked this question: "To us American Lutherans, the merger of such diverse denominations seems odd. Can you tell me how and why it came about?" He immediately responded, "Three things: 1) We came to the awareness that Jesus unites us more than any human divisions can divide us. 2) We came to the conclusion that we would grow closer together, faster, by worshiping together, praying together, studying scripture together and serving together, than we would by talking to each other. And 3) When you are two percent of your country's population [Christians in India], you can no longer afford to fight European battles."

The unity of the people of God under the one Lordship of Christ is not merely an article of faith. It must be practiced, lived out, enfleshed in structures and deeds. CCM is an ecumenical breakthrough because it has placed the unity and mission of the church ahead of defending particular structures and guarding theological turf. The theological,

liturgical and missiological life of the ECUSA and the ELCA
are so compatible that there can be no justification for
denying a deeper, fuller intertwining of our life together.

FOR THE SAKE OF MISSION

Things have changed in the United States in the last
fifty years. Our families rarely model the Cleaver family on
early television's "Leave it to Beaver." Our culture no
longer assumes people care about being Christian, or even
religious. Mass media does not produce epics around biblical
stories. Last year the ELCA and ECUSA celebrated a joint
Christmas Eve service that was to be broadcast nationwide
on CBS television. When I tuned in to watch the service, I
discovered that our local station decided to run an old
movie instead. And I live in a "Lutheran town," Madison,
Wisconsin.

But Madison also has a Buddhist Temple, and not far
away in a suburb of Milwaukee a Hindu Temple was dedi-
cated this year. Wisconsin has both Islamic and Wiccan
chaplains (as well as Christian) in their prison system. And
Madison is in the "heartland" of the country. Other parts
of the United States have experienced an even more radical religious transition within the last fifty years. The
strong Christian churches of the 1950s have declined in
members and in social influence. The fastest growing religions in the United States are not Christian. Denominational bickering hinders proclamation of the gospel to an
ever more secular society, a society where religious influence is less and less Christian.

Scholars often interpret Jesus' "High Priestly Prayer"
(John 17) in elevated, theological terms. I see it as a prayer
of anguish. Knowing that he is about to suffer a painful
death, Jesus agonizes over the possibility that it will make
no difference. It is one thing to die. It is another thing to

die for no ultimate purpose. The unity of the disciples is critical, not for their sake; it is critical for the world. It is critical for the very people for whom Jesus dies. He prays, "that the world may believe that you [the Father] have sent me."

How is the world to believe in the grace, mercy, and justice of God, when we who proclaim the gospel are not gracious, merciful, or just to each other? How can we convince the world that Jesus is Lord, when we are more passionate about church structure or theological nuances than we are about finding a way to make the gospel clear to those who do not believe? The division of the church is a scandal because it trivializes the death of Jesus. We are more concerned that other Christians live in our image than that the world lives in God's image. We seek to elevate ourselves by demeaning others in the faith, rather than being instruments of elevating a fallen world through the grace of a loving God. "European [theological] battles" matter more than people coming to know and believe in Jesus as the one whom the Father sent to redeem the world. We denounce the speck in the eye of another Christian without acknowledging the log in our own. Our division is a sin. We rarely repent. We do not even anguish over our separation. Often we justify it.

It is no accident that the agreement was renamed, *Called to Common Mission* (italics mine). It is our common mission that calls us, summons us, beckons us, to find ways to bridge that which separates us. We dare not settle for anything less than organic unity. That is our eternal destiny. It must also be our temporal quest, for it is in time, the here and now, that we must do mission. To elevate that which causes disagreement over that which is redemptive is to trivialize the cross.

THAT THE WORLD MAY BELIEVE

But has CCM made a difference? Have things changed since the agreement was approved? Will the risks being run be offset by the concrete gains being made?

In the nine months I have served as the ELCA's Interim Director for the Department for Ecumenical Affairs, I have been amazed at the impact of the ELCA's full communion agreements in our churchwide organization. Parallel heads of departments in our separate communions interact with each other. Communication concerning plans and problems is common. We have involved our partners (we also have full communion agreements with three Reformed communions and the Moravian Church in America) in our evangelism strategy, worship planning, and mission development. Cooperation in global mission work is widespread. Where we can work together, we are trying. New ways and ideas are being generated. In fact, one ecumenical officer recently asked the ELCA to back off a little. "We are a smaller church, and we cannot have so many people involved in ELCA projects, as grateful as we are for your invitations."

In terms of CCM specifically, we are considering common ways of training new bishops and of continuing education for bishops. A common means of support and review of bishops will be developed and considered. Discussions are beginning on the diaconate, as both churches are attempting to understand this biblical office more fully. Representatives of the ECUSA have been invited to be involved in the development of a number of our major programs. Churches in other countries, birthed from our two denominations, are working more closely on common witness.

But not enough will happen if it only happens in our national, church-wide planning. I called several ELCA bishops in various parts of the country to ask this simple question, "What difference has CCM made on the territory of your synod?" I was pleasantly surprised at the response.

There were some common threads. Many talked about the sharing of clergy. In some instances the sharing was of talents and skills in multi-staff congregations. In some others a pastor or priest was called to serve as solo cleric to a congregation of the other communion. In some cases the same person serves a Lutheran and an Episcopal congregation meeting in the same building. The greatest joy for some bishops was the availability of clergy of one communion to serve in part-time situations in the other communion, especially in isolated, rural communities. "It has given new life and hope to our smaller congregations," one bishop remarked.

But it is not only in rural congregations that the need is evident. Bishop Robert Rimbo (Southeast Michigan Synod) speaks of two congregations in the inner city of Detroit, neither capable of supporting their own full-time clergyperson. Faith Memorial Lutheran Church has been vacant for seven years. Trinity Episcopal Church has been vacant for five years. Just two blocks apart, they are calling a Lutheran pastor to serve them both. The reason the person is Lutheran is the hope that a Presbyterian congregation that meets at Trinity might also become involved, as they too have been vacant for some time. As the ELCA is in full communion with the Presbyterian Church, USA, that pastor could serve them as well. "It will make a mighty difference," Bishop Rimbo enthuses.

Some Lutheran deacons are receiving training through the Episcopal Church's General Theological Seminary in New York City. Some Episcopal deacons are attending the Lutheran Seminary in Philadelphia, and there is a possibility that an Episcopal layperson might endow the chair of an Episcopal professor at the seminary. The Lutheran Seminary in Austin is on the campus of the Episcopal seminary, and CCM is making greater coordination of their work possible.

I heard of common mission planning, including working together to develop new congregations that would express both Lutheran and Episcopal worship styles. Ascension-St. Matthew's Church, a joint fellowship of Lutherans and Episcopalians, served by an Episcopal priest, is a ministry intentionally reaching out to proclaim the gospel among the Mormon population of Price, Utah. The development of youth ministries was common, including the calling of trained youth ministers to serve the youth of both Episcopal and Lutheran congregations. A number of the synods spoke of sharing of campus ministries. As one bishop said, "Neither of us have the money to be everywhere." An Episcopal priest has been called to serve the Lutheran congregation in the Colorado Women's Correctional Facility. Joint mission outreach to the people of "Little Havana" in Miami has the blessing of both the Episcopal and Lutheran bishops. A joint ministry to migrant workers is significant in Maryland. A very active Lutheran layperson is hoping to develop an ELCA congregation in Aspen, Colorado. Because land is so expensive in Aspen, they are seeking to worship in a thriving Episcopal congregation's building.

While it is possible to tell story after story, and I only spoke with eight of the sixty-five ELCA bishops, what was most profound was the attitude. A sense of collegiality is clear. One bishop said, "The nearest ELCA bishop is five hours away. The Episcopal bishops of my area are my support group, a group of people who understand and who care." Many of the bishops spoke of mutual hospitality and collegiality, of celebrating the eucharist and preaching at each other's assemblies/conventions. Several spoke of the joy of participating in and having official responsibility at the consecration of new Episcopal bishops. They spoke of joint bible-studies and pericope study groups among their clergy. Various women's groups are beginning to practice hospitality with each other.

WORTH THE RISK?

This is a pivotal time in the world of ecumenism. For some, changes in and challenges to the conciliar movement point to an ominous future, a time when the ecumenical gains of the last fifty years are at risk. For others they signify a time when the Holy Spirit is shaking foundations and doing new and wonderful things. National and worldwide organizations are under consideration that will include significant Christian communions not currently in conciliar organizations. Other dynamics are evident. The ECUSA is part of *Churches Uniting in Christ*, nine protestant denominations seeking to find a multilateral way to full communion. The ECUSA also maintains a number of bilateral dialogues. The ELCA is in full communion discussions with the United Methodists and in dialogues that hope to lay the groundwork for full communion with the Orthodox and Roman Catholics.

It has been but three years since *Called to Common Mission* was passed by the ELCA, only two years since it was accepted by the ECUSA. Much is just beginning. One would have expected little concrete activity in this brief time, maybe some discussion and planning. Yet it is clear that many things are happening, both locally and nationally. Of course, there is much, much more to do. It will be at least ten years before we will know the impact of *Called to Common Mission*, and maybe not even then. In the world of the Spirit, we often do not know the full impact of something for generations. And yet, as Bishop Theodore Schneider (Metropolitan Washington, D.C., Synod) has said, "We are on the cusp of really exciting things. There is tremendous theological and emotional affinity between us."

Has CCM been worth the risk? On an abstract, theological level, the answer must be, "Of course." Doing the will of God is usually risky but always worth it. Recognizing our essential oneness for the sake of mission, that the world may believe, is the will of the One who humbled himself, died, and conquered death for the sake of the world. After viewing what has been accomplished in so little time, I would also answer a resounding "Yes!" on a missional and pragmatic level. While CCM has just begun to impact our life together, I am convinced that the beginning has been vital, strong, and God-pleasing. *Soli Deo Gloria!*

5

PLANTING IN UNCERTAIN STORIES

The Ritual Roots of Ecumenical Life

J. NEIL ALEXANDER

The history of ecumenical relations between Lutherans and Episcopalians in the United States is a well-rehearsed tale of two churches. It is the story of two dance partners that twist and shout, pull each other close, step on one another's toes, but never fully let go of one another. At the end of each dance there is a courteous, celebratory bow that is an act of profound fellowship and reverence. I learned a couple of these dance steps when I was a Lutheran seminarian in the 1970s. I remember, for example, being drilled by one professor in the main points of theology among the Calvinists, the Zwinglians, the Wesleyans, and the Romans, among others; and while he pointed out the imperfections in these positions vis-à-vis Lutheran theology, at least these traditions had a theology. Episcopalians and other Anglicans, of course, were believed to have no theology worthy of discussion, a curious position indeed since the principal textbook for introduction to systematic theology was

written by John Macquarrie, the distinguished *Anglican* theologian.[1] This professor's position stood in stark contrast
with that of another professor who regularly organized
field trips to Trinity Episcopal Church in Columbia, where
in those days one could regularly be treated to the finest
liturgical preaching available in the midlands of South
Carolina.[2]

The church at the time was still pregnant with the
Lutheran Book of Worship (LBW). The first-year liturgy
class was concerned primarily with *The Service Book and
Hymnal, 1958* (SBH). Class notes from those years record
how the faculty lauded the great tradition of Lutheran
liturgical music: hymns, chorales, cantatas, and unparal-
leled organ literature for church use. Despite this great tradition, however, we learned that the largest percentage of
service music in the SBH was, in fact, Anglican chant, chosen
because of its accessibility for congregational use and its
durability for frequent repetition. So prevalent was the use
of Anglican service music, particularly Anglican chant,
among American Lutherans in those days, that I suspect it
would not be too difficult to prove that the singing Lutherans
were by and large singing more Anglican music than their
largely non-singing Episcopalian counterparts.

Another question that was the stuff of lively conversation and debate was the influence of the Book of Common
Prayer on the Common Service tradition of English-speaking
American Lutheranism. The final decades of the nineteenth century and the first couple of decades of the twentieth were for both Lutherans and Episcopalians a time of
rich liturgical fermentation. In both churches significant
scholars from a variety of theological disciplines stepped
forward to ply their trades in service to the worship of the
church. One need only mention the names of Henry Eyster
Jacobs and Edward Traill Horn among the Lutherans, and

William Augustus Muhlenburg and William Reed Huntington among the Episcopalians to make the point. The influence of the renewal movements that burst forth from the heart of nineteenth-century romanticism that had such a profound influence on Lutheran and Anglican churches in Germany and England, was now being felt in the United States.[3]

At the heart of these movements was the desire for a renewed ecclesiology. Post-enlightenment rationalism combined with American frontier individualism had struck at the roots of the traditional, and I believe biblical, view of the church as a new community in Christ whose common life is defined by word, water, wine and bread.[4] This longing for renewed ecclesiology spawned reforming movements both among Lutherans and Episcopalians. These efforts sought to re-center the life of the church around word and font and word and table as clearly as it was centered in word and pulpit. This ecclesial reform was not in the first place interested in liturgy and sacraments, but all inquiry into the nature of the church eventually leads to the core realities of her life: baptism, eucharist, and ministry. It is, of course, impossible to speak very long of these sacramental foci without spilling over into matters of liturgy, music, architecture, and the related arts. The reader might find it helpful to imagine a mobile with three large dangles (baptism, eucharist, and ministry) and many smaller ones (liturgy, music, architecture, etc.). When you jiggle one, they all begin to move.

In both traditions, these "high churchmen," if I may be permitted that somewhat Victorian expression, are properly so-called not because of any particular commitment to precious liturgy, to romantically retrieved medieval aesthetics, or to the spiritual muscularity of the gothic revival. They were high churchmen precisely because they possessed a high view of the church and placed enormous value on the centrality of baptism, eucharist, and ministry. Many who followed their lead found themselves sidetracked into matters of ritualism and liturgical antiquarianism. This could have been predicted, perhaps, yet it was the full expression of the church, or better, the expression of the fullness of the church, that was at the heart of the movement.

An explanatory note on terminology: A moment ago, I might well have said that these early leaders of modern liturgical renewal "placed enormous value on the centrality of word and sacrament." That is true enough, but it lacks, I believe, some essential precision. "Word and sacrament" is an old and cherished phrase dear to us all and, like all such phrases, its familiarity may be inoculating us from its full range of meaning. In my experience, "word" is too quickly reduced to "preaching," and "sacrament" too quickly is reduced to "holy communion." While both associations are true, perhaps even primary, both are richer than such quick reduction implies.

When I was a newly minted parish pastor of the North Carolina Synod of the Lutheran Church in America, in practical terms "word" meant "preacher," and "sacrament" meant that I could now "do communion." I soon found myself serving an old Augustana Synod parish in the New Jersey Synod with a rich sacramental piety, and a long tradition of catholic liturgy, evangelical preaching, and rich sacred music. The people committed to my pastoral care taught me so much about the church I could never have learned in seminary. This was a parish that kept lavish baptismal feasts long before the framers of the LBW urged the church in that direction. I confess that I arrived from seminary with a rather utilitarian view of the baptismal rite, but the people quickly helped me see that for them the sacrament of holy baptism was not a casual ceremony to be accomplished. It was the people of the parish who helped me understand something of what it meant to come among them as the bearer of a promising word and the public embodiment of a promising tradition. It was the people who taught me that leading their parades to the font, enfolding their children in my arms, getting everyone nearby soaking wet, smearing christic grease on baby's faces, and giving hot, burning candles to infants *was as much about word* as anything I could ever say from the pulpit!

It was this same congregation that taught me something about the sacrament of holy preaching. I entered the preaching ministry armed with Hebrew and Greek, drilled in exegesis, and coached in the preparation and delivery of sermons. In spite of my seminary formation, however, I arrived in my parish with a non-sacramental view preaching. As a novice preacher, I was focused on "what the text said" and "what I was going to say about it." The Sunday propers all contained some sort of "spiritual truth," I assumed, a "word to live by," and it was my job somehow to tell the folks about it. This all began to change one day about a year into my life in the parish. A member of the congregation invited me to join him for lunch at his workplace in New York City. He had arranged for a table for two by a wall of windows with a panoramic view of the surrounding skyscrapers. Once we had ordered our meal, he got right to the point: "Pastor, I want to talk with you about your preaching." I noticed that the look on his face and the tone of his voice did not match. "Your sermons are very interesting, pastor, but you preach the text, not the gospel. I don't come to church for information; I come to hear a saving word."

I feel certain that I responded to his exhortation, but I cannot remember whether I was agreeable or defensive.

What I do know is that our conversation set in motion an inquiry that continues unabated to this day: *How is it that I give people Jesus from the pulpit, using words that are the elements of his real and risen presence among us, just as I give them Jesus under the forms of bread and wine at the table?* My suggestion, therefore, that baptism, eucharist, and ministry might be a better way to speak of those things at the heart of the church's renewal (than simply the phrase "word and sacrament,") is an attempt to be faithful to the somewhat richer picture that inspired those on whose shoulders much of the modern liturgical and ecumenical movements first rested.

Now back to the larger story. These late-nineteenth- and early-twentieth-century scholars of church, sacraments, and liturgy, both Lutherans and Episcopalians, unquestionably set the table for the rich developments we continue to enjoy. Both of our churches will be indebted to them forever for their pioneering work. Before we follow the trajectory they launched for the twentieth century, it is probably important to remind ourselves, in outline, of some of what they inherited.

Lutherans and Anglicans have had awareness of each other's rites and theologies of baptism, eucharist, and ministry since the sixteenth century. This did not take the form of official ecumenical dialogues like those we have known in the latter half of the twentieth century. National identities, and English-German-Scandinavian language barriers, had at least as much to do with slowing the pace of ecumenical rapprochement as anything theological or ecclesial. It is, therefore, more useful to speak of a process of liturgical exchange that was there from the very beginning. I am convinced that part of the "comfort zone" Lutherans and Anglicans experience with each other is related to the fact that our reformers deeply loved and respected the liturgical inheritance of the western catholic tradition. Neither the Lutheran Reformation nor the Church of England's departure from the authority of the papacy was, in the first order, about sacraments and liturgy. In both cases liturgical reform came quickly, precisely because it was so central to the church's identity, but in neither case was the inherited liturgy the first cause of reform.

Both Doctor Luther and Archbishop Cranmer show abundant evidence of being reluctant reformers and caring pastors when it comes to liturgical matters. That is not to say, of course, that their protestant principles did not come into conflict with their catholic inheritance at any number of points. It is to say that if you read Dr. Luther's commentary in the *Formula Missae* of 1523 and the *Deutsche Messe* of 1526, not to mention the *Invocavit* sermons of 1522, you will find a hesitant hand in these matters.[5] Similarly, a careful analysis of the liturgical work of Archbishop Cranmer from the mid-1530s through the first Book of Common Prayer in 1549 and the second Prayer Book in 1552, will reveal a careful process of liturgical evolution that deeply respects the inherited tradition.[6] Although one can certainly find exceptions among Lutherans and Anglicans in the sixteenth century, even in the heat of anti-Roman, protestant sentiments, both churches maintained a love and respect for "the great tradition" and never sought to dismiss it out of hand as did many of the more radical reformers.

The first wave of liturgical exchange took place in the sixteenth century and moved in a Lutheran-to-Anglican direction. The influence of the Lutheran liturgical reform was transported to England largely by way of the *Kirchenordnungen* of Bugenhagen, Dietrich, Melanchthon, and Bucer.[7] One such church order, prepared for the evangelically sympathetic Catholic Archbishop of Cologne, Hermann von Wied, between 1543 and 1547, we know to have had a clear influence on Archbishop Cranmer's preparation of the *Order for Communion, 1548*, and the First Book of Common Prayer, 1549.[7] This Cologne Church Order provided Cranmer with the idea of a preparatory service for the Saturday before those Sundays on which communion was to be received, two lengthy exhortations on the proper preparation for and proper reception of communion, confession, comfortable words, and absolution, all before the Introit (the psalm chant that began the liturgy proper). These are but a few of the items that influenced the revision of the liturgy in England by way of the Lutheran church orders. Cranmer and his associates never adopted wholesale the more radical liturgical reform on the continent—Lutheran or Reformed—but the influence of the Lutheran church orders is unmistakable.

Another gift of the Lutheran tradition to the Anglican is Dr. Luther's *Taufbüchlein* revision of the thanksgiving over the water, lovingly known as "the flood prayer." In fact, Luther's recasting of the flood prayer has on balance faired better in revisions of the Book of Common Prayer (see BCP, pp. 306-307) than it has over the same period in the liturgical books of Lutheranism; and from an Anglican perspective, translating and adapting the flood prayer may well be Dr. Luther's most enduring, if not most important, contribution to liturgical revision.

Perhaps the clearest difference between the Lutheran and Anglican traditions in the sixteenth century relates to the matter of celebrating the eucharist. Both traditions eventually had to deal with the theological and pastoral problems they inherited in the canon of the medieval Roman mass. Luther's solution was to isolate the words of institution (the "bare *verba*"), leaving only the slightest hint of thanksgiving and removing any lingering sense of supplication together. Luther's evangelical reinterpretation of the words of institution have long struck me as being among the great theological treasures of the reformation.[9] At the same time, it seems only fair to point out that Luther's reduction of eucharistic praying to little more than the bare *verba* brings to its obvious conclusion a trajectory that was launched in the fourth century by Bishop Ambrose of Milan.

It was Bishop Ambrose who in his major work on the sacraments responded to the question that has dogged western catholic thought from that day to this. "So let us explain," Ambrose wrote, "how that which is bread can be the body of Christ. And by what words and by whose sayings does consecration take place? The Lord Jesus! For all the other things which are said in the earlier parts are said by the bishop: praise is offered to God; prayer is made for the people, when the time comes for the venerated sacrament to be accomplished, the bishop no longer uses his own words, but uses the words of Christ to accomplish this sacrament.... Before it is consecrated, it is bread; but when the words of Christ are added, it is the body of Christ.... And before the words of Christ, the cup is full of wine and water; when the words of Christ have been employed, blood is created, which redeems his people. So you see in what ways the word of Christ has power to change everything."[10]

Bishop Ambrose's solution became the tipping point that launched a new way of thinking about how to interpret the eucharistic action. Before Ambrose, the overwhelming body of evidence points to the bread and wine "becoming for us the body and blood of our Lord Jesus Christ" as a consequence of the church's faithful prayer of thanksgiving. Although a fair amount of variation exists in early eucharistic prayers, some fairly stable theological ideas are at work.

Principal among these is what I call the "syntax of eucharistic praying." Building upon the ancient meal prayers and statutory blessings of the Jewish tradition, early Christians seem to have maintained a simple prayer form that was used not only at the Lord's table for eucharistic prayer, but appears to have been foundational throughout the life of prayer. This simple structure—thanksgiving, supplication, doxology—provides the basis for prayer that is both deeply theological and highly practical. The theological idea could not be more straightforward: in response to the creating, redeeming, and sustaining actions of God towards us, our first and only meaningful response is gratitude. Gratitude for grace, we might say. It is on the basis of making that thank-offering to God, that we, as individuals or as faith communities, dare to supplicate, dare to place our needs and desires before God in prayer. Then, having dared to supplicate, not on our own merits, but in thankful remembrance of the graciousness of God, we hedge our bets, as it were, in a profound declaration of doxology: *Come what may, O lover of souls, you alone are God, holy and true, and to you belongs all honor, praise, and glory, from before time and forevermore.*

The position of Bishop Ambrose represents a major blow to the profound simplicity and theological clarity of early eucharistic praying. By focusing on the words of institution, Ambrose sets in motion a new way of thinking that will, over time, diminish thanksgiving for the grace-filled benefits of our creation and redemption, and will recenter the eucharist on supplication, not only for the consecration of the bread and wine, but supplication for pretty much everything. By the time the developed Roman canon of the mass is in place—a document that cannot be dated with precision but for our purposes we'll say late sixth century—the thanksgiving has been almost totally eclipsed by supplication.

This creates for the church an unusual theological problem—a laundry list of supplications without any theological foundation, that is to say thanksgiving, upon which to make that supplication. There are several results of this problem that should be noted. When supplication no longer has as its underpinning the thankful praise of the people of God, then another starting point must be sought. In my judgment, this defect in the church's principal prayer—thanksgiving playing second fiddle to supplication—opened the way in the Middle Ages to the making of theologies that focused upon the priest as the chief consecrator of the eucharist; not the word, nor the thankful praise of the Christian assembly, but the priest held the consecratory power.

This went hand-in-hand with changing theologies about the nature of the church and the role of the baptized in the eucharistic assembly. Over time the picture shifts from thanksgiving centered in the people at prayer to supplication that only a priest is qualified to offer, thereby reducing the laity more and more to a position as spectators in their own rites. I am not naïve enough to believe that the loss of thanksgiving in the central prayer of the church and the resultant centrality of supplication is to blame for all of the theological and pastoral problems of the church in the Middle Ages. I do believe, however, that the impact of this has been severely understated in the general historical literature of the period. The fact that in the churches of the eastern rites the eucharistic prayers never lost the priority of thanksgiving over supplication is surely telling. The eastern rite *anaphoras* (eucharistic prayers) never centered an act of consecration in the words of institution alone, but balanced the words of institution with an explicit invocation of the Holy Spirit (*epiklesis*). The eastern rites also have tended to think of the entire eucharistic action as consecratory as opposed to assigning consecration to a particular part of the great prayer. Although there are other factors for sure, these aspects contributed greatly to the fact that eastern christianity has never been plagued with non-participatory rites to the degree that was known in the Latin west. The eastern rites never suffered from theologies of priestly power concentrated in one order of ministry to the exclusion of the assembly to the same degree that was known in the Latin west, they have been spared that great aberration of the catholic tradition known as "low mass," and they have escaped western theology's relentless fascination with the shelf-life of the real presence.

What I find interesting about this is that Bishop Ambrose in the fourth century isolates the words of institution as consecratory words and gives a defense of that position that to my ears could well have been written by Dr. Luther. Bishop Ambrose's position is a departure from much of what had preceded him and contributes to the obsession in western eucharistic theology with the "moment of consecration" and who possesses the power to effect it. This line of thought, while it certainly didn't *cause* the liturgical, sacramental, and theological havoc of the millennium between Ambrose and Luther, unquestionably contributed to it.

In the end, Dr. Luther looks to the same point—the words of institution—and with a similar argument tries to bring to an end what Bishop Ambrose had launched a millennium before. In defense of Dr. Luther's reform of the canon of the mass, some have been inclined to argue that his "liturgical surgery" that left exposed the words of institution was, in fact, radical surgery based on his evangelical insights. In others words, Luther intentionally departed from what had gone before him. By contrast, I am more inclined to argue that Dr. Luther simply took an understanding of consecration by the power of the word (achieved by the recitation of the words of institution) that had been brewing in the Latin rite since Bishop Ambrose, and pushed it toward its obvious conclusion. To put this another way, some would look at Luther's isolation of the bare *verba* and say, "Oh, how protestant." I, by contrast, look at it and say, "Oh, how catholic."

The alternative to Dr. Luther's "bare *verba*" approach would have been the creation of an evangelical eucharistic prayer that blessed God "for our creation, preservation, and all the blessings of this life; but above all for God's immeasurable love in the redemption of the world by our Lord Jesus Christ, for the means of grace, and for the hope of glory," as the general thanksgiving of the Book of Common Prayer (101) so eloquently puts it. An evangelical eucharistic prayer might have restored the priority of thanksgiving over supplication and thereby reminded us that it is always God who is blessed, always God who is the object of blessing. Whether we are speaking of bread and wine, marriages, buildings, our time and our possessions, or corned beef and beer, these things are blessed (set apart for our use) as a consequence of our having blessed God for them, held them before God in thankful remembrance, and made a thank offering in response to God's goodness. As one colleague often quipped, "When you bless something, what you are doing is saying something nice to God about it."

In 1523, in his first attempt to reform the liturgy, Ulrich Zwingli sought to create just such a eucharistic prayer. After the eucharistic dialogue and sanctus, he proposed four prayers that were to be prayed in place of the canon of the Roman mass. The first called to mind the history of salvation that came to a climax in the recitation of the Lord's prayer. The second prayer contained a hint of an invocation of the Holy Spirit and prayed that those receiving the Lord's supper might be quickened by the Spirit's power. The third prayer confessed Jesus Christ and recalled his atoning work, while the fourth prayer was a prayer for the worthy reception of the sacrament that led to the words of institution.[11]

As you might imagine, Zwingli's good deed did not go unpunished. It was too radical for the conservatives who desired a solution more like Luther, and not radical enough for others who seemed to have thought that it was still too much like the medieval mass they were trying to escape. What we don't know is how the faithful felt about it, but I suspect it might have faired better there than among those making the decisions.

In shaping the eucharistic rite of the reformed Church of England, Archbishop Cranmer led the church through a series of graduated changes. In 1548, Cranmer provided an order for communion. This was not so much a eucharistic rite as it was a procedure for receiving Holy Communion, sort of a "service within the service," "to be inserted in the Latin Mass of the English Use after the consecration of the elements and the communion of the priest."[12] Its purpose was to restore the cup to the laity and to encourage the more frequent reception of communion by those who received no more than once a year, if that often. This order consisted of a number of elements, the descendants of which can still be seen in the Book of Common Prayer of today. An invitation to communion ("Ye that do truly and earnestly repent you of your sin..."), the confession of sin ("Almighty God, Father of our Lord Jesus Christ, maker of all things, judge of all men...."), an absolution ("Almighty

God, our heavenly Father, who of his great mercy hath promised forgiveness of sins to all those who with hearty repentance and true faith turn unto him..."), the comfortable words of scripture to assure the faithful of their forgiveness in Jesus Christ; and a prayer of humble access ("We do not presume to come to this thy table, O merciful Lord, trusting in our own righteousness, but in thy manifold and great mercies..."). All of these elements were incorporated in the eucharistic rite of the first Book of Common Prayer of 1549.

Although the eucharist of the first prayer book shows many of the marks of both the Lutheran church orders and the influence of the reformed tradition on the continent, it also bears marks of continuity with the medieval Roman canon. After the eucharistic dialogue, the proper preface, and the sanctus, the rite continues with a long, supplicatory prayer that lacks any serious attempt at thanksgiving. This leads into a rehearsal of the saving work of Christ and an invocation of the Holy Spirit for the consecration of the elements, leading directly to the words of institution. The prayer continues after the words of institution to an *anamnesis*-like section that captures some elements of thanksgiving, but continues to be weak in its expression of the fullness of thanksgiving as the theological foundation for the entirety of the eucharistic prayer.

While containing a great deal of evangelical language, the ritual structure of the prayer continues to suggest only a partially reformed understanding of the eucharist. This is understandable, of course, because as noted earlier, liturgy and sacraments were not, in the first order, the front-burner issues of the Church of England's departure from the authority of the papacy. There were still plenty of clergy and people in the Church of England who saw little reason to change the liturgy they had inherited, save perhaps its translation into English.

The Prayer Book of 1549 was only the first step in Archbishop Cranmer's reform. The second Book of Common Prayer came out only three years later, in 1552, and there we see the full flowering of the reformed influence on the English Church. In this rite, after a brief recollection of the saving work of Christ, containing no element of praise or thanksgiving, there is a prayer for worthy reception that ends with the words of institution. The rite then proceeds immediately to the reception of the elements, implying (and I believe ritualizing) a highly receptionist view that is totally dependent upon the faith of the believer and suggesting that apart from such faith there is no sacrament. If the eucharistic service proper left any doubts about its receptionist quality, a rubric in the book settles the question: "Whatever bread and wine are left over are to be given to the Curate for his own use."

Although what I am about to say requires a few more caveats than can easily be managed in a brief essay, it is not unreasonable to think of the 1549 Book in continuity with its catholic past, despite the introduction of some evangelical elements; and to think of the 1552 Book as a skip across the more conservative position of the Lutheran tradition and indicative of the full bloom of Zwinglian-esque receptionist theology. This sort of either/or position—more "catholic" than the Lutherans or as "protestant" as the Zwinglians—was not a position that the English Church could long sustain.

In 1559, the new monarch, Elizabeth I, released a third Book of Common Prayer, the Book that often bears her name.[13] The Queen was a deeply religious woman who showed evidence of being well read in both catholic and protestant theology. She was astute enough as a politician to understand that holding her kingdom together meant holding the Church of England together, and that meant finding a *via media*, a middle way, that honored the substance of England's catholic heritage while claiming the evangelical witness of the protestant reformation.

With respect to the eucharist, Elizabeth ordered several small but effective changes in her prayer book as a way of creating this *via media*. What is at stake here, of course, is the proper understanding of the role of faith in the sacramental transaction. In what sense is there an objective understanding of the presence of Christ in the elements of bread and wine, and what is the role of faith in apprehending that presence? Elizabeth's most notable innovation combined the "catholic" words of administration from the 1549 Book ("The body of our Lord Jesus Christ, which was given for thee, preserve thy body and soul unto everlasting life") with the more "protestant" words from the 1552 Book ("Take and eat this, in remembrance that Christ died for thee, and feed on him in thy heart by faith with thanksgiving"). Elizabeth thereby merges two opposing views and creates a middle way between them. Taking a position that is more nearly like the Lutheran position than it is to any other, Elizabeth maintains with the more protestant side a clear role for the faith of the believer in the reception of the sacrament, while at the same time, with Dr. Luther, she gives the edge to the catholic conviction of the objective presence of Christ in the elements of bread and wine, as a gift of grace upon which to cling in full assurance when personal faith is weak and most in need of the sacrament. I am not the first Anglican theologian who has come to the conclusion that, at least with respect to the eucharist, Her Sovereign Majesty Elizabeth I, was a Lutheran, or something very nearly like one.

The attempt to stake out a *via media* in these and so many other matters, has been "the bane and blessing, the pain and pleasure" of the Anglican way. There always have been, and there continue to be, Anglicans who cling to old catholic ways that would make many Roman Catholics uncomfortable. At the same time there are evangelicals within the Anglican fold that would make many a protestant uneasy, if not downright frightened. But Anglicanism's constant search and seizure of a middle way lands most of us in a comfort zone not unlike that of the Lutheran tradition, a place that seeks to preserve the best of both the catholic and evangelical traditions.

This has been particularly true of the Episcopal Church in the United States. Prior to the American Revolution, Anglican churches in the colonies were missionary outposts of the Church of England and under the pastoral supervision of the Bishop of London. The English Prayer Book of 1662 provided the form and order of the church's worship. In the eighteenth century, Anglicanism in England and Scotland experienced a resurgence of interest in the ancient church and the writings of the fathers, and a love affair developed between Anglicanism and the churches of the Christian east. The story of the love affair is exciting at many levels, but well outside the scope of this essay. Suffice to say that this love of the ancient church, and the liturgy and spirituality of Eastern Orthodoxy, added still other partners into the mix of the Anglican conversation. No longer are we talking only of finding a middle way between the poles of our western catholic and protestant experiences. Now we have added the writings of the ancient church that seem to speak of a catholic faith that was broad, gracious, and inclusive, and possessed of a generosity of spirit that somehow was lost through the centuries. To this was added an increasingly deep affection and respect for the theological and spiritual depth of the Orthodox traditions. It was from this highly enriched form of eighteenth-century Anglicanism, mediated through the tiny Episcopal Church of Scotland, that the Episcopal Church in the United States developed. The first American Book of Common Prayer was issued in 1789, the same year of our nation's Constitution, and benefited from the richness of eighteenth-century Anglicanism in ways that the English Church with its continued insistence on its seventeenth-century Prayer Book has to this day never fully enjoyed.

We must note particularly the eucharistic prayer of the 1789 American Prayer Book, which benefited enormously from the marvelous patristic and Eastern rite influences of the eighteenth century. For the first time in the history of the Anglican tradition, at least since 1549, a full eucharistic prayer stood at the center of the rite. It is a prayer that has at its heart a clear thanksgiving for our creation and redemption in Jesus Christ that climaxes in the recitation of the words of institution. The prayer continues by calling to thankful remembrance the sufferings, death, resurrection, and promised coming of our Lord Jesus Christ as the only basis upon we can offer anything whatsoever to God, even our praise and thanksgiving. Having dared, on the basis of the merits of the savior, to offer to God the sacrifice of praise and thanksgiving, the prayer beseeches God to bless and sanctify, by word and the Holy Spirit, the gifts of bread and wine that we may be partakers of his body and blood.[14]

The restoration of a full eucharistic prayer (as much by historical accident as by intent, perhaps), has spared the Episcopal Church in the United States from the incessant re-fighting of the protestant reformation that continues to plague other parts of world Anglicanism when the topic of eucharistic theology re-emerges. The prayer enshrines an evangelical-catholic theology of the eucharist that satisfies all but the most ideologically-driven viewpoints.

We have noted the dependence of Archbishop Cranmer upon Dr. Luther and the church orders of sixteenth-century Lutheranism when he set out to reform the worship of the Church of England. Although there were other sources available to him, the influence of the Lutheran sources is unquestionable and the reformed liturgy of the Church of England would have looked very different if the Lutheran materials had not been spread out on the Archbishop's desk. As time went on, other liturgical exchanges between the traditions took place to shape our common life and help to create the "comfort zone" that exists between us in these matters. We know, for example, that English-speaking Lutherans in London in the eighteenth century used various orders from the Book of Common Prayer for their services rather than simply translations of the German Lutheran equivalents, and that similar practices were known among Lutherans in the colonies in those cases where some worship in English was necessary even if German continued to be the principal language of the congregation.

As a former pastor of the Evangelical Lutheran Church in Canada, I was a frequent visitor to the historic Lutheran parishes in the maritime province of Nova Scotia where communities of German Lutherans ministered to and alongside British loyalists, and found it necessary to have their own version of the Book of Common Prayer to complement their German liturgical services. Although still bearing many of the longtime marks of Lutheran liturgy, it can hardly be doubted that the framers of the Common Service[15] tradition looked to the Book of Common Prayer for guidance on how to talk to God in English. The Lutheran *Common Service Book* adopted wholesale the Prayer Book translations of many of the historical collects and prayers, as well as of the creeds and biblical canticles. As Professor

Luther D. Reed, the great Lutheran liturgiologist of the middle part of the twentieth century, put it, "In supplying the English dress for much of the material common to both communions, the Prayer Book repaid in the nineteenth century the debt which its framers owed to the Lutheran church orders of the sixteenth century....The general spirit and tone of the Common Service and the Common Service Book were definitely influenced by the character and quality of the older English liturgy. They expressed the same churchly feeling in forms of incomparable literary value."[16]

We noted earlier that in the late-nineteenth- and early-twentieth-centuries significant fermentation was going on in both churches around these matters. Some significant figures and their protégés in both churches were very much aware of each other's work. William Augustus Muhlenberg, the Episcopal descendant of Henry Melchior Muhlenberg, was deeply interested in, and influenced by, his Lutheran roots. Somewhat later, Luther Dotterer Reed held the Book of Common Prayer in high regard. A recent doctoral dissertation, in a hard-fought argument, has sought to redeem Luther Dotterer Reed from the frequent accusation that he was a closet Anglican (largely due to the fact that the *Service Book and Hymnal, 1958*, of which he was a principal architect, has something of an Anglican liturgical aesthetic about it), and to prove to the contrary that Reed was a card-carrying confessional Lutheran of the first order.[17] Frankly, it never occurred to me to think that Luther Reed was anything but a faithful Lutheran pastor, theologian, and seminary professor. At the same time, it is hard not to detect Reed's strong affection for the Anglican liturgical tradition. Reed's love of the language of the Prayer Book and his personal affinity for a sort of romanticized Anglican ecclesial aesthetic is unmistakable.[18]

At the time the 1960s were in full blush, the cultural shifts in American life, the progress of the ecumenical movement, and perhaps most important of all, the Second Vatican Council of the Roman Church, all combined to jumpstart another round of liturgical renewal. This time something new happened. The decades of the 1930s, 1940s, and 1950s were times of rebirth in historical studies, particularly related to liturgy and sacraments. For much of the time since the reformation, historians of Christian worship had spent most of their efforts rallying the data to support the status quo of their church's theological positions. The gradual freeing of Roman Catholic scholarship in the decades before Vatican II, and the gradual shifts in our ecumenical conversations that emphasized our likenesses rather than our differences, created the climate for the free exchange of common ground. No longer were we sneaking peeks at each other's work under the cover of darkness. Now we were engaging one another in the full light of day. Without turning our backs on our denominational histories, we were pursuing common history, common prayers, common ritual structures, and common theologies that could be described less clearly as Roman, or Lutheran, or Anglican, or Reformed, but as apostolic, catholic, and evangelical.

This period of liturgical and sacramental renewal through which most of us have lived, or perhaps survived, is not in the first order about liturgy and sacraments. It is about the church, that new community in Christ once again being reborn in the power of the Holy Spirit and finding its center in baptism, eucharist, and ministry. It is no accident that the 1979 Book of Common Prayer of the Episcopal Church and the *Lutheran Book of Worship* (used by the majority of North American Lutherans) bear so many similarities. They both embody a kind of practical ecumenism that grows out of a kind of practical ecclesiology. They are more alike than they are different because we are more alike than we are different, and as long as baptism, eucharist, and ministry remain at the heart of our common life, I can see no reason to believe that it will not continue to be so, until He comes.

NOTES

[1] John Macquarrie, *Principles of Christian Theology*, Second Edition (New York: Charles Scribner's Sons, 1977).

[2] Trinity Church, now Trinity Cathedral, is the seat of the Episcopal Bishop of Upper South Carolina. The Cathedral is located across the street from the Capitol of South Carolina and it has played a significant role in the history of Columbia in particular, and the State of South Carolina more generally.

[3] A particularly engaging treatment of this material may be found in R. William Franklin, *Nineteenth Century Churches: The History of New Catholicism in Württemberg, England, and France* (New York: Garland, 1987).

[4] I have argued this more extensively in "In Time and Community: Individualism and the Body of Christ," in *Time and Community: Essays in Honor of Thomas J. Talley*, ed. J. Neil Alexander (Washington, D.C.: Pastoral Press, 1990).

[5] English texts of *Formula Missae et Communionis, 1523,* and *Deutsche Messe, 1526,* may be found in Martin Luther, *Luther's Works* [American Edition], Vol. 53 (Philadelphia: Fortress, various dates); and the *Invocavit Sermons, 1522,* Vol. 51.

[6] There is a vast amount of literature on the liturgical reforms of Thomas Cranmer and the early Prayer Books of the Anglican tradition. A useful place to begin is Geoffrey J. Cuming, *A History of Anglican Liturgy,* Second Edition (London: Macmillan, 1982); and E. C. Ratcliff's "The Liturgical Work of Archbishop Cranmer" in A. H. Couratin and D. H. Tripp, eds., *Liturgical Studies/E. C. Ratcliff* (London: SPCK, 1976).

[7] The German texts of the church orders are available in critical editions. For a fine discussion in English of the influence of the church orders on subsequent Lutheran liturgy, see Frank C. Senn's, *Christian Liturgy: Catholic and Evangelical* (Minneapolis: Fortress Press, 1997), 323-356.

[8] The relevant portions of these texts, together with commentary, are most conveniently found in R. C. D. Jasper and G. J. Cuming, *Prayers of the Eucharist: Early and Reformed* (New York: Pueblo, 1987), 219-249. Another convenient edition of the Anglican texts is found in Colin Buchanan, ed., *Eucharistic Liturgies of Edward VI: A Text for Students* (Grove Liturgical Study 34) (Nottingham, England: Grove Books, 1983).

[9] This may be seen in a variety of treatises and sermons. The fullest exposition of this aspect of Luther's theology may be found in his *A Treatise on the New Testament, that is, the Holy Mass, 1520. Luther's Works*, Vol. 35, 75-112. A brief source is *Luther's Large Catechism, Part Five: The Lord's Supper,* in *The Book of Concord: The Confessions of the Evangelical Lutheran Church*, ed. Theodore G. Tappert (Philadelphia: Fortress Press, 1959), 447-457.

[10] Ambrose of Milan, *On the Sacraments (De sacramentis).* The relevant passages can be found in Jasper and Cuming, *Prayers,* 114-146. See also, Edward Yarnold, *The Awe-Inspiring Rites of Initiation: Baptismal Homilies of the Fourth Century* (Slough [U.K.]: St. Paul Publications, 1972), 133-141.

[11] The prayers of Zwingli may be seen in Jasper and Cuming, *Prayers,* 181-188.

[12] See note 8 above.

[13] The best edition for study purposes is *The Book of Common Prayer, 1559: The Elizabethan Prayer Book,* ed. John E. Booty (Charlottesville, Virginia: The University of Virginia Press, 1976) (published for The Folger Shakespeare Library). It includes a fine historical essay by Booty.

[14] The literature on the history and theology of eucharistic praying is enormous. A brief review of the main themes, with attention to the Anglican Prayer Books, is found in Byron D. Stuhlman, *A Good and Joyful Thing: The Evolution of the Eucharistic Prayer* (New York: Church Publishing, 2000).

[15] The Common Service was created in 1888 by representatives of several Lutheran Churches as a model rite for English-speaking Lutherans in North America. It formed the basis of *The Common Service Book, 1918. The Service Book and Hymnal, 1958,* also stands in the Common Service tradition.

[16] Luther D. Reed, *The Lutheran Liturgy: A Study of the Common Liturgy of the Lutheran Church in America* (Philadelphia: Muhlenberg Press, 1947), 195.

[17] Ronald Miller, What Language Shall I Borrow? Three of the Vernaculars of Luther Dotterer Reed (Unpublished Ph.D. dissertation, Drew University, 2000).

[18] This is particularly visible in Dr. Reed's volume of pastoral liturgy, *Worship: A Study in Corporate Devotion* (Philadelphia: Muhlenberg Press, 1959).

6

BISHOPS: WHY BOTHER?

The Chicago-Lambeth Quadrilateral as
Anglican Ecumenical Starting Point*

ROBERT BOAK SLOCUM

OVERVIEW

The question about bishops and apostolic ministry in an ecumenical context—like all ecumenical questions for Episcopalians and other Anglicans—is properly referred to the Chicago-Lambeth Quadrilateral at the outset of discussion. The Chicago-Lambeth Quadrilateral has served as the primary reference point and working document of the Anglican Communion for ecumenical Christian reunion. It identifies four essential elements for Christian unity in terms of scriptures, creeds, sacraments, and the historic episcopate. The Quadrilateral is based on the ecumenical thought and leadership of William Reed Huntington, an Episcopal priest who was the moving force behind approval of the Quadrilateral by the House of Bishops of the 1886

---

* This essay is a revised version of an article that appeared in the *Journal of Ecumenical Studies* (Fall, 1996, copyright 1996), reprinted with permission from the *Journal of Ecumenical Studies*.

General Convention of the Episcopal Church. Huntington has been described as "the Episcopal Church's leading proponent of Church unity and prayer book revision" in the late nineteenth century.[1] The Quadrilateral was subsequently approved with modifications by the Lambeth Conference of 1888 and finally reaffirmed in its Lambeth form by the General Convention of the Episcopal Church in 1895. The Quadrilateral has been at the heart of Anglican ecumenical discussions and relationships since its approval. Interpretation of the meaning of the Quadrilateral has undergone considerable development in its more than 100-year history. This essay considers the unfolding and development of the Quadrilateral in terms of official church statements and the writings of other Anglican theologians. Particular attention is given to the meaning of the historic episcopate (which has required and received the most attention) to answer the question why we "bother" and care so much about the historic episcopate relative to ecumenical relationships. The Episcopal understanding of the historic episcopate is quite possibly the most challenging point for engagement with the Evangelical Lutheran Church in America to discover common mission. The future ecumenical relationships of the Episcopal Church and the cause of church unity with respect to Anglicanism will likewise hinge on the Quadrilateral as developed and applied.

HISTORICAL BACKGROUND AND INTRODUCTION

The Chicago-Lambeth Quadrilateral states the four Anglican essentials for a reunited Christian church. The statement was originally approved by the House of Bishops of the 1886 General Convention of the Episcopal Church meeting in Chicago and subsequently approved by the

Lambeth Conference of 1888 with modifications. The statement became the primary ecumenical working document for the Anglican Communion.

The Chicago version of the Quadrilateral offers an ecumenical statement of purpose and introduction that states that the Episcopal Church is "ready in the spirit of love and humility to forego all preferences of her own" concerning things of human ordering or choice "relating to modes of worship and discipline, or to traditional customs." The Episcopal Church "does not seek to absorb other Communions, but rather, co-operating with them on the basis of a common Faith and Order, to discountenance schism, to heal the wounds of the Body of Christ, and to promote the charity which is the chief of Christian graces and the visible manifestation of Christ to the world."[2] However, the statement of purpose warns, Christian unity

> ...can be restored only by the return of all Christian communions to the principles of unity exemplified by the undivided Catholic Church during the first ages of its existence; which principles we believe to be the substantial deposit of Christian Faith and Order committed by Christ and his Apostles to the Church unto the end of the world, and therefore incapable of compromise or surrender by those who have been ordained to be its stewards and trustees for the common and equal benefit of all men.[3]

The Chicago statement then lists the four "inherent parts of this sacred deposit," which are "essential" for the restoration of Christian unity:

> 1. The Holy Scriptures of the Old and New Testament as the revealed Word of God.
> 2. The Nicene Creed as the sufficient statement of the Christian Faith.
> 3. The two Sacraments,—Baptism and the Supper of the Lord,—ministered with unfailing use of Christ's words of institution and of the elements ordained by Him.

> 4. The Historic Episcopate, locally adapted in the
> methods of its administration to the varying needs of
> the nations and peoples called of God into the unity of
> His Church.[4]

The Quadrilateral was not enacted by the House of
Deputies at the 1886 General Convention in Chicago, but
it was "incorporated in a general plan referred for study
and action to a newly created Joint Commission on Christian
Reunion." It was passed in a modified form as "Resolution
II" of the Lambeth Conference of 1888. At Lambeth the
four essential and "inherent parts" of the sacred deposit of
the faith were termed "Articles." The introductory statement of purpose of the Chicago version of the Quadrilateral
was deleted and replaced by a simple statement that "the
following Articles supply a basis on which approach may
be by God's blessing made towards Home Reunion."[5]

The Lambeth modifications include language from Article
VI of the Articles of Religion that the scriptures of the First
and Second Testaments contain "all things necessary to
salvation." The Lambeth version also states that the scriptures provide "the rule and ultimate standard of faith." The
Lambeth resolution affirms the Nicene Creed as the "sufficient statement of the Christian faith," but it also adds the
"Apostles' Creed, as the Baptismal Symbol" to the creedal
article of the Quadrilateral. The Lambeth version adds the
statement that the dominical sacraments of baptism and
the Lord's Supper were "ordained by Christ Himself." The
article concerning the historic episcopate was not altered
at Lambeth.[6] Gillian R. Evans has noted that "the bishops
of 1888 saw their 'articles' as serving their ecumenical purpose best by saying the minimum, so as to be 'free from all
questions of doubtful controversy' and thus acceptable as
widely as possible."[7]

The Chicago version of the Quadrilateral continued for
some time to be the "official" basis for ecumenical activity

by the Episcopal Church. The Episcopal Church's Commission on Christian Unity was continued by resolutions at the 1889 and 1892 General Conventions, which authorized the Commission "to confer with all or any similar commissions for the restoration of the unity of the Church on the basis of those things declared essential elements of such basis [for reunion] by the House of Bishops" at the Chicago General Convention of 1886. Finally, in 1895, the Commission on Christian Unity was continued with the goal of seeking Christian unity on the basis of "the principles enunciated throughout the Declaration of the House of Bishops made at Chicago in 1886, and as re-affirmed by the Lambeth Conference of 1888."[8] Thus, for the first time, in 1895, the entire General Convention of the Episcopal Church affirmed and owned the Quadrilateral in the form in which it had been finalized at Lambeth in 1888.

DIFFERENT PERSPECTIVES AND AGENDAS CONCERNING THE QUADRILATERAL

The fact of an official statement of principles for ecumenical Christian reunion in any form was a major first step for the churches of the Anglican Communion. However, there have been different understandings of the nature and purpose of the Quadrilateral from its inception. John Woolverton notes in his 1984 article on the Quadrilateral and the Lambeth Conference reactions to the Quadrilateral in its first century:

> Behind the constant reiterations of the four points has been a debate about whether the Quadrilateral was a *terminus ad quem*, that is a conclusion to which unity talks should proceed or whether it was a *terminus a quo*, an agreement to be reached before we would commence to talk about unity with others and from which greater demands for agreement and conformity would naturally follow.[9]

Different goals and purposes for the Quadrilateral can be seen in the Chicago General Convention of 1886 and the Lambeth Conference of 1888. The Quadrilateral was first proposed by William Reed Huntington (1838-1909), an Episcopal priest, scholar, and leader of the House of Deputies. Prior to the Chicago General Convention, he proposed the Quadrilateral in his 1870 book, *The Church-Idea: An Essay Towards Unity.*[10]

Huntington wanted "to make Anglicanism the basis of a Church of the Reconciliation," but he felt it was "necessary to determine what Anglicanism pure and simple is." In this regard, he recognized a sharp distinction between Anglicanism and the current practice of the Church of England. Huntington noted that Anglicanism must be stripped of "the picturesque costume which English life has thrown around it." In contrast, he concluded that the true Anglican position lies "foursquare" on the Holy Scriptures "as the Word of God," the "Primitive Creeds as the Rule of Faith," the "two Sacraments ordained by Christ himself," and the "Episcopate as the key-stone of Governmental Unity." Huntington blamed the "English State-Church" for having "muffled these first principles in a cloud of non-essentials," causing "the loss of half her children." In view of the English muddle of Anglicanism, he asked, rhetorically, "what if it can be shown that here in America we have an opportunity to give that [Anglican] principle the only fair trial it has ever had?"[11]

Huntington's purpose was neither confessional nor limited to a particular ethnic heritage. Woolverton finds that Huntington wanted his four "points" to provide the basis to "draw attention to those essentials around which all churches might eventually unite"; to "overcome the high church/low church divisions in the Anglican communion" by a return to the fundamentals without "insisting upon any interpretation of scripture, creeds, sacraments, and above all episcopacy"; and to "persuade his own Episcopal church to become for America the 'Church of the Reconciliation.'"[12]

Huntington was anything but confessional in his approach. J. Robert Wright has noted that Huntington believed American national church unification "was to be accomplished on the basis of the Quadrilateral's four points *rather than* upon the time-honored quasi-confessional Anglican doctrinal basis of the Thirty-Nine Articles."[13] Huntington states in The Church-Idea that the articles should "not continue to be considered. . .one of the essentials of the Anglican position." He was also willing to dispense with the Anglican Prayer Book tradition of uniformity in worship.[14]

At the 1907 General Convention, Huntington's efforts to remove the Thirty-Nine Articles from the Episcopal Book of Common Prayer and to write the Quadrilateral into the preamble of the Episcopal Church Constitution were unsuccessful.[15] Nevertheless, he definitely influenced the understanding of the Quadrilateral at the Chicago General Convention in 1886. Evans noted that the bishops at the Chicago Convention were concerned with reunion "of a diversity of Christian communions in their own land, rather than with the communion of Anglican churches scattered throughout the world. They addressed themselves 'especially to our fellow-Christians of the different Communions in this land.' They spoke of a 'Christian unity' of 'all Christian communions.'"[16] The bishops at Chicago followed Huntington's lead.

The bishops at the Lambeth Conference of 1888, however, saw the Quadrilateral as the basis for "Home Reunion" of *English-speaking* peoples of various Christian faiths throughout the world. Henry Chadwick has stated, "By Home Reunion the English bishops meant the reconciliation of Protestant Nonconformists to the ministry and liturgy of the Church of England, or, in other words, the old ideal of a 'national' church with essential marks of Catholic continuity but including all Christians in one Christian nation in allegiance to the Crown."[17] To achieve this goal of an English-speaking Home Reunion, Chadwick explained, "The Quadrilateral stated minimum conditions for establishing even partial and imperfect communion, and stripped things down to that skeletal structure which perhaps a moderate Nonconformist might think possible as a basis for discussion."[18]

> Similarly, Evans notes that the bishops at Lambeth had an "ecumenical intention," but we need to be clear about the way they saw it. The Quadrilateral was a statement of the foundation principles of an Anglican church. . .in a British Empire which still confidently embraced much of the world and where it was possible to talk of "Home Reunion," that is, to put first the practical need to hold together Anglican churches in widely differing conditions all over the world.[19]

The goals of the Lambeth Conference for the Quadrilateral were an imperial and ethnic unity of English-speaking Christians, while the Chicago General Convention sought a national unity of all Christians. From the beginning, there were differing goals for the Quadrilateral. The sharing of common mission by Lutherans and Episcopalians would certainly be consistent with the hopes of the bishops in Chicago.

DEVELOPMENT AND UNFOLDING OF THE QUADRILATERAL: ANGLICAN AND EPISCOPAL STATEMENTS CONCERNING THE "HISTORIC EPISCOPATE"

There was a growing understanding of the meaning and application of the Quadrilateral in the years following its framing. Evans notes that when the framers of the Chicago-Lambeth Quadrilateral offered the four articles as a contribution to ecumenical understanding, they "fed them into a process in which they *must* undergo change and development in expression in order the better to state the central truths they sought to encapsulate."[20] This process of development is most evident concerning the historic episcopate.

The Quadrilateral's article on the episcopate certainly needed development. Arthur Vogel, a bishop in the Episcopal Church, stated that the historic episcopate is "the most disputed element of the Quadrilateral" and that "the terse statement of the Quadrilateral's on the 'Historic Episcopate' has caused such a large volume of discussion because the concept was not defined, and because the idea of being able locally to adopt the episcopate to varying situations offered no limit to the adaptations and variations which might be produced."[21]

Evans explains that the lack of doctrinal definition for the fourth article on episcopacy was intentional on the part of the drafters of the Quadrilateral. She notes that "Dr. Vincent, assistant bishop of Southern Ohio, was anxious in the debates of the 1880s to make it plain that the phrase 'the historic episcopate' was chosen precisely because it was intended to avoid saying anything 'of a doctrinal nature.'" Vincent recalled, "'That phrase "the Historic Episcopate" was deliberately chosen as declaring not a doctrine, but a fact, and as being general enough to include all variants.'"[22]

An ecumenical statement that is "general enough to include all variants" also may cause problems. The variants need to be worked through to some degree of clarity and consensus before the statement can be the basis for significant ecumenical results. In terms of the need for development and clarification of the fourth article, Vogel states:

> When commentaries on the Quadrilateral are com-
> pared, however, the first feature to strike the attentive
> reader may be how much more explication the fourth
> principle seems to require than the other three. In the
> "Statement of Faith and Order" passed by the Episcopal
> Church's General Convention of 1949, over five times
> as much space is spent on the "Historic Episcopate" as
> is spent on any of the other three principles.[23]

The rather terse and "matter of fact" article on the historic episcopate needed development. The intense attention given to this article can also be seen to reflect the
importance of the historic episcopate for Anglican identity
and practice.

The ecclesiological "climate" in the Anglican Communion
was conducive for further reflection on episcopacy in the
years following publication of the Quadrilateral. Chadwick
states:

> The prominence of concern for the Old Catholics at
> the [Lambeth] Conference of 1897 may evidently
> reflect a deeper realization of the truth that Anglican
> ecumenism could not hope for much success if it were
> constructed on the basis of liberal Protestant ecclesi-
> ology; and the committee of the 1908 conference
> roundly declared "there can be no fulfillment of the
> Divine purpose in any scheme of reunion which does
> not ultimately include the great Latin Church of the
> West, with which our history has been so closely asso-
> ciated in the past, and to which we are still bound by
> many ties of common faith and tradition."[24]

Admittedly, the prospects for ecumenical relationship
with "the great Latin Church of the West" were limited at
this time due to the Roman Catholic view of the invalidity
of Anglican orders.[25] Nevertheless, the prominent concern
for the Old Catholics and Roman Catholics stated implicitly
the importance of episcopacy for future Anglican ecumenical discussions.

Reflection and comment on the episcopate became very explicit in the years following World War I with the "Appeal to All Christian People" of the 1920 Lambeth Conference. The Appeal restated the Quadrilateral's four points without mentioning the Quadrilateral by name. Although the Appeal acknowledged "the spiritual reality of the ministries of those Communions which do not possess the Episcopate," it urged, "we believe that the visible unity of the Church will be found to involve the whole-hearted acceptance of. . . A ministry acknowledged by every part of the Church as possessing not only the inward call of the Spirit, but also the commission of Christ and the authority of the whole body." The Appeal then asked, "May we not reasonably claim that the Episcopate is the one means of providing such a ministry?" This claim was supported by the statement, "we submit that considerations alike of history and of present experience justify the claim which we make on behalf of the Episcopate. Moreover, we would urge that it is now and will prove to be in the future the best instrument for maintaining the unity and continuity of the Church."[26]

The purpose of the Appeal's claim concerning the episcopacy was clearly ecumenical. The Appeal concluded that

> we eagerly look forward to the day when through its acceptance in a united Church we may all share in that grace which is pledged to the members of the whole body in the apostolic rite of the laying-on-of-hands, and in the joy and fellowship of a Eucharist in which as one Family we may together, without any doubtfulness of mind, offer to the one Lord our worship and service.[27]

The Appeal of the 1920 Lambeth Conference reflected considerable development concerning the role of episcopacy in Anglican ecumenical activity.

This development concerning Anglican episcopacy in an ecumenical context was continued in 1923 at a Lambeth Palace joint conference of Nonconformist divines and representatives of the Church of England. Although the Church of England representatives refused to declare non-episcopal ministries to be "invalid," they regarded the Preface to the Ordinal of 1662 as more than "a local rule of discipline for the Church of England." The Ordinal was seen "as enshrining a principle of order that Anglicans could not break without painful consequences both for relations with Rome and orthodoxy and for the internal coherence of the Anglican Communion."[28]

Chadwick notes that the Church of England representatives at the 1923 joint conference "envisaged the real possibility of an internal Anglican schism if the ordinal's requirement of episcopal ordination were to be set aside or made optional." In a statement that recalls the Quadrilateral, Chadwick concludes that the 1923 text "is a significant expression of the view that the Anglican Communion does not possess freedom to treat essential matters of order with any more liberty than could be applied to the doctrines of the creed or the use of the two sacraments of the gospel and the Bible."[29]

Continuing development concerning the episcopate was evident in the Lambeth Report of 1930, which stated, "The Historic Episcopate as we understand it goes behind the perversions of history to the original conception of the Apostolic Ministry."[30] Woolverton notes that significant parts of the 1930 Lambeth Report were "reiterated and enlarged upon" by the "Statement of Faith and Order" from the Report of the Joint Commission on Approaches to Unity to the 1949 General Convention of the Episcopal Church.[31] The 1949 Statement of Faith and Order quotes the appeal to patristic tradition of the 1930 Lambeth Report concerning episcopacy:

Whatever variety of system may have existed in addition in the earlier age, it is universally agreed that by the end of the second century episcopacy had no effective rival. Among all the controversies of the fourth and fifth centuries the episcopal ministry was never a subject of dispute. . . . If the Episcopate, as we find it established universally by the end of the second century, was the result of a process of adaptation and growth in the organism of the Church, that would be no evidence that it lacked divine authority, but rather that the life of the Spirit within the Church had found it to be the most appropriate organ for the functions which it discharged.[32]

Appealing to New Testament tradition to defend and define the role of ordained ministry in the church, the 1949 statement considered the historic episcopate in light of the mutuality of ministerial service and responsibility in the church of the New Testament:

The Church is set before us in the New Testament as a body of believers having within it, as its recognized focus of unity, of teaching and of authority, the Apostolate, which owed its origin to the action of the Lord Himself. There was not first an Apostolate which gathered a body of believers about itself; nor was there a completely structureless collection of believers which gave authority to the Apostles to speak and act on its behalf. From the first there was the fellowship of believers finding its unity in the Twelve. Thus the New Testament bears witness to the principle of a distinctive ministry, as an original element, but not the sole constitutive element, in the life of the Church.[33]

The 1949 statement noted that Anglican formularies define "ministers within this historic stream as 'Ministers of Apostolic Succession.'" Although no judgments were made concerning other ministries, Woolverton concludes, this statement meant that for Anglicans "the theory of apostolic succession could not be excluded."[34]

The statement expanded the meaning of the Quadrilateral's "Historic Episcopate" to specify the apostolicity of the threefold ordained ministry in the church. "It should be clear," the statement urges,

> that while acceptance of the "Historic Episcopate" may not involve acceptance of any one formulation of the doctrine of the ministry, it does involve acceptance, in the form of a fact, of the three-fold ministry of bishops, priests, and deacons, and the acceptance of it also as accompanied by the claim that it is a ministerial succession tracing back to the "Apostles' time."[35]

Evans found the 1949 statement to be an exposition that "moves away from the extreme simplicity of the Chicago-Lambeth formulations." It contrasts with the language and emphasis of the Quadrilateral. The statement "places the emphasis upon 'response' and 'reception' and the reciprocal movement of God's self-revelation and Christian understanding. It reflects the attitudes of a less authoritarian age, or perhaps it would be more accurate to say, of an age when Christian authority was beginning to be understood rather differently."[36] Evans's conclusion about authority seems directly related to the statement's discussion of mutuality of ministries and authority concerning the historic episcopate. The 1949 statement reflected a considerable development concerning episcopacy in Anglican ecclesiology and ecumenical activity.

Further development concerning the Quadrilateral and episcopacy was evident at the 1982 General Convention in New Orleans. The 1982 resolution considered the Quadrilateral both in terms of Anglican identity and ecumenical relations. The 1982 text reaffirmed the Quadrilateral "as a statement of basic principles which express our own unity, and as a statement of essential principles for organic unity with other churches."[37]

The 1982 text also presents "an explication of that basic document" of the Quadrilateral, including a developed view of episcopacy in light of the full meaning of apostolicity. The text considers the historic episcopate in light of the ministries of all baptized persons in the church, while also taking into account the church's scriptural and traditional sources of authority. The text states:

> Apostolicity is evidenced in continuity with the teaching, the ministry, and the mission of the apostles. Apostolic teaching must, under the guidance of the Holy Spirit, be founded upon the Holy Scriptures and the ancient fathers and creeds, making its proclamation of Jesus Christ and his Gospel for each age consistent with those sources, not merely reproducing them in a transmission of verbal identity. Apostolic ministry exists to promote, safeguard and serve apostolic teaching. All Christians are called to this ministry by their Baptism. In order to serve, lead and enable this ministry, some are set apart and ordained in the historic orders of Bishop, Presbyter, and Deacon. We understand the Historic Episcopate as central to this apostolic ministry and essential to the reunion of the Church.[38]

The explication also identifies the role of episcopacy in the continuity of the church's mission through time. The text explains this role in functional terms, noting:

> Apostolic mission is itself a succession of apostolic teaching and ministry inherited from the past and carried into the present and future. Bishops in apostolic succession are, therefore, the focus and personal symbols of this inheritance and mission as they preach and teach the Gospel and summon the people of God to their mission of worship and service.[39]

However, it is important to note that the 1982 statement recognizes the apostolic ministry to be larger than the historic episcopate. All Christians are understood to share in the apostolic ministry of the church by baptism.

As stated in the 1949 statement, the ministry of the apostles was distinctive and an original element, but not "the sole constitutive element" in the life of the church. James E. Griffiss has described the distinction between apostolic ministry and historic episcopate as a "most significant" development in the official statements and other theological writings of the Anglican Communion concerning ecumenical relations. In view of this distinction, he states, "now it was possible to say more clearly that apostolic ministry is the fundamental ministry which derives from Christ himself as the High Priest who reconciles the world to God through his life, death and resurrection."[40]

The 1982 statement reflects considerable development of the original Quadrilateral concerning the historic episcopate, especially with respect to apostolic continuity and the interdependence of the ministries of all baptized persons in the church. Margaret O'Gara, in a Roman Catholic response to Wright's centenary essay, "Heritage and Vision," notes the "increasing sophistication or nuanced distinctions which the Quadrilateral elicited within the Anglican Communion and within the American Episcopal church during its one hundred years. . . . especially in the Quadrilateral's fourth point, the point that emphasizes the importance of the episcopate within the work of reunion of the church."[41]

Regarding the relationship of apostolic teaching, ministry, and mission relative to apostolic continuity in the 1982 statement, O'Gara concludes:

> This understanding of the episcopate within the context of apostolicity is not seen as any less a conviction of the importance of the episcopate: indeed, in 1982 the episcopate is called "essential" for reunion. But the reason for its essential character is explained more carefully, with more nuances. It is a long way from the simple lists that included the episcopate in 1886 and 1888.[42]

The meaning of the historic episcopate has undergone considerable development since the framing of the Quadrilateral, as evidenced by the subsequent statements of the Anglican Communion and the Episcopal Church.

Development of the meaning of the historic episcopate has also gone hand-in-hand with commitment to its importance in the life of the church. Ephraim Radner notes—with apparent amusement—that "episcopacy is central to who we are as Episcopalians" and the central place of episcopacy "has always surprised people, despite our denomination's name." He identifies the Episcopal Church's "basic claim concerning bishops" in terms of the Quadrilateral's listing the "'historic episcopate, locally adapted' as an 'inherent part of the sacred deposit' of the 'Christian Faith and Order committed by Christ and the Apostles to the Church unto the end of the world,' and 'essential' to the restored unity of the Church." Radner urges that the Quadrilateral's affirmation of the essential role of the historic episcopate has given rise to "a revolution in ecumenical discussion" (even if it is not a fully appreciated "ecumenical revolution"), as evidenced by the 1982 Lima Statement of the Faith and Order Commission of the World Council of Churches, on *Baptism, Eucharist, and Ministry*. Relative to this Statement, Radner notes that "among the agreed-upon assertions was the fact that, 'among the gifts [of the Spirit for the Church] is the ministry of the *episcope*'—that is, 'oversight'—'which is *necessary* [emphasis added by Radner] for expressing and guarding the unity of the body; every church has need of this ministry of unity, in some particular form, in order that it can be the Church of God, the single Body of Christ, a sign of the whole's unity in the Kingdom' (*Ministry*, c. 23)." Although Radner admits that the Lima Statement does not identify the historic episcopate as "an explicit element of the 'essence' of the Church, it does recommend its explicit adoption, and indeed, could be interpreted as implicitly defining some 'local adaptation' as part of that essence."[43] Clearly, for Radner, the historic episcopate is essential in Anglicanism and influential in ecumenical discussions reaching beyond the boundaries of the Anglican Communion. In this sense, the historic episcopate is alive and well.

DEVELOPMENT AND UNFOLDING OF THE QUADRILATERAL: REFLECTIONS CONCERNING THE "HISTORIC EPISCOPATE" BY ANGLICAN THEOLOGIANS

The Quadrilateral has been considered by other Anglican theologians whose writings reflect the development of the historic episcopate in Anglican thought, identity, and ecumenical activity. This development is considered in a sampling of theological themes presented by Charles P. Price, Arthur A. Vogel, and John Macquarrie concerning the Quadrilateral.

Price has emphasized the role of the episcopate in the dynamic process of maintaining apostolic continuity between the past, present, and future of the church's life. He uses a literary analogy to explain the problem of continuity in the church: "The Red Queen in *Alice Through the Looking Glass* said that in her race, you had to run as fast as you could to stay in the same place." Similarly, Price urges, "In our Christian race, theology has to change precisely in order to communicate the same message." In this regard, the historic episcopate serves to "regulate and supervise the change, so that it does not alter beyond recognition."[44]

The flexibility needed for this ministry of "regulating and supervising" theological change is available in the historic episcopate, which is distinctive among the points of the Quadrilateral. Price explains that the episcopate "operates quite differently from the other three Lambeth items. It involves a human factor, which is its virtue and strength on the one hand and its peril and risk on the other. It accounts for continuity through time and change in the transmission of the apostolic message."[45] Price has clearly identified the dynamic role of the historic episcopate in the apostolic continuity of the church.

Although the episcopate's responsibility for "regulating and supervising" theological change is not seriously disputed, this apostolic ministry should be placed in the context of the apostolic life, ministry, mission, and theological reflection of the whole church. Theologically speaking, the episcopate speaks on behalf of the whole apostolic community to insure the apostolic continuity of the church in and through the process of theological change. Practically speaking, it is advisable for the episcopate to have the full benefit of the experience and theological reflection of the whole church before attempting to say anything to preserve apostolic continuity. Price offers an important insight concerning the role of the historic episcopate in theological change and apostolic continuity.

Vogel describes the meaning of the historic episcopate in incarnational terms, urging that "the key word is 'historic.' The 'Historic Episcopate' is another mark of God's having truly entered history; it is another way in which God's mystery is confronted in the human world." He explains that the "historic" of "Historic Episcopate" reflects God's gift and indicates God's action in history. Showing appreciation for the role and context of episcopacy in community, Vogel emphasizes the episcopacy's calling for service in the community rather than lordship over others. He states that "the church is a community of service, not a society of rulers and ruled. Because the spirit of the one who came to serve rather than to be served fills the Christian community of faith, there is no need for the presence of Christ, the Head of the Church, to be passed from one person to another in a delegated manner."[46] However, the apostolic ministry does serve to signify Christ's ubiquitous risen presence to the community.

The historic episcopate, with other ministerial orders, also identifies "special servants of the church to the church." The episcopacy may then be understood in terms of ordination that focuses and unites the whole church's vocation to service. Vogel explains that the historic episcopate is a focus for the unity of the Christian community, "but, if the nature of the episcopate is fully understood, it focuses a oneness of *service*, not lordship, through time and space." In this regard, the themes of Vogel's theology prove to be deeply interconnected, as the historic episcopate "reveals the mystical body's nature to itself in a sacramental manner: the ordained ministry, as an apostolic ministry, points beyond itself both to God and to the nature of God's people."[47]

Vogel's essay leads to important conclusions that reflect significant development of thought concerning the historic episcopate. The episcopate is "incarnational" and sacramental. It signifies for the community in time and space the source of the community's life in Christ. It also represents the nature of the community's vocation and identity in service. In this way, the episcopate *is* the focus of unity for the church. It is also the focus for drawing together and enabling the diverse ministries of the baptized who share the church's apostolic mission. In this way, the apostolicity of the community is continued.

Macquarrie has understood the four "notes" of the church (one, holy, catholic, apostolic) to be signified or embodied in terms of the four points of the Quadrilateral: The church's unity is signified and embodied by the Bible, and the church's holiness is visibly embodied by its sacramental life (with special respect and reverence given to "the forms which are rooted in the Bible and which have been developed in the Church's tradition and proved of value in her devotional life").[48] The church's catholicity is embodied in "the catholic creeds, especially the Apostles' and Nicene; and also the pronouncements of the universally recognized councils of the Church, such as those of Nicaea and Chalcedon,"[49] and the church's apostolicity is embodied in the episcopacy.

Macquarrie explains, "The apostolic Church is the authentic Church, continuing the teaching and practice of the apostles, who had been 'eyewitnesses' of the events proclaimed in the Church's message" and who were "commissioned by Christ himself."[50] Macquarrie (like Price) has understood the church's apostolicity in terms of continuity through time. Although the church must change "in many ways," Macquarrie urges that "it can claim to be the Church of Jesus Christ only if it has retained at least a minimal degree of continuity with Christ, first through his apostles and then through the generations of their successors." The inner meaning of the church's apostolicity is its "constancy in the faith of the apostles," which the episcopacy protects by "ensuring the continuity of that heritage of faith and practice which was likewise transmitted by the apostles."[51]

Macquarrie's identification of the four notes of the church with the Quadrilateral has not gone unchallenged.[52]

CONCLUSION: THE QUADRILATERAL'S CONTINUING ECUMENICAL USEFULNESS AND DEVELOPMENT

The Quadrilateral remains the standard for the ecumenical relations of the Anglican Communion, including the Episcopal Church. Its continuing importance is evidenced by Peter Day in a letter written to the members of the Joint Commission on Ecumenical Relations and the Episcopal members of the Lutheran-Episcopal Dialogue on January 25, 1973, when he was Ecumenical Officer of the Episcopal Church. In responding to a report of recent Lutheran-Episcopal conversations, Day wrote, "Perhaps the most controversial issue for Episcopalians is whether the degree of recognition accorded to non-episcopal Lutheran ordinations and Eucharistic celebrations is within the meaning of Point IV of the Chicago-Lambeth Quadrilateral."[53] Day's comment was prescient concerning issues that would prove challenging and would have to be faced in later ecumenical efforts involving the common mission of the Evangelical Lutheran Church in America and the Episcopal Church.

The Quadrilateral continues to be the Anglican foundation for ecumenical relations. Wright notes that "Every General Convention from 1934 to 1964 instructed the Episcopal Church's Joint Commission on Approaches to Unity to conduct its ecumenical conversations 'on the basis of the Chicago-Lambeth Quadrilateral.'"[54] He explains that

> every time a proposal has come from some unofficial group, from some official commission, or from elsewhere in the Episcopal Church to replace the Chicago-Lambeth Quadrilateral, or to alter its fourth point in the light of apparently more recent scholarly and ecumenical realities, the General Convention has

> always demurred and returned to a reaffirmation of
> the Quadrilateral in its 1888 form as the starting point
> for the Episcopal Church's participation in the ecu-
> menical movement. This is the authority that it still
> seems to hold[55]

Macquarrie likewise concludes that the Quadrilateral "still remains the basic minimum required for any possible reunion."[56]

Interpretation of the Quadrilateral's meaning also continues to develop as it is used in ecumenical contexts. It was noted with reference to the historic episcopate in ecumenical discussions of the Episcopal Church with the Evangelical Lutheran Church in America[57] and with the Orthodox Church in Russia. At the 1992 Moscow Consultation of the Joint Coordinating Committee of the Episcopal Church and the Orthodox Church in Russia, Richard A. Norris of the Episcopal Church appeals to the Quadrilateral in his paper on "Bishops, Succession, and the Apostolicity of the Church."[58] In summary, he suggests that

> the apostolicity of the church's life and its unity with
> its own origins does not consist merely or solely in the
> succession of bishops but in the organic continuity of
> a "concatenated set of institutions—Scriptures, the
> Apostles' and Nicene Creeds, the two Gospel Sacra-
> ments, and Historic Episcopate" which support each
> other and are mutually interrelated.[59]

Norris's use of the Quadrilateral reflects its vitality and ongoing development in ecumenical dialogue.

We may hope that the application of the Quadrilateral will continue in its process of development and evolution—especially as the Lutheran and Episcopal Churches explore the possibilities for ecumenical mission. The Quadrilateral's principles should be much more than a "litmus test" or minimum requirement for ecumenical relationships. Vogel states that the principles of the Quadrilateral should "call us beyond ourselves." When they are seen as "marks of God's presence in and presence to the church," Vogel concludes, "the principles of the Quadrilateral immediately move us into the mystery of our salvation and reveal the structure of our most intimate life with God. They are not just tests one community can give to another to see whether they may both be called by the same name."[60] Vogel's understanding reflects development concerning the meaning and appropriate use of the Quadrilateral. As this development continues, the Quadrilateral can continue to be the Anglican instrument for deepening, clarifying, articulating, and sharing with others "our most intimate life with God." This can certainly prove true as Lutherans and Episcopalians continue to discover common mission.

NOTES

[1] Stuart H. Hoke, "Broken Fragments: William Reed Huntington's Personal Quest for Unity," *Anglican and Episcopal History* 69 (June, 2000): 211.

[2] "Text of the Chicago-Lambeth Quadrilateral," in J. Robert Wright, ed., *Quadrilateral at One Hundred, Essays on the Centenary of the Chicago-Lambeth Quadrilateral, 1886/88-1986/88, Anglican Theological Review* Supplemental Series 10 (March, 1988)(Cincinnati, OH: Forward Movement Publications, 1988), vii. Wright's significant collection of essays on the Quadrilateral serves as a major source for this study.

[3] "Text of the Chicago-Lambeth Quadrilateral," vii.

[4] "Text of the Chicago-Lambeth Quadrilateral," viii. It is noteworthy that the text identifies *two* sacraments.

[5] "Text of the Chicago-Lambeth Quadrilateral," viii.

[6] "Text of the Chicago-Lambeth Quadrilateral," viii-ix.

[7] Gillian R. Evans, "'Permanence in the Revealed Truth and Continuous Exploration of Its Meaning,'" in Wright, *Quadrilateral at one Hundred*, 112.

[8] J. Robert Wright, "Heritage and Vision: The Chicago-Lambeth Quadrilateral," in Wright, *Quadrilateral at One Hundred*, 29-30.

[9] John F. Woolverton, "The Chicago-Lambeth Quadrilateral and the Lambeth Conferences," *Historical Magazine of the Protestant Episcopal Church* 53 (June, 1984): 101. Woolverton states that "Anglo-catholic Anglicans have traditionally opted" for the *terminus a quo* position.

[10] Wright, "Heritage and Vision," 8-9. Huntington's first proposal of the Quadrilateral may have been at ecumenical clergy gatherings in Worcester, Massachusetts, in the 1860s. He co-founded this ecumenical clergy fellowship with a priest from St. Paul's Roman Catholic parish in Worcester while serving as rector of All Saints Church, Worcester. Woolverton notes that the term "Quadrilateral" for Huntington's "four-sided ecclesiological figure" was borrowed "from the system of fortress cities in Lombardy comprised of Mantua, Verona, Peschiera, and Legano which figured in the Napoleonic wars and which, from 1815 to 1859, provided Austria with a means of keeping northern Italy under her control." Woolverton, "The Chicago-Lambeth Quadrilateral," 98.

[11] Wright, "Heritage and Vision," 9-10, quoting Huntington's *The Church-Idea: An Essay Towards Unity* (1870), 155-157.

[12] Woolverton, "The Chicago-Lambeth Quadrilateral," 98.

[13] Wright, "Heritage and Vision," 12 (emphasis in original).

[14] Wright, "Heritage and Vision," 12.

[15] Wright, "Heritage and Vision," 12. Ironically, the Quadrilateral now follows the Articles of Religion in the "Historical Documents" section at the back of the *Book of Common Prayer* of the Episcopal Church (876-878).

[16] Evans, "Permanence," 112.

[17] Henry Chadwick, "The Quadrilateral in England," in Wright, *Quadrilateral at One Hundred*, 140.

[18] Chadwick, "The Quadrilateral in England," 141.

[19] Evans, "Permanence," 111-112.

[20] Evans, "Permanence," 125 (emphasis in original).

[21] Arthur A. Vogel, "Chicago-Lambeth Quadrilateral: Yardstick or Mirror?" in Wright, *Quadrilateral at One Hundred*, 136-137. Vogel served as Bishop of West Missouri.

[22] Evans, "Permanence," 118-119.

[23] Vogel, "Chicago-Lambeth Quadrilateral," 136.

[24] Chadwick, "Quadrilateral in England," 146.

[25] Chadwick, "Quadrilateral in England," 146-147.

[26] Wright, "Heritage and Vision," 26.

[27] Wright, "Heritage and Vision," 26.

[28] Chadwick, "Quadrilateral in England," 149.

[29] Chadwick, "Quadrilateral in England," 149.

[30] John F. Woolverton, "Huntington's Quadrilateral—A Critical Study," *Church History* 39 (June, 1970): 199. Woolverton comments dryly that this statement was made "with something less than historical acuity."

[31] Woolverton, "Huntington's Quadrilateral," 199.

[32] Wright, "Heritage and Vision," 35.

[33] Wright, "Heritage and Vision," 34.

[34] Woolverton, "Huntington's Quadrilateral," 199.

[35] Wright, "Heritage and Vision," 34.

[36] Evans, "Permanence," 116. Evans states that "if we put the 1949 statement and the report of ARCIC I on authority side by side with the formulations of 1886-88 it is obvious at once that the tone of the 1949 statement is much closer to ARCIC than to the Quadrilateral."

[37] Wright, "Heritage and Vision," 41.

[38] Wright, "Heritage and Vision," 42. This statement concerning apostolicity and apostolic ministry is virtually identical to an earlier unofficial statement on principles of unity. James E. Griffiss notes that in 1978 the Episcopal Church began "a major theological evaluation" of its ecumenical conversations. The theologians and ecumenical consultants involved in the evaluation wanted "to state once again on what basis the Episcopal Church, as a province of the Anglican Communion, could reach doctrinal consensus with other traditions," and felt that the Quadrilateral "needed elaboration and development in consideration of the new issues which have arisen" since it was proposed. James E. Griffiss, *Church, Ministry, and Unity: A Divine Commission* [Oxford: Basil Blackwell, 1983], 91-93. This unofficial statement on principles of unity was published as "The Detroit Report: National Ecumenical Consultation of the Episcopal Church, Farmington Hills, Michigan (Detroit), 5-9 November 1978," in J. Robert Wright, ed., *A Communion of Communions: One Eucharistic Fellowship—The Detroit Report and Papers*

of the Triennial Ecumenical Study of the Episcopal Church, 1976-1979, A Crossroad Book (New York: Seabury Press, 1979), 1-29, with the proposed "principles for unity with other churches" at 16-17.

[39] Wright, "Heritage and Vision," 42.

[40] Griffiss, *Church, Ministry, and Unity*, 56. He quotes the 1949 statement at 56-57.

[41] Margaret O'Gara, "The Episcopate, the Universal Primacy, and the Growth of Understanding: A Roman Catholic Response to Robert Wright," in Wright, *Quadrilateral at One Hundred*, 48.

[42] O'Gara, "The Episcopate, the Universal Primacy, and the Growth of Understanding," 49.

[43] Ephraim Radner, "Bad Bishops: A Key to Anglican Ecclesiology," *Anglican Theological Review* 82 (Spring, 2000): 322-323.

[44] Charles P. Price, "Whence, Whither, and What? Reflections on the Hundredth Anniversary," in Wright, *Quadrilateral at One Hundred*, 92.

[45] Price, "Whence, Whither, and What? Reflections on the Hundredth Anniversary," 93.

[46] Vogel, "Chicago-Lambeth Quadrilateral," 137-138.

[47] Vogel, "Chicago-Lambeth Quadrilateral," 138-139.

[48] John Macquarrie, *Principles of Christian Theology*, Second Edition (New York: Charles Scribner's Sons, 1977), 407; see, generally, 401-413.

[49] Macquarrie, *Principles of Christian Theology*, 407.

[50] Macquarrie, *Principles of Christian Theology*, 409.

[51] Macquarrie, *Principles of Christian Theology*, 410.

[52] See Price, "Whence, Whither, and What?" at 86-87. Price disagrees with Macquarrie, stating, "One recognizes something artificial and mechanical about this direct one-to-one identification between the several Lambeth articles and the several notes of the church—which are as old as the Nicene-Constantinopolitan Creed itself" (87).

[53] Don S. Armentrout, "Lutheran-Episcopal Conversations in the Nineteenth Century," *Historical Magazine of the Protestant Episcopal Church* 44 (June, 1975): 186-187.

[54] Wright, "Heritage and Vision," 39.

[55] Wright, "Heritage and Vision," 42-43.

[56] Macquarrie, *Principles of Christian Theology*, 412.

[57] William A. Norgren and William G. Rusch, eds., *"Toward Full Communion" and "Concordat of Agreement," Lutheran-Episcopal Dialogue, Series III* (Minneapolis, MN: Augsburg Publishing Co./Cincinnati, OH: Forward Movement Publications, 1991), 65-68 (paras. 3-65). This statement also quoted the rewording of the Quadrilateral by the bishops of the 1920 Lambeth Conference in "An Appeal to All Christian People," and considered the "deliberate but steady" responses to this Appeal.

[58] Richard A. Norris, Jr., "Bishops, Succession, and the Apostolicity of the Church [Third Paper]," in J. Robert Wright, ed., *On Being a Bishop: Papers on Episcopacy from the Moscow Consultation, 1992* (New York: Church Hymnal Corporation, 1993), 59-62. Papers on episcopacy from the Moscow Consultation of June 22-27, 1992, of the Joint Coordinating Committee for practical cooperation and bilateral relations between the Episcopal Church and the Orthodox Church in Russia were published in *On Being a Bishop*.

[59] "Joint Working Document: Summary of the Moscow Papers and Review of the Discussions [III. The Rev. Canon Prof. Richard A. Norris—'Bishops, Succession, and the Apostolicity of the Church'],'" in Wright, *On Being a Bishop*, 217-218.

[60] Vogel, "Chicago-Lambeth Quadrilateral," 128.

7

CALLED TO COMMON MISSION

Some Marginal Questions

REGINALD H. FULLER

INTRODUCTION

Why marginal? Because my questions concern the problems of a common ministry rather than our common mission. All the same, a common ministry is necessary in the service of common mission. Ministry is subservient to the gospel.

My first direct contact with Lutheranism was in 1938. In that year I "came down" from Cambridge and went to Tübingen for a year of post-graduate studies. Like most of my Anglican contemporaries I had assumed that the Lutherans were similar to our own Nonconformists (Methodists, Congregationalists, etc.), or at best like our own low-church Evangelicals. I was in for a surprise! Even in Württemberg, where they were Lutheran in Confession but Reformed in liturgy, they faithfully observed the church year, always preached from the lectionary, and observed the liturgical colors of the season. In Hannover and Bavaria they had a full liturgy. Crucifixes, stone altars, and in Bavaria albs were everywhere. The *Benedictus qui venit* and the *Agnus Dei*, abhorred by English Evangelicals, were in common use. All in all, Lutherans had as strong a sense of being church as had most Anglicans. The one thing, however, they seemed to lack was episcopacy in apostolic succession. Even in Sweden where they had it, as Archbishop Södorblom said, "we have it as though we had it not." I came away from Tübingen resolved to do all I could for the rest of my life to bring our two traditions together.

My attempt to carry out that resolve culminated in participation in Lutheran Episcopal Dialogue (LED) I and II, and in the world-wide Anglican-Lutheran Conversations. I remember two highlights of those dialogues, both of them concerning the subject of ministry. One highlight was our common recognition that ordination was a sacramental rite. The Lutherans did not use that language, but like us believed that ordination was an ecclesial act through which God acted, calling, commissioning, and empowering ministers for the proclamation of the word and ministration of the sacraments. The other highlight concerns the apostolicity of the church. Anglicans had generally understood the church's apostolicity to be dependent on the succession of our bishops in ordination from the apostles. This was not a Tractarian innovation, as sometimes supposed, but a concept worked out in seventeenth-century Britain in controversy with Presbyterianism and Independency. It was rediscovered independently in the American colonies by the Yale Seven, who having studied the Church Fathers came to believe that their congregational orders were invalid, and sailed to England to receive Episcopal ordination.[1] However, my teacher at Cambridge, Sir Edwyn Hoskyns, had held a wider conception of apostolicity. For him, it was not merely a matter of the validity of the sacraments, but concerned the truth of the gospel. At the Anglo-Catholic Congress of 1930 he delivered a lecture on the Apostolicity of the Church in which he made this remarkable point:

> In our modern controversy we Catholics are not concerned primarily with a question of organization. We are concerned with the nature of the Gospel . . . Taught by the New Testament, we are bound to think of the Episcopate as preserving the witness of the Apostles, and to demand this of the Bishops. The Bishops are not mystical persons to whom we owe some undefined mysterious obedience. The Bishops are responsible to bear witness to Jesus Christ, the Son of God, and to hold the Church to that witness.[2]

I had further learned in my Tübingen days that Lutherans were equally concerned with apostolicity in Hoskyns' sense of fidelity to the gospel, and was sure that such an understanding of episcopacy would be acceptable to our Lutheran partners in dialogue. This proved to be the case; and three of us, the late Jules Moreau, Robert Jensen, and myself produced a statement which was accepted not only by LED in this country, but by the worldwide dialogue, and ultimately by the Lima Report of the World Council of Churches.

It was for me a matter of rejoicing when LED III culminated in the statement on Common Mission, which led to full communion between ELCA and ECUSA. But I feel obliged to raise certain questions with the Called to Common Mission (CCM) document, all of them concerning the ministry, which I suggest call for further discussion.

MINISTRY OF THE BAPTIZED AND ORDAINED MINISTRY

In paragraph 6 of CCM we read: "We together affirm that all members of Christ's church are commissioned for ministry through baptism." This same paragraph goes on to give thanks "for the renewed discovery" of the centrality of the ministry of all the baptized in both our churches. What does centrality mean in this context? What are the implications of this claim for understanding the nature of the ordained ministry? Later on, in paragraph 7, the ordained ministry is described as "instruments of God's grace in the service of God's people, possessing not only the inward call of the Spirit but also Christ's commission." The same paragraph goes on to speak of the "one [sic] ministry of Word and Sacrament." It is not clear how the ministry of the baptized relates to the ministry of the ordained. The word "centrality" in paragraph 6 and the word "one" call for clarification. As I see it, there are two different kinds of ministry in the church. There is the ministry of word and sacrament grounded in the commission of the risen Christ, a ministry which makes the once-for-all redemptive event effectively present for participation through word and sacrament, and there is the response of the believing community, which is called to serve Christ in the world, through loving their neighbors, striving for justice and peace, and witnessing to Christ by their personal testimony, I would argue, not by authoritative proclamation of word and sacrament. It would be better to speak of the *general* ministry of the baptized and the *special* ministry of the ordained. This distinction would call into question much loose talk nowadays about *all* being ministers. As one of my colleagues (W. H. Gilbert) observed after a sermon along these lines, "when everyone is somebody, no one is anybody."[3]

This distinction between general and special ministry is, I believe, supported by scripture. In the synoptic gospels people generally respond to Jesus' eschatological message by faith and discipleship, whereas certain individuals are selected from that company (the Twelve, and in Luke, the Seventy or Seventy-two) and specially commissioned to carry that same message further afield. In Paul's list of the gifts of the Spirit in 1 Corinthians, three gifts are specified as exercised by particular persons—apostles, prophets and teachers—whereas the other gifts are exercised by individuals with no particular designation. The deutero-Pauline author of Ephesians similarly lists the designated apostles, prophets, etc. (i.e., the *special* ministries), whose task is to equip the saints (i.e., the baptized), for *general* ministry. [4]

Incidentally, the distinction between general and special ministries may help clarify the problem of lay presidency at the eucharist, which is on the verge of implementation by the diocese of Sydney, Australia, and, as I understand, practiced in certain situations by the Lutherans. When lay presidents are duly authorized by competent ecclesiastical authority (in our case, by the diocesan bishop), this may preserve the special character of the ordained ministry as commissioned "from above," and thus bearing the authority of Christ himself. Special ministry is not derived from baptism, but by the special commission of Christ himself. Lay presidency would of course be sanctioned only in special circumstances.

PRIEST AND PRESBYTER

Paragraph 7 of the Concordat implies that in Anglicanism the terms "presbyter" and "priest" are equivalent designations of our second order of ministry, referring to the same ministers Lutherans normally call "pastors." While etymologically the English word "priest" is derived from the Greek word *presbyteros*, it can also be used to translate the

Latin *sacerdos* (Greek, *hiereus*). While there are Anglicans who would reject the word "priest" in the sense of *sacerdos*, we have a long-standing tradition of recognizing a sacerdotal aspect of the ministry, carefully defined and nuanced so as not to deny the sole priesthood of Christ. When a new rector or vicar is instituted by a bishop, the Latin formula which speaks of *meum sacerdotium et tuum* ("my priesthood and yours") is used. Anglicans often speak of "ministerial priesthood."[5] What is at stake here is the sacrificial aspect of the eucharist—hence our second question is not exclusively concerned with the ministry as such.

Since the time of Luther, who eliminated from the eucharistic liturgy everything that "stank of oblation," Lutherans have been allergic to any idea of eucharist sacrifice. This was understandable at the time of the Reformation. Prior to Vatican II, the Roman liturgy emphasized sacrifice to excess, and it needed to be pruned down and properly defined so as not to suggest a repetition of Christ's sacrifice. Under the impact of newly discovered patristic writings, the Caroline divines recovered a sacrificial understanding of the eucharist. While holding firmly to the once-for-all sacrifice of Calvary, so eloquently expressed in the exordium of Cranmer's eucharistic prayer, they viewed Christ's high-priestly work as continued in heaven through his intercession for the church below, pleading his sacrifice to the Father. This heavenly intercession was "externalized" in the church on earth as it celebrated the eucharist. Such a view was expressed pictorially in an eighteenth-century engraving which shows an Anglican priest with wig, full-length surplice, and (Oxford MA) hood, standing at the north side of the altar (as was the custom in those days), while in heaven above the ascended Christ, similarly attired (there is almost a suggestion of an Oxford MA hood on his shoulders!) stands at the north side of the heavenly altar and pleads his once-for-all sacrifice on Calvary. It is indeed ironic that when the eastward position was being introduced by the ritualists in the mid-nineteenth century, the evangelicals clung to the old Laudian high church north-end position on the ground that it denied the sacrificial aspect of the eucharist. This sacrificial understanding of the eucharist is expressed in much Anglican hymnody. Take for instance Charles Wesley's hymn:

> Victim Divine, thy grace we claim
> While thus thy precious death we show;
> Once offered up, a spotless Lamb,
> In thy great temple here below,
> Thou didst for all mankind atone,
>
> And standest now before the throne.
> Thou standest in the holiest place,
> As now for guilty sinners slain,
> Thy blood of sprinkling speaks and praise
> All-prevalent for helpless man;
> Thy blood is still our ransom found,
> And spreads salvation all around.
>
> We need not now go up to heaven
> To bring the long-sought Saviour down:
> Thou art to all already given,
> Thou dost e'en now thy banquet crown;
> To every faithful soul appear,
> And show thy real presence here.
> (*New English Hymnal*, 309)

In the nineteenth century Dean Burgon, a self-described "primitive Tractarian" (i.e., he welcomed the Tracts so long as they reasserted traditional Anglican doctrine, but came to the parting of the ways when they introduced un-Anglican ideas) justified the north side position from Leviticus 1:11, "It [the sacrificial animal] shall be slaughtered on the north side of the altar before the Lord." A familiar hymn included in the Episcopal *Hymnal 1982* by a later Tractarian, William Bright (Hymn 337) contains the words:

We here present, we here spread forth to thee,
that only offering perfect in thine eyes,
the one true, pure, immortal sacrifice.

An American Lutheran New Testament scholar, J. H. Elliott, has distinguished between the Exodus priesthood of the people of Israel as a whole (Exod. 19:1) and the Levitical priesthood of the tabernacle or temple. The Exodus priesthood was expressed in daily living, the Levitical in temple sacrifices. Each type of priesthood is taken up in the New Testament. The Exodus type appears in 1 Peter 2:1-10; and Revelation 1:6, 5:10. The Leviticus type is fulfilled in Christ's eternal high priesthood, but as we have argued, visibly represented in the ministerial priesthood on earth. As O. C. Quick put it, Christ's high priesthood is "externalized" in the eucharist.[6]

In LED I (meeting appropriately at the Missouri Lutheran Concordia Seminary in St. Louis), we discussed the real presence at great length, and it was difficult to convince our Missouri partners in dialogue that we really believe in the real presence. Incidentally, Episcopalians should never say that the Lutherans believe in consubstantiation. In my experience they never use that word, they always speak of the real presence. Unfortunately, we never got around to discussing the eucharistic sacrifice, and this is a subject that calls for greater clarification, especially in connection with ministerial priesthood.

In conclusion, we might say that the term "presbyter" defines the *order* of ministry while priest/*sacerdos* points to the *function* of the president at the eucharist, whether bishop or priest.

THE HISTORIC EPISCOPATE

CCM's proposal to suspend the 1662 restriction of the Anglican Ordinal requiring invariable ordination by bishops in the historical succession was accepted with little difficulty by General Convention, it being understood that all the future ELCA ordinations would be performed within the succession. Since then, however, ELCA has decided to permit exceptions to this rule. Paragraph 20 of the Concordat has stated that "a bishop shall regularly preside and participate in the laying-on-of-hands of all clergy." The word "regularly" is to be interpreted to mean "usually, though not invariably." This of course creates difficulties for many Episcopalians. Since the seventeenth century three different theological interpretations of the historical episcopate have been current among us, the *esse*, the *bene esse*, and the *plene esse*, by which is meant that the episcopate is of the essence of the church, that it is desirable though not necessary, and that it belongs to the fullness of the church. Since my seminary days I have held to the *plene esse* view.[7]

At seminary I became friendly with a German refugee pastor who was preparing for ordination in the Church of England. He had no intention of denying the reality of his Lutheran orders but had to wrestle with the meaning for him of Anglican ordination. With the help of George Bell, the ecumenically minded Bishop of Chichester, my friend and I came to interpret his Anglican ordination as an *Ergänzung* (supplementation or making whole) of his previous ordination as a pastor in the Lutheran church. Holding that view as I have for over sixty years it has not been easy for me to accept the proposal to suspend the Preface to the Ordination Rites, which requires "ordination with the laying on of hands by bishops who are themselves duly qualified to confer Holy Orders" (BCP, 510). I have had no difficulty in recognizing Lutheran pastors as true ministers of Christ, and have gladly received communion in their own churches. But I have difficulties in receiving communion from non-episcopally ordained ministers in my own church. Initially I argued to myself that the intention that all future ordinations would be within the succession was sufficient justification for the present temporary arrangement. It was a sort of realized eschatology. But the prospect of future presbyteral ordinations raises the question of the commitment of the ELCA to the historic episcopate. J. Robert Wright has argued that the Chicago-Lambeth Quadrilateral requires only the acceptance of the historical episcopate and not necessarily exclusive episcopal ordination within the succession. Such an argument I find totally incomprehensible. It is calculated only to encourage the view that bishops have a merely bureaucratic role, and not a sacramental one. What does "historic" episcopate mean if the bishop is not the primary minister of *word and sacrament* (including the sacramental rite of ordination)? I fear that insufficient attention has been paid in our dialogue to the sacramentality of the bishop's office. Are we ready for full communion at this moment in time?

NOTES

[1] The pre-Tractarian origin of apostolic succession as an Anglican doctrine is attested by the American Prayer Books from 1789 until 1979. In the office for the Institution of Ministers we find the phrase "hast promised to be with Ministers of Apostolic succession."

[2] E. C. Hoskyns, "The Apostolicity of the Church-I" in *Report of the Anglo-Catholic Congress*, ed. Kenneth Ingram and F. Lesie Cross (Westminster: Catholic Literature Association, 1930).

[3] I disagree with those (mainly Roman Catholics) who hold that there is only an ordained ministry, the rest of the baptized being merely passive recipients of their ministrations.

[4] John N. Collins, "A Ministry for Tomorrow's Church" *Journal Of Ecumenical Studies* 32.2 (Spring, 1995), from whom I have learnt much in preparing this part of my paper, rightly seeks to reassert the distinctiveness of the ordained ministry. But in my opinion he goes too far in reverting to the older punctuation of Ephesians 4:12: "Equip the saints for the work of ministry." This makes the passage refer exclusively to the special ministry, rather than a recognition that the ordained ministry equips all the baptized for their general ministry.

[5] Note the classic Anglican work on the priesthood, R. C. Moberly, *Ministerial Priesthood* (London: Longmans, Green, 1897).

[6] See Oliver Chase Quick, *The Christian Sacraments* (London: Nisbet, 1952), 198.

[7] See Kenneth Carey, ed., *The Historic Episcopate and the Fullness of the Church* (Westminster: Dacre, 1954).

8

THE LESSONS OF *CALLED TO COMMON MISSION*

GEORGE H. TAVARD

The communion that has been established between the Episcopal Church and the Evangelical Lutheran Church in America along the lines of *Called to Common Mission* is not, one must admit, what the Orthodox Church or the Catholic Church would recognize as full communion. In this paper I plan to look at the background of the agreement in the ecumenical history of the twentieth century, to show that the Common Mission makes sense at the present moment of the ecumenical movement; and to suggest that it holds a promise, not only for Anglicans and Lutherans, but also for the multiplying network of relations between all the classical Christian churches.

THE BACKGROUND

The adoption of the decree on ecumenism, *Unitatis redintegratio,* by Vatican Council II inaugurated a new phase in inter-church relations. This was characterized by the multiplication of bilateral dialogues between churches, which supplemented and enlivened the multilateral dialogues of the World Council of Churches, notably in the Faith and Order Commission. As these dialogues bore fruit in joint statements, new forms of communion emerged within the broad communion of all Christians in baptism. The common search for the will of God concerning long-standing divisions among believers is already an experience of communion.

The ferment that was at work in the Roman Catholic Church at the time of the Council may have been at work even in the margins of classical Christianity. The mushrooming of new movements and sects outside the churches was not unlike the turmoil that exploded in the Roman Catholic Church in the implementation of the conciliar constitutions and decrees. Among these movements I would count the fissiparous creation of "Africa-instituted Churches." It may be more controversial to see a similar emulation at work in the zone of influence that the Unification Church opened for a while around itself when it took the bold step of bringing together a great variety of theologies and religions, as in the "God Conference" that met several times in the 1980s. It is difficult to believe that these disparate events were unrelated, though the debate on how what influenced what could go on for a long time.

In any case it is self-evident that sooner or later the churches that entered in dialogue at the end of Vatican Council II were bound to face the problem of implementing the results of their new familiarity and solidarity. The many joint statements that have embodied several degrees of agreement and consensus could well be left on the shelves as a resource for future generations. And there are those, in practically all churches, who think that it would be prudent to leave them there. Were this course of action adopted by the churches, it is likely that from time to time some of the ideas expressed in those statements would come back to the surface and at least astonish the many pious people who believe that their own church has faithfully carried on the teachings of Jesus and the practices that the Apostles established before the end of the first century.

In concrete life the agreements that have followed a common search for historical and theological truth cannot remain fruitless. Whatever can be officially done to dispose of them cannot stifle their inner dynamics, any more than the formula can kill the meaning or the letter can kill the spirit. There lies in them a latent capacity to transform formal structures that are no longer really alive. Churches that have been in dialogue together are unavoidably faced with the question: What should we do when a dialogue commission judges that it has done the work assigned to it, and that it has fundamentally overcome the reasons that brought about the divisions of the sixteenth century?

This is precisely the point where all churches, including the Roman Catholic and the Orthodox, should learn a lesson from *Called to Common Mission* that is being implemented among Episcopalians and Lutherans.

THE MEANING

When it is seen in a broad context of intense ecumenical dialogues, the agreement of communion between Episcopalians and Lutherans takes on a special meaning. The peculiarities of the Anglican-Roman Catholic conversations have themselves contributed to this meaning. Shortly after Vatican II Pope Paul VI and Archbishop of Canterbury Michael Ramsey created the Anglican-Roman Catholic International Commission (ARCIC) to study and make recommendations on the best way to overcome the chief theological problems on which Anglicans and Roman

Catholics separated in the sixteenth century. The overall plan for such a dialogue was established in January 1968, by the Preparatory Commission that composed the *Malta Report*. Following this, ARCIC met over a period of twelve years. It presented its *Final Report* to the pope and the archbishop in 1983.

The *Final Report* clearly formulated the conviction of the members of ARCIC that in regard to the eucharist, to ministry, and to ordination, they had reached substantial agreement. In context substantial agreement meant that they had agreed on all that they considered essential, and that remaining problems could be solved "on the principles here established." The *Final Report* also registered considerable progress in regard to the nature and scope of the ministry of the bishop of Rome as primate of the universal church.

By 1983 the pope was John Paul II, and the archbishop was Robert Runcie. This change of the guard at the highest level could not be without influence on the official reception of the *Final Report*. John Paul II came from another background than did Paul VI, had other personal and pastoral experiences, and presumably entertained different views of a possible convergence of the churches. The critical judgment that was passed on the *Final Report* by the Roman Congregation for the Doctrine of the Faith, acting on behalf of John Paul II, unveiled a fundamental ecumenical question: *How can the authorities in each church be persuaded to act when the theologians who have been entrusted with the task of ecumenical research determine that the divisions of the Reformation have lost their justification?* Although some of its members were aware of the problem, I had failed to foresee how the process of reception could do justice to its work.

The critique of the *Final Report* by the organ that is in charge of supervising the teaching of doctrine in the

Catholic Church accidentally raised a basic question of trust. After the report was composed, John Paul II received the members of ARCIC. The co-chairs went in first. They returned some fifteen minutes later, enthusiastic, expecting a prompt endorsement of the report. They evidently thought that they had received a promise. And this promise did not correspond to what effectively happened.

In any case, ARCIC-I was dissolved; and its pioneer work was placed politely on the shelves. Since ARCIC-I no longer existed, it could not appeal for a better comprehension of its work. ARCIC-II pursued the dialogue, unavoidably, however, without sharing the illusion of ARCIC-I that its joint statements would be approved and proven true by implementation.

It was partly as a result of the lack of reception of ARCIC-I that some Anglicans and some Lutherans began to fear that any process of agreement with Rome would be made impossible by the reliance of the pope on the judgment of the Congregation for the Doctrine of the Faith. In this case it seemed better, though ideally less urgent, to concentrate on a progressive reunion of the churches of the Reformation. Even for those who did not reach such a conclusion, the difficulties of obtaining a doctrinal agreement with the Roman authorities seemed overwhelming. Would it ever be possible to reshape the structures of Roman Catholicism in view of an eventual reunion? Major as they were, these difficulties should not delay the rapprochements that may be possible among the churches which in one way or another honored the heritage of the Reformers.

WHAT IS COMMUNION?

The churches of England, of Scotland, and of Ireland, and the churches that have been born of them since the Reformation, have always formed a communion of churches; on the model of the catholic church before the separations. The churches issued from the Lutheran movement in Germany and Scandinavia were originally parallel churches that recognized in one another the gospel preached and the sacraments properly administered according to the gospel. Whether they all together constituted a communion of churches could be a moot point, which was not raised explicitly until most of these churches experienced fellowship and mutual assistance in the Lutheran World Federation (LWF). Then the question whether the LWF was a communion could be properly asked. Precisely, in 1990 the LWF changed its constitution so as to identify itself as a communion of churches, which despite a few missing churches that did not wish to join, could be considered the worldwide Lutheran Communion. This identification was explained and clarified in a study of *The Church as Communion* that ended in 1996.

As it was defined in this document, communion is grounded in participation by faith in the life and mutuality of the Holy Trinity (n. 6). Such a communion is necessarily open to all who also participate in the Triune God. It is thereby turned to all diversities that are compatible with catholicity and unity (n. 14). It entailed a commitment to mission; and part of this mission is "to move beyond our limited and often inward looking forms of congregational and ecclesial life" (n. 19). Such an understanding of communion could only be fostered by the increasing cooperation between Lutherans and Anglicans.

LUTHERANS AND OTHER CHRISTIANS

The broad process of dialogue that was at work among European Lutherans since the formation of the LWF in 1947 raised early the crucial question: Where should dialogue lead? The answer was obvious. After discussions among theologians it should lead to decisions and actions by the authorities of the churches. Doctrinal agreements should not be ranked as theoretical speculation. They are the opening toward a pastoral horizon. The question of implementation was thus faced squarely in two dialogues in which Lutheran churches were engaged.

Chronologically first, the Leuenburg agreement was reached between Lutheran and Reformed theologians in Germany in September 1971, presented to the churches in March 1973, and adopted by Lutheran and Reformed Churches in October 1974. Henceforth the churches that would subscribe to it would be in communion while keeping their administrative structures and the theological accents of their tradition.

The international dialogue between the Lutheran World Federation and the Roman Catholic Church, which started at the same time as ARCIC-I, issued common statements on *The Gospel and the Church* (1972) and on the *Eucharist* (1979), and then turned its attention to the more difficult problem of reunion between Lutherans and Roman Catholics. The report *Facing Unity* (1985) described several "models of union," and envisioned a growth toward church fellowship through a progressive communion in faith, sacraments, and service. While the report was not received officially, it opened the way to an ecumenical study of the anathemas of the sixteenth century on the question of justification. The relevant canons of the Council of Trent and of the Formula of Concord were judged to be no longer church-dividing. An evaluation of this conclusion by the Pontifical Council for the Unity of

Christians and the Congregation for the Doctrine of the Faith bore fruit when, on October 31, 1999, the Catholic Church and the Lutheran World Federation signed their Common Declaration on Justification by Faith.

In a way that was broadly parallel with this, Lutherans in several countries carried on conversations with Reformed Churches, the Moravian Church, the Methodist Church, and Churches of the Anglican Communion. The result has been remarkable, since several agreements of full communion have been passed: the Porvoo Common Statement (October, 1992) that links the Anglican Churches in the British Isles and the Lutheran Churches in Scandinavia and the Baltic States; a relationship of full communion between the ELCA and the Reformed Church in America, the Presbyterian Church USA, and the United Church of Christ (August, 1997); and a similar relationship between the ELCA and the Moravian Church (1999).

EPISCOPALIANS AND LUTHERANS

Dialogues took place at the same time between Lutherans and the Anglican Communion at the international level and in the United States. In the USA the dialogue was initiated by the General Convention of the Episcopal Church in 1967. It started effectively in October 1969, with what was then the Lutheran Council in the USA. A first series of meetings produced a Progress Report in 1973. A second series, begun in 1976, ended in 1980 with a Report and Recommendations, in which the Lutheran Church, Missouri Synod, could not join. Constituted in 1982, the ELCA soon picked up the recommendations made in 1980. In 1982, agreement was reached with the Episcopal Church that a third series of dialogues should seek ways for the two churches to arrive at full communion. Several reports came from this phase of the dialogue: *Implications of the Gospel* (1998), *Toward Full Communion*

(January 1991), and a proposal for full communion that was entitled, *Concordat of Agreement* (January 1991). After further extensive discussions the proposal was reworded by the ELCA. The new form, *Called to Common Mission,* was finally adopted by the two churches in 1999.

A close attention is now paid throughout the churches to the doctrine of *koinonia.* On the one hand the World Council of Churches has long considered its member-churches as being in a relationship of developing communion. On the other hand, the dialogues of Roman Catholics with Anglicans, Lutherans, and Disciples have published joint studies of the ecclesiology of communion. These are not academic exercises. The findings are grounded in the biblical descriptions of discipleship, in the traditions of the churches, and also in the very experience of dialogue across denominations. In fact all the ecumenical dialogues have made it possible to experience communion in Christ where it was not formerly deemed possible, namely across the institutional boundaries of churches. And when this is truly experienced collectively, and not only by individuals who may be particularly sensitive to certain types of relationships, then decisions and actions at the highest level of authority become imperative. In their different contexts *Called to Common Mission* and the *Joint Declaration on the Doctrine of Justification* have shown that a decision is possible by the leadership of the churches when it has been adequately prepared.

THE PROMISE

Reconciliation requires the desire to be reconciled. This is true of churches as it is of persons. The implications of arguments vary according to their context. They lead to understanding when they are explained among friends, and to hostility when among rivals. Arguments that seem convincing in a hostile context are not persuasive among friends. This was one of the problems at Westminster and in Rome, when Leo XIII in 1896 pronounced his condemnation of Anglican ordinations. And today the argumentation of the apostolic letter *Apostolicae curae* seems empty of substance when the Archbishop of Canterbury accompanies the Pope at the official opening of the great jubilee of the year 2000! It is because Episcopalians and American Lutherans have lived close to one another and have been able to appreciate the similarities of their worship, their teaching, and their social commitment, that they have been able to arrive at full communion.

Doctrine does not thereby lose its importance. On the contrary, the agreement is made possible by the conviction that the churches concerned share the same doctrine about God, the revelation in Christ, and the nature and purpose of the church. Admittedly, the Anglican tradition has focused its formulation of doctrine on the liturgical embodiment of it, in keeping with the patristic principle, *lex orandi lex credendi* (the rule of prayer is the rule of belief). One should not be misled by expressions like "the essentials," or "the fundamental articles" of the faith, that were commonly used by the Caroline divines. They do not designate a small hard core outside of which there would only be individual opinions. They correspond to what a more ontological way of speaking would call the essence of the faith. It is "the substance," the "same sense and same judgment" to which John XXIII referred, in September 1962, in the inaugural address of Vatican Council II, "The substance of the ancient doctrine contained in the deposit of faith is one thing, another the formulation in which it is clothed, taking account, as to forms and proportions, of the needs of a chiefly pastoral teaching and style, yet in the same sense and with the same judgment" *(eodem tamen sensu eademque sententia).* Analogically, many formulations of the faith at the time of the Reformation—in the *Confession of Augsburg,* in the *Heidelberg Catechism* and the Calvinist Confessions, in the Book of Common Prayer and the Thirty-nine Articles, and also in the decrees of the Council of Trent—were to one another, at the time, like the Creed of Nicaea interpreted in the many languages of the world. The creed does not sound the same at all when one hears it in Latin, English, and ki-Swahili. It nevertheless expresses the same identical faith in three linguistic systems. Admittedly, the differences that must be overcome today for the disunited churches to come together as one communion are more than linguistic. Four centuries of separate life have left profound marks on the ethos, the practice, and the self-understanding of each church.

One should not be misled at this point by a recent debate about the expression that appears in the decree on ecumenism of Vatican Council II: "Western Churches and Ecclesial Communities." When he introduced this text to the Vatican Council on October 7, 1964, the Archbishop of Westminster, John Carmel Heenan, declared explicitly: As we use these terms, "we do not at all enter the disputed question of what is required for a Christian community to be theologically called a Church." He thus limited the meaning of the text; and it was with this meaning that the Council adopted it and Paul VI promulgated it.

Beyond temporary setbacks there remains the promise of the unity for which Jesus prayed. In baptism the churches are one communion. In eschatological hope and prayer they anticipate their restored oneness. In between they must continue to search for eucharistic unity. That this is possible is the promise that is now carried by Episcopalians and Lutherans together.

9
STEPS TO COMMON MISSION

A Narrative Chronology

Don S. Armentrout

On October 4, 1967, a bilateral dialogue was authorized between the Lutheran Council in the United States of America (LCUSA) and the Episcopal Church in the United States of America (ECUSA). The Lutheran Council consisted of the American Lutheran Church (ALC), the Lutheran Church in America (LCA) and the Lutheran Church-Missouri Synod (LC-MS). The first series of the dialogue went from October 14, 1969, until June 1, 1972. The Lutheran participants in the dialogue were named by the Division of Theological Studies of the Lutheran Council in the United States of America, and the Episcopal participants were named by the Joint Commission on Ecumenical Relations of the Episcopal Church. This first series of the dialogue is known as LED I. The agreement, recommendations and papers were published under the title *Lutheran-Episcopal Dialogue: A Progress Report* (1972).

Agreement was reached on the following fundamentals of church life and doctrine:

a. The primacy and authority of the Holy Scriptures
b. The doctrine of the Apostles' and Nicene Creeds
c. Justification by grace through faith as affirmed by both the Lutheran Confessions and the Anglican Book of Common Prayer and Thirty-Nine Articles of Religion
d. The doctrine and practice of Baptism
e. Fundamental agreement on the Holy Eucharist, though with some differences in emphasis.[1]

The recommendations included "Continuing joint theological study and conversation, at a level similar to that of the conversations just concluded, with such arrangements for broad discussion as will assure influence on the thought and practice of both communions.[2]

The second series of the dialogue met from January 28-31, 1976, until November 8, 1980, and is known as LED II. The proceedings were published under the title *Lutheran-Episcopal Dialogue: Report and Recommendations* (1991) (another title for the proceedings is *The Report of the Lutheran-Episcopal Dialogue, Second Series, 1976-1980*). One of the major recommendations was "That, because of the consensus achieved in the discussion of LED I and II on the chief doctrines of the Christian faith, our respective bodies work out a policy of interim eucharistic hospitality so that Episcopalians may be welcomed at Lutheran altars and that Lutherans may be welcomed at Episcopalian altars."[3]

In September 1982, LED II reached its climax when four American churches passed identical recommendations in their general conventions. The Episcopal Church, the American Lutheran Church, the Lutheran Church in America, and the Association of Evangelical Lutheran Churches (AELC)[4] voted to enter a new kind of relationship known as Interim Sharing of the Eucharist.

The four denominations agreed that "the basic teaching of each respective church is consonant with the Gospel and is sufficiently compatible with the teaching of this church that a relationship of Interim Sharing of the Eucharist is hereby established."[5] Several guidelines spelled out how this would happen and what it would look like. The Episcopal Church would extend a special welcome to members of the three Lutheran bodies "to receive Holy Communion" in it and the three Lutheran bodies would do the same with regard to members of the Episcopal Church. It was clearly noted that "this does not intend to signify that final recognition of each other's Eucharists or ministries has yet been achieved."[6] The heart of the document was guideline 4b:

> Recognize that bishops of dioceses of the Episcopal Church and bishops/presidents of the Lutheran districts/synods may by mutual agreement extend the regulations of church discipline to permit common, joint celebration of the Eucharist in their jurisdictions. This is appropriate in particular situations where the said authorities deem that local conditions are appropriate for the sharing of worship jointly by congregations of the respective churches. The presence of an ordained minister of each participating church at the altar in this way reflects the presence of two or more churches expressing unity in faith and baptism as well as the remaining divisions which they seek to overcome; however, this does not imply rejection or final recognition of either church's Eucharist or ministry. In such circumstances the eucharistic prayer will be one from the Lutheran Book of Worship or the Book of Common Prayer as authorized jointly by the bishop of the Episcopal diocese and the bishops/presidents of the corresponding Lutheran districts/synods.[7]

This meant that clergy of one denomination could stand with, but not in the place of, clergy of another denomination. Full intercommunion means that clergy of one denomination may stand in the place of clergy of the other denomination. The term, "Interim Sharing of the Eucharist," was a new expression to describe a new relationship, based on a sufficient, not total, mutual recognition of eucharistic teaching.

On May 3, 1983, the Executive Council of the Lutheran Church in America adopted guidelines for implementing "Interim Sharing of the Eucharist." Among the guidelines were the following: "Consideration should be given to the following models of service: When the service is in an Episcopal church, an Episcopal rite [will] be used with an Episcopal priest as presiding minister and when the service is in a Lutheran Church, a Lutheran service [will] be used with a Lutheran pastor as presiding minister. It is appropriate for the guest Episcopal or Lutheran minister to be the preacher." "Ministers should be vested in the manner appropriate to their tradition." "Worship materials from both traditions can be employed, but an amalgamation of Lutheran and Episcopal rites should not occur." "Since the eucharistic prayer is required in the Episcopal tradition and an option in the Lutheran tradition, Lutherans should employ a eucharistic prayer. This prayer is to come from the Book of Common Prayer if an Episcopal priest is the presiding minister or from the *Lutheran Book of Worship* if a Lutheran pastor is the presiding minister." "During the Great Thanksgiving, ministers from both traditions should be present at the altar. There should be only one presiding minister. Only this person should recite the eucharistic prayer. Concelebration by word or gesture is precluded." "Ministers of both traditions should take part in the distribution of communion."[8]

The fifth section of the *Agreement* stated: "Authorize and establish a third series of Lutheran-Episcopal Dialogues for the discussion of any other outstanding questions that must be resolved before full communion (*communio in sacris*/altar and pulpit fellowship) can be established between the respective churches, e.g., implications of the Gospel, historic episcopate, and ordering of ministry (bishops, priests, and deacons) in the total context of apostolicity."[9]

The third series of the dialogue, known as LED III, ran from December 4, 1983, until December 31, 2000, when *Called to Common Mission* went into effect. The first topic considered was implications of the gospel. After over four years of dialogue, *Implications of the Gospel* was published.[10] It illustrated the converging theological scholarship in both of the churches.

On January 1, 1988, the ELCA came into being. It was formed by a merger of the American Lutheran Church, the Association of Evangelical Lutheran Churches, and the Lutheran Church in America. From this time on the dialogue was between the Episcopal Church and the Evangelical Lutheran Church in America.

The remaining issue for LED III to discuss was the historic episcopate and the ordering of ministry (bishops, priests, and deacons) in the context of apostolicity. The major issue that had divided Lutherans and Episcopalians since the sixteenth-century Reformation was polity or order. During the sixteenth century, the Lutherans in Germany dropped the historic episcopate, but the Church of England continued it. This meant that Lutheran and Episcopalians were divided over the issue of polity. LED III continued to address that issue and on January 6, 1991, issued "Concordat of Agreement Between the Episcopal Church and the Evangelical Lutheran Church in America." This was a plan to overcome the polity issues.

The Book of Common Prayer, in "An Outline of the Faith commonly called the Catechism," states (855) that "The ministers of the Church are lay persons, bishops, priests, and deacons." These are the four orders of the church. At the level of laypersons there is complete reconciliation between Lutherans and Episcopalians. Because of baptism nothing divides Lutheran laypersons from Episcopal laypersons. At the level of bishops there is a lack of reconciliation between Lutherans and Episcopalians. Lutheran bishops and Episcopal bishops have been divided over the issue of the historic episcopate. The Church of England continued the historic episcopate during the sixteenth-century English Reformation and then passed it on to the Episcopal Church in the United States with the consecration of Samuel Seabury. The Lutherans in Germany dropped the historic episcopate primarily because no Roman Catholic bishops joined the Lutheran movement.

At the level of the episcopate, ELCA bishops and Episcopal Church bishops are not reconciled. The same is true with regard to the order of presbyter (priest/pastor). The "Preface to the Ordination Rites" in the Book of Common Prayer states (510), "The persons who are chosen and recognized by the Church as being called by God to the ordained ministry are admitted to these sacred orders by solemn prayer and the laying on of episcopal hands. . . . No persons are allowed to exercise the offices of bishop, priest, or deacon in this Church unless they are so ordained, or have already received ordination with the laying on of hands by bishops who are themselves duly qualified to confer Holy Orders." With regard to deacons there is also a lack of reconciliation. The Episcopal Church ordains deacons, but the Evangelical Lutheran Church in America does not.

Later in 1991, LED III published *"Toward Full Communion"* and *"Concordat of Agreement," Lutheran–Episcopal Dialogue, Series III. "Toward Full Communion"* traces the work of the dialogues until 1991, and *"Concordat*

of Agreement" describes the basis and several actions of
each church that would bring them into full communion.
On November 10, 1991, the Joint Lutheran-Episcopal
Coordinating Committee was appointed. It consisted of
eight members from the Episcopal Church and nine members from the ELCA. The coordinating committee was
charged with responsibility for implementing the following
goals:

1. To assist the two churches in understanding and in
    moving towards full communion, and in the reception
    of *The Concordat of Agreement* and its accompanying
    theological document *Toward Full Communion.*

2. To continue to explore and to recommend ways of
    implementing the 1982 Joint Agreement, including
    Implications of the Gospel.

3. To assist in developing processes and resources for a
    study of the above-mentioned documents.

4. To interpret the relationship between full communion
    and mission, as set forth in the above-mentioned
    documents.

5. To facilitate communication among all expressions of
    the two churches (national, synodical, diocesan, local)
    regarding proposals put forth by LED III, responses to
    the proposals, and implications of the proposals.

6. To assist in the interpretation of the proposals put
    forth by LED III within the wider ecumenical context,
    seeking comments and responses from other ecu-
    menical partners; comments and responses from
    inter-Anglican bodies (e.g., ACC) and inter-Lutheran
    bodies (e.g., LWF); and to be sensitive to areas of
    dissent and concern within our two churches.[11]

At first there was little conversation about and discussion of this last LED III document. What got the discussion
going was a joint meeting on October 3-8, 1996, of the
House of Bishops of the Episcopal Church and the Conference of Bishops of the Evangelical Lutheran Church in America at Mountain Laurel Lodge, White Haven, Pennsylvania. At

the conclusion of the meeting H. George Anderson, presiding bishop of the ELCA, and Edmond L. Browning, presiding bishop of the Episcopal Church, issued the "Mountain Laurel Communique" endorsing the "Concordat of Agreement." In it they noted that "We stand on the threshold of an exciting new possibility—namely, the declaration of full communion between our churches and the mutual recognition of the authenticity of the ordained ministries presently existing in our two churches." They added, "Unity and mission are organically linked in the Body of Christ, the church. . . . We remind our churches that our search for a fuller expression of visible unity is for the sake of living and sharing the gospel."[12] At this meeting the ELCA bishops drew up a list of twelve recommendations and forwarded them to the Joint Lutheran-Episcopal Coordinating Committee. The coordinating committee met October 31-November 3, 1996, and issued a final revision of the "Concordat of Agreement."

On July 16-25, 1997, the 72nd General Convention of the Episcopal Church met in Philadelphia and overwhelmingly passed the "Concordat of Agreement." The House of Bishops passed it by 98 percent and the House of Deputies by 95.5 percent. The Churchwide Assembly (which is a unicameral body) of the Evangelical Lutheran Church in America also met in Philadelphia, August 14-20, 1997, and voted in favor of the "Concordat" 684 to 381, but that was six votes short of the needed two-thirds majority. It received 66.1 percent of the vote. After defeating the "Concordat" the Assembly passed the following resolution:

> RESOLVED, that the Evangelical Lutheran Church in America seeks conversations with The Episcopal Church, building on the degree of consensus achieved at this assembly and addressing concerns that emerged during consideration of the Concordat of Agreement. The aim of these conversations is to bring to the Churchwide Assembly a revised proposal for full communion. . . .[13]

Following the Churchwide Assembly, the Church Council of the ELCA voted "To request that the Office of the Presiding Bishop of the Evangelical Lutheran Church in America work with the counterpart in The Episcopal Church in developing a revised and rewritten *Concordat of Agreement*, using clear, down-to-earth language and including the rationale for its conclusions and recommendations; and to authorize the presiding bishop, in consultation with the Executive Committee of the Church Council, to appoint a small drafting team to be informed by a panel of advisors in that endeavor, with the understanding that an effort will be made in the composition of the team and panel to reflect the diversity of opinion on this matter within this church."[14]

The three Lutheran members of the drafting team were Martin E. Marty, chairman; Todd W. Nichol; and Michael J. Root. The three Episcopal members were C. Christopher Epting, William A. Norgren, and J. Robert Wright. On April 9, 1998, the drafting team issued a draft proposal to be studied by the churches. It was entitled *Called to Common Mission: A Lutheran Proposal for a Revision of the Concordat of Agreement*. On October 14-15, 1998, the drafting team met and revised this document. Then on November 13-16, 1998, the ELCA Church Council met and voted to transmit the October draft of the document to the next Churchwide Assembly.

Called to Common Mission differs from the *Concordat of Agreement* in a number of ways. The first concerns how to reconcile Lutheran bishops and Episcopal bishops. The *Concordat* required that three Episcopal bishops must participate in the ordaining and consecrating of future Lutheran bishops. *Called to Common Mission* requires that three bishops in the historic episcopate will preside at the installation[15] of a new Lutheran bishop. These bishops will be invited from the churches of the Lutheran communion which share in the historic episcopate. Also, a bishop from the Episcopal Church will participate in the installation.

In the Episcopal Church a bishop does not serve a stated term, but has "life tenure" in the sense that he or she is a bishop for life, regardless of office. Lutheran bishops will be installed for a six-year term and can be reelected. Their tenure in office and identity as bishop may be terminated by retirement, resignation, disciplinary action, or conclusion of term.

Called to Common Mission does not refer to the three-fold order of ministry (bishops, priests, and deacons) as the *Concordat* did. The Lutherans will continue not to ordain deacons.

Meanwhile, Lutheran opposition to *Called to Common Mission* was growing. On February 8-9, 1999, a conference of about 200 Lutherans was held at St. Andrew's Lutheran Church, Mahtomedi, Minnesota, to plan ways to oppose *Called to Common Mission*. The meeting was entitled "Upholding Lutheran Confessions," and it passed the "Mahtomedi Resolution." The resolution was a recommendation that the 1999 Churchwide Assembly reject the document *Called to Common Mission*. Congregations, conferences, and synods opposed to *Called to Common Mission* were invited to sign the resolution, and it was forwarded to ELCA headquarters in Chicago. "Upholding Lutheran Confessions 2" was held at St. Andrew's, Mahtomedi, May 10-11, 1999.

The ELCA Churchwide Assembly met at Denver, August 16-22, 1999, and passed *Called to Common Mission* 716 (69.3 percent) to 317 (30.7 percent). On August 26, 1999, A. L. Barry, president of the Lutheran Church-Missouri Synod, expressed the profound regret of the LC-MS for this action.

On November 15-16, 1999, a WordAlone National Gathering was held at Roseville Lutheran Church, St. Paul, Minnesota, to oppose *Called to Common Mission*. The gathering elected Roger Eigenfeld, pastor of St. Andrew's Lutheran Church, Mahtomedi, Minnesota, interim chair. Then on February 16-18, 2000, 18 members of the ELCA met in Milwaukee and adopted the "Common Ground Resolution." This resolution read in part:

> Whereas the Evangelical Lutheran Church in America has adopted at its 1999 Churchwide Assembly in Denver, Colorado, the requirement that all future ELCA bishops must be installed into the Episcopal historic episcopate and all future pastors must be ordained by ELCA bishops, And whereas these requirements have forced me/us to participate in practices which I/we, in good conscience, cannot believe and hereby refuse to accept;
>
> I, we, the undersigned. . .
>
> Do hereby pledge to resist and not comply with any and all efforts to impose the requirement of accepting an historic episcopate upon the members, congregations, . . . pastors and bishops of the ELCA and do hereby join the company of like-minded brothers and sisters in Christ in the WordAlone Network for the purpose of carrying forth mission, ministry, worship and service in an organization free of the historic episcopate.[16]

On March 6, 2000, the ELCA Conference of Bishops adopted a Pastoral Letter on Implementation of *Called to Common Mission*. In it the bishops stated: ". . . we invite the exploration of possible ways to allow a synodical bishop, in unusual circumstances and with appropriate consultation, to authorize another ELCA pastor to preside at an ordination." On March 26-29, 2000, the Constituting Convention of the WordAlone Network was held at St. Andrew's Lutheran Church, Mahtomedi, and elected Roger C. Eigenfeld president.

The 73rd General Convention of the Episcopal Church
met at Denver and passed *Called to Common Mission*
overwhelmingly. It was to go into effect on January 1,
2001.

The WordAlone Network met at St. Andrew's Church,
Mahtomedi, on November 9-11, 2000, and heard about a
new association to be formed, Lutheran Congregations in
Mission for Christ (LCMC). This was to be an umbrella
organization for churches opposed to *Called to Common
Mission*.

On January 6, 2001, the Epiphany of Our Lord Jesus
Christ, Lutherans and Episcopalians inaugurated full communion with a service at the Cathedral of St. Peter and St.
Paul (the National Cathedral) in Washington, D.C. Presiding Bishop Frank Griswold preached and stressed the centrality of baptism for both denominations.

The ELCA Conference of Bishops met March 1-6, 2001,
and unanimously approved a proposed bylaw change to the
ELCA constitution that would permit synod bishops to
authorize another ELCA pastor to preside at an ordination.
On March 9-11, 2001, the Board of the Division for Ministry (ELCA) met and approved guidelines that would help
the ELCA implement a bylaw being considered to permit
ordinations "in unusual circumstances." On March 10, the
Board voted 10-7 to send the following text to the Church
Council of the ELCA. The text of the changed bylaw,
7.13.17, reads:

> Ordinations in unusual circumstances. For pastoral
> reasons in unusual circumstances a synodical bishop
> may provide for the ordination of another pastor of
> the Evangelical Lutheran Church in America of an
> approved candidate who has received and accepted a
> properly issued, duly attested letter of call for the
> office of ordained ministry. Prior to authorization of
> such an ordination, the bishop of the synod of the can-
> didate's first call shall consult with the presiding bishop

as this church's ecumenical officer and shall seek the advice of the Synod Council. The pastoral decision of the synod bishop shall be informed by guidelines developed by the Division for Ministry, reviewed by the Conference of Bishops and adopted by the Church Council.

On March 20, 2001, Presiding Bishop Frank T. Griswold of the Episcopal Church wrote a letter to ELCA Presiding Bishop H. George Anderson. Griswold expressed his concerns about the bylaw changes:

> While recognizing the pastoral concern which prompts this proposed bylaw, I am concerned that it seems to compromise the ELCA's voted intention as a church "to enter the ministry of the historic episcopate" (CCM, para. 18), especially with regard to its voted "provision that a bishop shall regularly preside and participate in the laying-on-of-hands at the ordination of all clergy" (CCM, para. 20).
>
> It was my understanding that the rationale of the ELCA for adding the word "regularly" to paragraph 20 of the original CCM text was that this word "does not imply the possibility of planned exceptions but allows for pastoral discretion in emergencies" (Section IV, page 10.4 of the 1999 ELCA Churchwide Assembly). Although such provision is virtually unknown in Anglican-Lutheran agreements anywhere in the world, the Episcopal Church agreed that it would understand the ELCA to be a church entering the historic episcopate so long as such emergency ordinations are not accepted for the purpose of interchangeability or reciprocity.
>
> This proposal for the ELCA seems to create two classes of clergy, it ensures that the argument over CCM will continue, it allows for denial of that which was previously agreed, it threatens the role of bishop as focus of unity in service to Word and Sacrament, and it could jeopardize future hopes of the ELCA for closer relations and full communion with the majority of other churches that already perform ordinations in the historic catholic tradition and thus do not acknowledge ordinations by pastors.

> Certainly none of us would want to see the "full" com-
> munion we have recently achieved be reduced to
> something like "partial" or "limited" communion.[17]

The ELCA Church Council approved the guidelines approved by the Board of the Division of Ministry on April 6-8, 2001.

Meanwhile, the Second Annual WordAlone Network Convention was held at Valley Cathedral, Phoenix, Arizona, March 25-27, 2002. At this meeting they adopted a constitution for a new Lutheran association, Lutheran Congregations in Mission for Christ (LCMC). This is an association for ELCA congregations opposed to *Called to Common Mission*. At this meeting the Rev. Sam Pascoe, an Episcopal priest, said, "What is happening among our two [denominations] is not only anti-Lutheran, it is anti-Anglican, [and] sub-Christian."[18] The first national convention of LCMC met at Westwood Lutheran Church, St. Louis Park, Minneapolis, Minnesota, October 26-27, 2001.

The ELCA Churchwide Assembly met at Indianapolis on August 8-14, 2001, and approved the bylaw that allows its bishops to delegate to other clergy their authority to ordain. The Episcopal Church has made it clear that ELCA clergy not ordained by a bishop will not be interchangeable with Episcopal clergy.

On July 20, 2002, Daniel Shaw was ordained pastor by another pastor, the Rev. Richard H. Foege, at Emmanuel Lutheran Church, Tacoma, Washington. Bishop William Chris Boerger of the Northeast Washington Synod of the ELCA granted the request for "ordination under unusual circumstances." This is the first exception made to the guidelines of *Called to Common Mission*.

Professor J. Robert Wright has stated most clearly the joint possibilities of *Called to Common Mission*:

This shared leadership and interaction may include, for example, sacramental sharing and common celebration of the Eucharist, interchangeability of clergy upon invitation, regular representation of the other church at each church's diocesan conventions or synodical assemblies, the symbolic presence and actual participation of bishops and others from time to time at major events in the life of the other church, representation of the church in each church's structures of mission, sharing of resources and programs and staff, periodic joint meetings of the Episcopal House of Bishops and the Lutheran Conference of Bishops as well as of other churchwide officers, regular consultations on the basis of common issues or overlapping regions, elimination of duplicated facilities, closer sharing of ecumenical dialogues, intentional prayer for each other at all levels, common planning for evangelization, clustering in sparsely populated areas, increased sharing of education at all levels (seminaries, retreats, instructional materials, parish programs), sharing of chaplaincies in military, medical, and prison ministries, common facing of ethical and social issues, and joint approaches to multi-cultural and multi-ethnic situations in urban areas.[19]

At the time of this writing, it remains to be seen what will be the impact of the WordAlone movement and the provision for Lutheran ordinations by those who are not bishops in the historic episcopate. Despite the tensions and uncertainties, there continues to be considerable enthusiasm for discovering common mission by the Lutheran and Episcopal Churches.

NOTES

[1] *Lutheran-Episcopal Dialogue: A Progress Report* (Cincinnati: Forward Movement, 1972), 23.

[2] Ibid., 24.

[3] *Lutheran-Episcopal Dialogue: Report and Recommendations* (Cincinnati: Forward Movement, 1981), 57.

[4] The constituting convention of the Association of Evangelical Lutheran Churches was held, December 4-5, 1976. The AELC was a group of moderates who left the Lutheran Church-Missouri Synod.

[5] *The Lutheran-Episcopal Agreement: Commentary and Guidelines* (Division for World Mission and Ecumenism, Lutheran Church in America, 1983), 8.

[6] Ibid., 8.

[7] Ibid., 8-9.

[8] Ibid., 15-16.

[9] Ibid., 13.

[10] *Implications of the Gospel: Lutheran-Episcopal Dialogue, Series III.* Edited by William A. Norgren and William G. Rusch (Cincinnati: Forward Movement; Minneapolis: Augsburg Fortress, 1988).

[11] *The Blue Book: Reports of the Committees, Commissions, Boards, and Agencies of the General Convention of the Episcopal Church. 71st General Convention, Indianapolis, Indiana, August, 1994* (New York: General Convention of the Episcopal Church, 1994), 177. AAC is the Anglican Consultative Council and LWF is the Lutheran World Federation.

[12] "Mountain Laurel Communique" (Unpublished paper).

[13] *Report of the Lutheran-Episcopal Drafting Team* (Chicago: Evangelical Lutheran Church in America, 1998), 4.

[14] Ibid.

[15] What the Episcopalians refer to as "consecration" the Lutherans call "installation."

[16] WordAlone Network flyer.

[17] Faxed copy of letter in writer's files.

[18] http://www.wordalone.org/lcmc/lcmc_press_release.htm

[19] J. Robert Wright, "Ecumenical Breakthrough between Episcopalians and Lutherans in the United States: An Ecclesiological Reflection, "*Internationale Kirchliche Zeitschrift* (2002): 200.

10

CALLED TO COMMON MISSION

A Lutheran Proposal for a Revision of the *Concordat of Agreement**

INTRODUCTION

Our churches have discovered afresh our unity in the gospel and our commitment to the mission to which God calls the church of Jesus Christ in every generation. Unity and mission are organically linked in the Body of Christ, the church. All baptized people are called to lives of faithful witness and service in the name of Jesus. Indeed, the baptized are nourished and sustained by Christ as encountered in word and sacrament. Our search for a fuller expression of visible unity is for the sake of living and sharing the gospel. Unity and mission are at the heart of the church's life, reflecting thereby an obedient response to the call of our Lord Jesus Christ.

Many years of thorough and conscientious dialogue have brought our churches to this moment. The history of

---

how far our churches have already traveled together is significant. It guides us on a common path toward the unity for which Christ prayed.

The purpose of this *Concordat of Agreement* is to achieve full communion between the Evangelical Lutheran Church in America and the Episcopal Church. Our churches have set this goal in response to our Lord's prayer that all may be one. Our growing unity is urgently required so that our churches will be empowered to engage more fully and more faithfully the mission of God in the world.

> I ask not only on behalf of these, but also on behalf of those who will believe in me through their word, that they may all be one. As you, Father, are in me and I am in you, may they also be in us, so that the world may believe that you have sent me (John 17:20-21).

The Concordat is the latest stage in a long history of ecumenical dialogue between the two churches. Although the issues that gave rise to the Protestant Reformation in England and on the European continent were dissimilar in some respects, Anglicans and Lutherans have long recognized something of themselves in each other, and our churches have never issued condemnations against one another. Liturgical and sacramental worship has always figured largely in the identity and character of each tradition. Moreover, the architects of reformation, both in England and on the continent, were concerned to uphold the catholic faith. Thus it is no surprise that official ecumenical conversations between Lutherans and Anglicans date back to the late nineteenth century.

The first official conversation in this century involving Anglicans and Lutherans in the U.S.A. took place in December 1935, between The Episcopal Church and The Augustana Evangelical Lutheran Church, a church with roots in Sweden. In 1969, the first of three rounds of Lutheran-Episcopal Dialogue began. Periodic reports were submitted to the Evangelical Lutheran Church in America and its predecessor bodies and to The Episcopal Church. Two final reports, *Implications of the Gospel* and *"Toward Full Communion" and "Concordat of Agreement,"* were submitted in 1988 and 1991 respectively.

Lutheran-Episcopal Dialogue was coordinated through the Lutheran World Federation and the Anglican Consultative Council with the Anglican-Lutheran International Conversations, the European Regional Commission, and the other national and local dialogues. Consultations were held as well with other churches and traditions in dialogue with Lutherans and Anglicans.

In 1996, the Nordic and Baltic Lutheran and the British and Irish Anglican churches entered communion on the basis of agreement in The Porvoo Common Statement. Earlier, in 1988, the Evangelical Lutheran Church in Germany and the Church of England agreed on steps to closer relations on the basis of The Meissen Declaration. Anglican and Lutheran churches in Canada, in Southern and Eastern Africa, and in Asia have initiated dialogue and begun to share in mission. These actions, and those that follow, help to prepare us and, indeed, other churches committed to the ecumenical movement, to move from our present separation into a relationship of full communion.

Official Text

CALLED TO COMMON MISSION:
A LUTHERAN PROPOSAL FOR A REVISION
OF THE *CONCORDAT OF AGREEMENT*

As Amended by the 1999 Churchwide Assembly of the
Evangelical Lutheran Church in America

[August 19, 1999]

1. The Lutheran-Episcopal Agreement of 1982 identified as
its goal the establishment of "full communion (*communio
in sacris*/altar and pulpit fellowship)" between The Episcopal Church and the churches that united to form the
Evangelical Lutheran Church in America. As the meaning
of full communion for purposes of this *Concordat of
Agreement*, both churches endorse in principle the definitions agreed to by the (international) Anglican-Lutheran
Joint Working Group at Cold Ash, Berkshire, England, in
1983, which they deem to be in full accord with their own
definitions given in the Evangelical Lutheran Church in
America's policy statement "Ecumenism: The Vision of the
Evangelical Lutheran Church in America" (1991), and in
the "Declaration on Unity" of The Episcopal Church
(1979). This agreement describes the relationship between
our two church bodies. It does not define the church,
which is a gift of God's grace.

2. We therefore understand full communion to be a relation between distinct churches in which each recognizes
the other as a catholic and apostolic church holding the
essentials of the Christian faith. Within this new relation,
churches become interdependent while remaining
autonomous. Full communion includes the establishment
locally and nationally of recognized organs of regular
consultation and communication, including episcopal

collegiality, to express and strengthen the fellowship and enable common witness, life, and service. Diversity is preserved, but this diversity is not static. Neither church seeks to remake the other in its own image, but each is open to the gifts of the other as it seeks to be faithful to Christ and his mission. They are together committed to a visible unity in the church's mission to proclaim the Word and administer the Sacraments.

3. The Episcopal Church agrees that in its General Convention, and the Evangelical Lutheran Church in America agrees that in its Churchwide Assembly, there shall be one vote to accept or reject, as a matter of verbal content as well as in principle, the full set of agreements to follow. If they are adopted by both churches, each church agrees to make those legislative, canonical, constitutional, and liturgical changes that are needed and appropriate for the full communion between the churches. In adopting this document, the Evangelical Lutheran Church in America and The Episcopal Church specifically acknowledge and declare that it has been correctly interpreted by the resolution of the Conference of Bishops of the Evangelical Lutheran Church in America, adopted at Tucson, Arizona, March 8, 1999.[1]

A. AGREEMENTS

AGREEMENT IN THE DOCTRINE OF THE FAITH

4. The Evangelical Lutheran Church in America and The Episcopal Church recognize in each other the essentials of the one catholic and apostolic faith as it is witnessed in the unaltered *Augsburg Confession*, the *Small Catechism*, and *The Book of Common Prayer* of 1979 (including "Ordination Rites" and "An Outline of the Faith"), and also

as it is summarized in part in *Implications of the Gospel* and *"Toward Full Communion"* and *"Concordat of Agreement,"* (containing the reports of Lutheran-Episcopal Dialogue III), the papers and official conversations of Lutheran-Episcopal Dialogue III, and the statements formulated by Lutheran-Episcopal Dialogues I and II. Each church also promises to encourage its people to study each other's basic documents.

5. We endorse the international Anglican-Lutheran doctrinal consensus which was summarized in *The Niagara Report* (1989) as follows: "We accept the authority of the canonical Scriptures of the Old and New Testaments. We read the Scriptures liturgically in the course of the church's year.

"We accept the Niceno-Constantinopolitan and Apostles' Creeds and confess the basic Trinitarian and Christological Dogmas to which these creeds testify. That is, we believe that Jesus of Nazareth is true God and true Man, and that God is authentically identified as Father, Son, and Holy Spirit.

"Anglicans and Lutherans use very similar orders of service for the Eucharist, for the Prayer Offices, for the administration of Baptism, for the rites of Marriage, Burial, and Confession and Absolution. We acknowledge in the liturgy both a celebration of salvation through Christ and a significant factor in forming the *consensus fidelium* [the consensus of the faithful]. We have many hymns, canticles, and collects in common.

"We believe that baptism with water in the name of the Triune God unites the one baptized with the death and resurrection of Jesus Christ, initiates into the one, holy, catholic and apostolic church, and confers the gracious gift of new life.

"We believe that the Body and Blood of Christ are truly present, distributed, and received under the forms of bread and wine in the Lord's Supper. We also believe that the grace of divine forgiveness offered in the sacrament is received with the thankful offering of ourselves for God's service.

"We believe and proclaim the gospel, that in Jesus Christ God loves and redeems the world. We share a common understanding of God's justifying grace, i.e. that we are accounted righteous and are made righteous before God only by grace through faith because of the merits of our Lord and Savior Jesus Christ, and not on account of our works or merit. Both our traditions affirm that justification leads and must lead to 'good works'; authentic faith issues in love.

"Anglicans and Lutherans believe that the church is not the creation of individual believers, but that it is constituted and sustained by the Triune God through God's saving action in Word and Sacraments. We believe that the church is sent into the world as sign, instrument, and foretaste of the kingdom of God. But we also recognize that the church stands in constant need of reform and renewal.

"We believe that all members of the church are called to participate in its apostolic mission. They are therefore given various ministries by the Holy Spirit. Within the community of the church the ordained ministry exists to serve the ministry of the whole people of God. We hold the ordained ministry of Word and Sacrament to be a gift of God to his church and therefore an office of divine institution.

"We believe that a ministry of pastoral oversight (*episkope*), exercised in personal, collegial, and communal ways, is necessary to witness to and safeguard the unity and apostolicity of the church.

"We share a common hope in the final consummation of the kingdom of God and believe that we are compelled to work for the establishment of justice and peace. The obligations of the kingdom are to govern our life in the church and our concern for the world. The Christian faith is that God has made peace through Jesus 'by the blood of his cross' (Colossians 1:20) so establishing the one valid center for the unity of the whole human family."

AGREEMENT IN MINISTRY

6. The ministry of the whole people of God forms the context for what is said here about all forms of ministry. We together affirm that all members of Christ's church are commissioned for ministry through baptism. All are called to represent Christ and his church; to bear witness to him wherever they may be; to carry on Christ's work of reconciliation in the world; and to participate in the life, worship, and governance of the church. We give thanks for a renewed discovery of the centrality of the ministry of all the baptized in both our churches. Our witness to the gospel and pursuit of peace, justice, and reconciliation in the world have been immeasurably strengthened. Because both our churches affirm this ministry which has already been treated in our previous dialogues, it is not here extensively addressed. Both churches need more adequately to realize the ministry of the baptized through discernment of gifts, education, equipping the saints for ministry, and seeking and serving Christ in all persons.

7. We acknowledge that one another's ordained ministries are and have been given by God to be instruments of God's grace in the service of God's people, and possess not only the inward call of the Spirit, but also Christ's commission through his body, the church. We acknowledge that personal, collegial, and communal oversight is embodied and exercised in both our churches in a diversity of forms, in fidelity to the teaching and mission of the apostles. We

agree that ordained ministers are called and set apart for the one ministry of Word and Sacrament, and that they do not cease thereby to share in the priesthood of all believers. They fulfill their particular ministries within the community of the faithful and not apart from it. The concept of the priesthood of all believers affirms the need for ordained ministry, while at the same time setting ministry in proper relationship to the laity. The Anglican tradition uses the terms "presbyter" and "priest" and the Lutheran tradition in America characteristically uses the term "pastor" for the same ordained ministry.

8. In order to give witness to the faith we share (see paragraphs 4 and 5 above), we agree that the one ordained ministry will be shared between the two churches in a common pattern for the sake of common mission. In the past, each church has sought and found ways to exercise the ordained ministry in faithfulness to the apostolic message and mission. Each has developed structures of oversight that serve the continuity of this ministry under God's Word. Within the future common pattern, the ministry of pastors/priests will be shared from the outset (see paragraph 16 below). Some functions of ordained deacons in The Episcopal Church and consecrated diaconal ministers and deaconesses in the Evangelical Lutheran Church in America can be shared insofar as they are called to be agents of the church in meeting needs, hopes, and concerns within church and society. The churches will over time come to share in the ministry of bishops in an evangelical, historic succession (see paragraph 19 below). This succession also is manifest in the churches' use of the apostolic scriptures, the confession of the ancient creeds, and the celebration of the sacraments instituted by our Lord. As our churches live in full communion, our

ordained ministries will still be regulated by the constitu-tional framework of each church.

9. Important expectations of each church for a shared ordained ministry will be realized at the beginning of our new relation: an immediate recognition by The Episcopal Church of presently existing ordained ministers within the Evangelical Lutheran Church in America and a commit-ment by the Evangelical Lutheran Church in America to receive and adapt an episcopate that will be shared. Both churches acknowledge that the diaconate, including its place within the threefold ministerial office and its rela-tionship with all other ministries, is in need of continuing exploration, renewal, and reform, which they pledge them-selves to undertake in consultation with one another. The ordination of deacons, deaconesses, or diaconal ministers by the Evangelical Lutheran Church in America is not required by this Concordat.

10. The New Testament describes a laying-on-of-hands to set persons apart for a variety of ministries. In the history of the church, many and various terms have been used to describe the rite by which a person becomes a bishop. In the English language these terms include: confecting, con-secrating, constituting, installing, making, ordaining, ordering. Both our traditions have used the term "conse-cration of bishops" for this same rite at some times. Today the Evangelical Lutheran Church in America uses the term "installation" while The Episcopal Church uses the word "ordination" for the rite by which a person becomes a bishop. What is involved in each case is the setting apart within the one ministry of Word and Sacrament of a per-son elected and called for the exercise of oversight (*episkope*) wider than the local congregation in the service of the gospel.

11. "Historic succession" refers to a tradition which goes back to the ancient church, in which bishops already in the succession install newly elected bishops with prayer and the laying-on-of-hands. At present The Episcopal Church has bishops in this historic succession, as do all the churches of the Anglican Communion, and the Evangelical Lutheran Church in America at present does not, although some member churches of the Lutheran World Federation do. The Chicago-Lambeth Quadrilateral of 1886/1888, the ecumenical policy of The Episcopal Church, refers to this tradition as "the historic episcopate." In the Lutheran Confessions, Article 14 of the Apology refers to this episcopal pattern by the phrase, "the ecclesiastical and canonical polity" which it is "our deep desire to maintain."

12. Commitment and Definition. As a result of their agreement in faith and in testimony of their full communion with one another, both churches now make the following commitment to share an episcopal succession that is both evangelical and historic. They promise to include regularly one or more bishops of the other church to participate in the laying-on-of-hands at the ordinations/installations of their own bishops as a sign, though not a guarantee, of the unity and apostolic continuity of the whole church. With the laying-on-of-hands by other bishops, such ordinations/ installations will involve prayer for the gift of the Holy Spirit. Both churches value and maintain a ministry of *episkope* as one of the ways, in the context of ordained ministries and of the whole people of God, in which the apostolic succession of the church is visibly expressed and personally symbolized in fidelity to the gospel through the ages. By such a liturgical statement the churches recognize that the bishop serves the diocese or synod through ties of collegiality and consultation that strengthen its links with the

universal church. It is also a liturgical expression of the full communion initiated by this Concordat, calling for mutual planning and common mission in each place. We agree that when persons duly called and elected are ordained/installed in this way, they are understood to join bishops already in this succession and thus to enter the historic episcopate.

13. While our two churches will come to share in the historic institution of the episcopate in the church (as defined in paragraph 12 above), each remains free to explore its particular interpretations of the ministry of bishops in evangelical and historic succession. Whenever possible, this should be done in consultation with one another. The Episcopal Church is free to maintain that sharing in the historic catholic episcopate, while not necessary for salvation or for recognition of another church as a church, is nonetheless necessary when Anglicans enter the relationship of full communion in order to link the local churches for mutual responsibility in the communion of the larger church. The Evangelical Lutheran Church in America is free to maintain that this same episcopate, although pastorally desirable when exercised in personal, collegial, and communal ways, is nonetheless not necessary for the relationship of full communion. Such freedom is evidenced by its communion with such non-episcopal churches as the Reformed churches of *A Formula of Agreement* and most churches within the Lutheran World Federation.

14. The two churches will acknowledge immediately the full authenticity of each other's ordained ministries (bishops, priests, and deacons in The Episcopal Church and pastors in the Evangelical Lutheran Church in America). The creation of a common and fully interchangeable ministry of bishops in full communion will occur with the incorporation of all

active bishops in the historic episcopal succession and the continuing process of collegial consultation in matters of Christian faith and life. For both churches, the relationship of full communion begins when both churches adopt this Concordat. For the Evangelical Lutheran Church in America, the characteristics of the goal of full communion—defined in its 1991 policy statement, "Ecumenism: The Vision of the Evangelical Lutheran Church in America" will be realized at this time. For The Episcopal Church, full communion, although begun at the same time, will not be fully realized until both churches determine that in the context of a common life and mission there is a shared ministry of bishops in the historic episcopate. For both churches, life in full communion entails more than legislative decisions and shared ministries. The people of both churches have to receive and share this relationship as they grow together in full communion.

B. ACTIONS OF THE EPISCOPAL CHURCH

15. The Episcopal Church by this Concordat recognizes the ministers ordained in the Evangelical Lutheran Church in America or its predecessor bodies as fully authentic. The Episcopal Church acknowledges that the pastors and bishops of the Evangelical Lutheran Church in America minister as pastors/priests within the Evangelical Lutheran Church in America and that the bishops of the Evangelical Lutheran Church in America are pastors/priests exercising a ministry of oversight (*episkope*) within its synods. Further, The Episcopal Church agrees that all bishops of the Evangelical Lutheran Church in America who are chosen after both churches pass this Concordat and installed within the ministry of the historic episcopate will be understood by The Episcopal Church as having been ordained into this ministry (see paragraph 18 below).

16. To enable the full communion that is coming into being by means of this Concordat, The Episcopal Church pledges to continue the process for enacting a temporary suspension, in this case only, of the seventeenth-century restriction that "no persons are allowed to exercise the offices of bishop, priest, or deacon in this Church unless they are so ordained, or have already received such ordination with the laying-on-of-hands by bishops who are themselves duly qualified to confer Holy Orders" ("Preface to the Ordination Rites," *The Book of Common Prayer*, p. 510). The purpose of this action, to declare this restriction inapplicable to the Evangelical Lutheran Church in America, will be to permit the full interchangeability and reciprocity of all its pastors as priests or presbyters within The Episcopal Church, without any further ordination or re-ordination or supplemental ordination whatsoever, subject always to canonically or constitutionally approved invitation. The purpose of temporarily suspending this restriction, which has been a constant requirement in Anglican polity since the Ordinal of 1662, is precisely in order to secure the future implementation of the ordinal's same principle in the sharing of ordained ministries. It is for this reason that The Episcopal Church can feel confident in taking this unprecedented step with regard to the Evangelical Lutheran Church in America.

17. The Episcopal Church acknowledges and seeks to receive the gifts of the Lutheran tradition which has consistently emphasized the primacy of the Word. The Episcopal Church therefore endorses the Lutheran affirmation that the historic catholic episcopate under the Word of God must always serve the gospel, and that the ultimate authority under which bishops preach and teach is the gospel itself (see *Augsburg Confession* 28. 21-23). In testimony and implementation thereof, The Episcopal Church

agrees to establish and welcome, either by itself or jointly with the Evangelical Lutheran Church in America, structures for collegial and periodic review of the ministry exercised by bishops with a view to evaluation, adaptation, improvement, and continual reform in the service of the gospel.

C. ACTIONS OF THE EVANGELICAL LUTHERAN CHURCH IN AMERICA

18. The Evangelical Lutheran Church in America agrees that all its bishops chosen after both churches pass this Concordat will be installed for pastoral service of the gospel with this church's intention to enter the ministry of the historic episcopate. They will be understood by The Episcopal Church as having been ordained into this ministry, even though tenure in office of the Presiding Bishop and synodical bishops may be terminated by retirement, resignation, disciplinary action, or conclusion of term. Any subsequent installation of a bishop so installed includes a prayer for the gift of the Holy Spirit without the laying-on-of-hands. The Evangelical Lutheran Church in America further agrees to revise its rite for the "installation of a Bishop" to reflect this understanding. A distinction between episcopal and pastoral ministries within the one office of Word and Sacrament is neither commanded nor forbidden by divine law (see *Apology of the Augsburg Confession* 14.1 and the *Treatise on the Power and Primacy of the Pope* 63). By thus freely accepting the historic episcopate, the Evangelical Lutheran Church in America does not thereby affirm that it is necessary for the unity of the church (*Augsburg Confession* 7.3).

19. In order to receive the historic episcopate, the Evangelical Lutheran Church in America pledges that, following

the adoption of this Concordat and in keeping with the collegiality and continuity of ordained ministry attested as early as Canon 4 of the First Ecumenical Council (Nicaea I, A.D. 325), at least three bishops already sharing in the sign of the episcopal succession will be invited to participate in the installation of its next Presiding Bishop through prayer for the gift of the Holy Spirit and with the laying-on-of-hands. These participating bishops will be invited from churches of the Lutheran communion which share in the historic episcopate. In addition, a bishop or bishops will be invited from The Episcopal Church to participate in the same way as a symbol of the full communion now shared. Synodical bishops elected and awaiting installation may be similarly installed at the same service, if they wish. Further, all other installations of bishops in the Evangelical Lutheran Church in America will be through prayer for the gift of the Holy Spirit and with the laying-on-of-hands by other bishops, at least three of whom are to be in the historic succession (see paragraph 12 above). Its liturgical rites will reflect these provisions.

20. In accord with the historic practice whereby the bishop is representative of the wider church, the Evangelical Lutheran Church in America agrees to make constitutional and liturgical provision that a bishop shall regularly preside and participate in the laying-on-of-hands at the ordination of all clergy. Pastors shall continue to participate with the bishop in the laying-on-of-hands at all ordinations of pastors. Such offices are to be exercised as servant ministry, and not for domination or arbitrary control. All the people of God have a true equality, dignity, and authority for building up the body of Christ.

21. The Evangelical Lutheran Church in America by this Concordat recognizes the bishops, priests, and deacons

ordained in The Episcopal Church as fully authentic ministers in their respective orders within The Episcopal Church and the bishops of The Episcopal Church as chief pastors in the historic succession exercising a ministry of oversight (*episkope*) within its dioceses.

D. ACTIONS OF BOTH CHURCHES

INTERCHANGEABILITY OF CLERGY: OCCASIONAL MINISTRY, EXTENDED SERVICE, TRANSFER

22. In this Concordat, the two churches declare that each believes the other to hold all the essentials of the Christian faith, although this does not require from either church acceptance of all doctrinal formulations of the other. Ordained ministers serving occasionally or for an extended period in the ministry of the other church will be expected to undergo the appropriate acceptance procedures of that church respecting always the internal discipline of each church. For the Evangelical Lutheran Church in America, such ministers will be expected to preach, teach, and administer the sacraments in a manner that is consistent with its "Confession of Faith" as written in chapter two of the Constitution, Bylaws, and Continuing Resolutions of the Evangelical Lutheran Church in America. For The Episcopal Church, such ministers will be expected to teach and act in a manner that is consistent with the doctrine, discipline, and worship of The Episcopal Church. Ordained ministers from either church seeking long-term ministry with primary responsibility in the other will be expected to apply for clergy transfer and to agree to the installation vow or declaration of conformity in the church to which she or he is applying to minister permanently.

JOINT COMMISSION

23. To assist in joint planning for mission, both churches authorize the establishment of a joint commission, fully accountable to the decision-making bodies of the two churches. Its purpose will be consultative, to facilitate mutual support and advice as well as common decision making through appropriate channels in fundamental matters that the churches may face together in the future. The joint commission will work with the appropriate boards, committees, commissions, and staff of the two churches concerning such ecumenical, doctrinal, pastoral, and liturgical matters as may arise, always subject to approval by the appropriate decision-making bodies of the two churches.

WIDER CONTEXT

24. In thus moving to establish, in geographically overlapping episcopates in collegial consultation, one ordained ministry open to women as well as to men, to married persons as well as to single persons, both churches agree that the historic catholic episcopate can be locally adapted and reformed in the service of the gospel. In this spirit they offer this Concordat and growth toward full communion for serious consideration among the churches of the Reformation as well as among the Orthodox and Roman Catholic churches. They pledge widespread consultation during the process at all stages. Each church promises to issue no official commentary on this text that has not been accepted by the joint commission as a legitimate interpretation thereof.

EXISTING RELATIONSHIPS

25. Each church agrees that the other church will continue to live in communion with all the churches with whom the latter is now in communion. The Evangelical Lutheran Church in America continues to be in full communion

(pulpit and altar fellowship) with all member churches of the Lutheran World Federation and with three of the Reformed family of churches (Presbyterian Church [U.S.A.], Reformed Church in America, and United Church of Christ). This Concordat does not imply or inaugurate any automatic communion between The Episcopal Church and those churches with whom the Evangelical Lutheran Church in America is in full communion. The Episcopal Church continues to be in full communion with all the Provinces of the Anglican Communion, with the Old Catholic Churches of Europe, with the united churches of the Indian subcontinent, with the Mar Thoma Church, and with the Philippine Independent Church. This Concordat does not imply or inaugurate any automatic communion between the Evangelical Lutheran Church in America and those churches with whom The Episcopal Church is in full communion.

OTHER DIALOGUES

26. Both churches agree that each will continue to engage in dialogue with other churches and traditions. Both churches agree to take each other and this Concordat into account at every stage in their dialogues with other churches and traditions. Where appropriate, both churches will seek to engage in joint dialogues. On the basis of this Concordat, both churches pledge that they will not enter into formal agreements with other churches and traditions without prior consultation with each other. At the same time both churches pledge that they will not impede the development of relationships and agreements with other churches and traditions with whom they have been in dialogue.

E. CONCLUSION

27. Recognizing each other as churches in which the gospel is truly preached and the holy sacraments duly administered, we receive with thanksgiving the gift of unity which is already given in Christ.

> He is the image of the invisible God, the firstborn of all creation; for in him all things in heaven and on earth were created, things visible and invisible, whether thrones or dominions or rulers or powers—all things have been created through him and for him. He himself is before all things, and in him all things hold together. He is the head of the body, the church; he is the beginning, the firstborn from the dead, so that he might come to have first place in everything. For in him all the fullness of God was pleased to dwell, and through him God was pleased to reconcile to himself all things, whether on earth or in heaven, by making peace through the blood of his cross (Colossians 1:15-20).

28. Repeatedly Christians have echoed the scriptural confession that the unity of the church is both Christ's own work and his call to us. It is therefore our task as well as his gift. We must "make every effort to maintain the unity of the Spirit in the bond of peace" (Ephesians 4:3). We pray that we may rely upon, and willingly receive from one another, the gifts Christ gives through his Spirit "for building up the body of Christ" in love (Ephesians 4:16).

29. We do not know to what new, recovered, or continuing tasks of mission this Concordat will lead our churches, but we give thanks to God for leading us to this point. We entrust ourselves to that leading in the future, confident that our full communion will be a witness to the gift and goal already present in Christ, "so that God may be all in all" (1 Corinthians 15:28). Entering full communion and thus removing limitations through mutual recognition of faith, sacraments, and ministries will bring new opportunities

and levels of shared evangelism, witness, and service. It is
the gift of Christ that we are sent as he has been sent (John
17:17-26), that our unity will be received and perceived as
we participate together in the mission of the Son in obedi-
ence to the Father through the power and presence of the
Holy Spirit.

> Now to him who by the power at work within us is able
> to accomplish abundantly far more than all we can ask
> or imagine, to him be glory in the church and in Christ
> Jesus to all generations, forever and ever. Amen
> (Ephesians 3:20-21).

---

[1] RESOLVED, that the Conference of Bishops affirm the
following understandings of "Called to Common Mission":

A. The Conference of Bishops understands that "Called
to Common Mission" contains:

1. no requirement that the Evangelical Lutheran
Church in America must eventually adopt the
three-fold order of ministry. Rather, "Called to Common Mission" recognizes that the present understanding of one ordained ministry in the Evangelical
Lutheran Church in America, including both pastors and bishops, may continue in effect;

2. no requirement that ELCA bishops be elected to
serve as synodical bishops for life. Rather, they will
continue to be elected and installed for six-year
terms, with eligibility for re-election, subject to
term limits, where applicable;

3. no defined role for the presiding bishop or synodical bishops after their tenure in office is completed;

4. no requirement that the Evangelical Lutheran
Church in America establish the office of deacon,
nor that they be ordained;

5. no requirement that priests of The Episcopal Church will serve congregations of the Evangelical Lutheran Church in America without the congregation's consent;

6. no requirement that the Ordinal (rules) of The Episcopal Church will apply to the Evangelical Lutheran Church in America;

7. no commitment to additional constitutional amendments or liturgical revisions other than those presented to the 1999 ELCA Churchwide Assembly (ELCA constitutional provisions 8.72.10-16.; 9.21.02.; 9.90.-9.91.02.; 10.31.a.9.; 10.81.01., and parallel provisions in synodical and congregational constitutions); and further

B. The Conference of Bishops has the expectation that:

1. ordinations of pastors will continue to be held at synodical worship services and in congregations, as is the present pattern;

2. the Evangelical Lutheran Church in America will continue to receive onto the roster of ordained ministers, without re-ordination, pastors from other traditions, some of whom will not have been ordained by a bishop in the historic episcopate;

3. following the adoption of "Called to Common Mission," if someone who has been received onto the roster of ordained ministers of the Evangelical Lutheran Church in America who was not ordained into the pastoral office in the historic episcopate is elected bishop and installed, he or she will be understood to be a bishop in the historic episcopate;

4. lay persons may continue to be licensed by the synodical bishop in unusual circumstances to administer the Sacraments of Baptism and Holy Communion as is the present practice of the Evangelical Lutheran Church in America;

5. "Definitions and Guidelines for Discipline of Ordained Ministers" will apply to priests of The Episcopal Church and ordained ministers of the Reformed churches serving ELCA congregations [under ELCA bylaw 8.71.15.b..."to live in a manner consistent with the ministerial policy of this church."];

6. the Evangelical Lutheran Church in America is not in any way changing its confessional stance that, "For the true unity of the Church it is enough to agree concerning the teaching of the Gospel and the administration of the sacraments" (Augsburg Confession, Article VII);

7. The Episcopal Church accepts fully, and without reservation, present Lutheran pastors and bishops who are not in the historic episcopal succession;

8. priests of The Episcopal Church and ordained ministers of the Reformed churches will not be asked to subscribe personally to the Confession of Faith of the Lutheran Church as their personal faith. They will be expected to recognize the agreement in faith of the churches and to preach and teach in a manner consistent with the Lutheran Confessions;

9. the Evangelical Lutheran Church in America receives the historic episcopal succession as a sign of and service to the continuity and unity of the

Church and in no way as a guarantee of the faithful transmission of the faith;

10. future decisions of the Evangelical Lutheran Church in America on matters of common concern will be made in consultation with churches with whom a relationship of full communion has been declared, but these decisions will not require their concurrence or approval;

11. future Churchwide Assemblies of the Evangelical Lutheran Church in America will be free to make whatever decisions they deem necessary after mutual consultation on matters related to full communion;

12. the joint commission [to which reference is made in "Called to Common Mission"] will have no authority over the appropriate decision-making bodies of the Evangelical Lutheran Church in America or The Episcopal Church; and

13. pastors of the Evangelical Lutheran Church in America will continue to preside at confirmations.

11

LUTHERAN-EPISCOPAL FESTIVALS AND COMMEMORATIONS*

ROBERT H. BUSCH

With Lutherans and Episcopalians now in full communion, we pray that God will guide our new relationship and that the Holy Spirit will lead us to ever greater cooperation. To this end, the people of Saint Peter's Lutheran Church in New York City now include the Archbishop of Canterbury, the Presiding Bishop of the Episcopal Church, and the Bishop of New York in our prayers every Sunday. We also include all the commemorations in both the Book of Common Prayer (1979) and *The Lutheran Book of Worship* (1978). All these remembrances are listed in our Sunday bulletins and are included in the Prayers of the People at each of the ten liturgies that we celebrate during the week. We invite all Episcopal and Lutheran congregations to join in this prayer cycle.

---

* This calendar originally appeared in *The Anglican* (October 2001), and it is reprinted with permission of *The Anglican*. It has been revised and updated for use here.

The following comparison of major festivals and other commemorations was taken from the *BCP* as updated through the 2000 General Convention, and from the *LBW*. Names added subsequent to these dates are not included. The Book of Common Prayer identifies Principal Feasts, Holy Days (including Feasts of our Lord and other Major Feasts) and Commemorations. The calendar in *The Lutheran Book of Worship has* three groupings: Principal Festivals, Lesser Festivals, and Commemorations. Episcopal Principal Feasts and Holy Days (including Feasts of our Lord and other Major Feasts) and Lutheran Principal Festivals are identified here in bold type. Episcopal commemorations presented for trial use appear in brackets. These commemorations will be included in the Episcopal calendar of the church year if approved by General Convention at a second reading. The Lutheran Lesser Festivals are in normal upper and lower case type, while Commemorations for both churches are in italics.

LUTHERAN BOOK OF WORSHIP	BOOK OF COMMON PRAYER

JANUARY

1	The Name of Jesus	The Holy Name of Our Lord Jesus Christ
2	*Johann Konrad Wilhelm Loehe,* *pastor, 1872*	
5	*Kaj Munk, martyr, 1944*	
6	The Epiphany of Our Lord	The Epiphany of Our Lord Jesus
9		Christ
10		*Julia Chester Emery, 1922*
12		*William Laud, Archbishop of*
12		*Canterbury, 1645*
13	*George Fox, renewer of Society, 1691*	*Aelred, Abbot of Rievaulx, 1167*
14	*Eivind Josef Breggrav, Bishop of Oslo,* *1959*	*Hilary, Bishop of Poitiers, 367*
15	*Martin Luther King, Jr, renewer/* *martyr, 1968*	
17		*Antony, Abbot in Egypt, 356*
18	The Confession of Saint Peter	**The Confession of Saint Peter the Apostle**
19	*Henry, Bishop of Uppsala,* *missionary/martyr*	*Wulfstan, Bishop of Worcester, 1095* *Fabian, Bishop and Martyr of Rome, 250*
20		*Agnes, Martyr at Rome, 304*
21		*Vincent, Deacon of Saragossa, and*
22		*Martyr, 304*
22		*Phillips Brooks, Bishop of Massachusetts,*
23		*1893*
25	The Conversion of Saint Paul	**The Conversion of Saint Paul the Apostle**
26	*Timothy, Titus and Silas*	*Timothy and Titus, Companions of* *Saint Paul*
27	*Lydia, Dorcas, and Phoebe*	*John Chrysostom, Bishop of* *Constantinople, 407*
28		*Thomas Aquinas, Priest and Friar, 1274*

FEBRUARY

1		*Brigid (Bride), 523*
2	The Presentation of Our Lord	**The Presentation of Our Lord Jesus** **Christ in the Temple**
3	*Ansgar, Archbishop of Hamburg, 865*	*Anskar, Archbishop of Hamburg,* *Missionary to Denmark and* *Sweden, 865*
4		*Cornelius the Centurion*
5	*The Martyrs of Japan, 1597*	*The Martyrs of Japan, 1597*
13		*Absalom Jones, Priest, 1818*
14	*Cyril, monk, 869: Methodius, bishop,* *865*	*Cyril, Monk, and Methodius, Bishop,* *Missionaries to the Slavs, 869, 885*
15		*Thomas Bray, Priest and Missionary, 1730*
18	*Martin Luther, renewer of the Church,* *1546*	
20	*Rasmus Jensen, first pastor in North* *America*	

23	*Polycarp, Bishop of Smyrna, martyr, 156*	**Polycarp, Bishop and Martyr of Smyrna, 156**
23	*Bartholomaeus Ziegenbalg, missionary, 1719*	
24	St. Matthias, Apostle	**Saint Matthias the Apostle**
25	*Elizabeth Fedde, deaconess*	
27		*George Herbert, Priest, 1633*

MARCH

1	*George Herbert, priest, 1633*	*David, Bishop of Menevia, Wales, c. 544*
2	*John Wesley, 1791, Charles Wesley, 1788*	*Chad, Bishop of Lichfield, 672*
3		*John and Charles Wesley, Priests, 1791, 1788*
7	*Perpetua and her companions, martyrs, 202*	*Perpetua and her Companions, Martyrs at Carthage, 202*
7	*Thomas Aquinas, teacher, 1274*	
9		*Gregory, Bishop of Nyssa, c. 394*
12	*Gregory the Great, Bishop of Rome, 604*	*Gregory the Great, Bishop of Rome, 604*
17	*Patrick, bishop, missionary to Ireland, 461*	*Patrick, Bishop and Missionary of Ireland, 461*
18		*Cyril, Bishop of Jerusalem, 386*
19	*Joseph, guardian of our Lord*	**Saint Joseph**
20		*Cuthbert, Bishop of Lindisfarne, 687*
21		*Thomas Ken, Bishop of Bath and Wells, 1711*
22	*Jonathan Edwards, teacher missionary, 1758*	*James De Koven, Priest, 1879*
23		*Gregory the Illuminator, Bishop and Missionary of Armenia, c. 332*
25	The Annunciation of Our Lord	**The Annunciation of Our Lord Jesus Christ to the Blessed Virgin Mary**
27		*Charles Henry Brent, Bishop of the Philippines, and of Western New York, 1929*
29	*Hans Nielsen Hauge, renewer of the Church, 1824*	*John Keble, Priest, 1866*
31	*John Donne, priest, 1631*	*John Donne, Priest, 1631*

APRIL

1		*Frederick Denison Maurice, Priest, 1872*
2		*James Lloyd Breck, Priest, 1876*
3		*Richard, Bishop of Chichester, 1253*
4		*Martin Luther King, Jr., Civil Rights Leader, 1968*
6	*Albrecht Dürer, painter, 1528*	

6	Michelangelo Buonarroti, artist, 1564	
8		William Augustus Muhlenberg, Priest, 1877
9	Dietrich Bonhoeffer, teacher, 1945	William Law, Priest, 1761
		Dietrich Bonhoeffer, 1945
10	Mikael Agricola, Bishop of Turku, 1557	
11		George Augustus Selwyn, Bishop of New Zealand and of Lichfield, 1878
19	Olavus Petri, priest, 1552	Alphege, Archbishop of Canterbury, and Martyr, 1012
19	Laurentius Petri, Archbishop of Uppsala, 1573	
21	Anselm, Archbishop of Canterbury, 1109	Anselm, Archbishop of Canterbury, 1109
23	Toyohiko Kagawa, renewer of society, 1960	
25	St. Mark, Evangelist	**Saint Mark the Evangelist**
29	Catherine of Siena, teacher, 1380	Catherine of Siena, 1380

MAY

1	St. Philip and St. James, Apostles	**Saint Philip and Saint James, Apostles**
2	Athanasius, Bishop of Alexandria, 373	Athanasius, Bishop of Alexandria, 373
4	Monica, mother of Augustine, 387	Monnica, Mother of Augustine of Hippo, 387
8		Dame Julian of Norwich, c. 1417
9		Gregory of Nazianzus, Bishop of Constantinople, 389
18	Erik, King of Sweden, martyr, 1160	
19	Dunstan, Archbishop of Canterbury, 988	Dunstan, Archbishop of Canterbury, 988
20		Alcuin, Deacon, and Abbot of Tours, 804
21	John Eliot, missionary to American Indians, 1690	
23	Ludwig Nommensen, missionary to Sumatra, 1918	
24	Nicolas Copernicus, 1543, teacher	Jackson Kemper, First Missionary Bishop in the United States, 1870
24	Leonard Euler, 1783, teacher	
25		Bede, the Venerable, Priest, and Monk of Jarrow, 735
26		Augustine, First Archbishop of Canterbury, 605
27	John Calvin, renewer of the Church, 1564	
29	Jiri Tranovský, hymnwriter, 1637	
31	The Visitations	**The Visitation of the Blessed Virgin Mary**

JUNE

1	*Justin, martyr at Rome, c. 165*	*Justin, Martyr at Rome, c. 167*
2		*The Martyrs of Lyons, 177*
3	*John XXIII, Bishop of Rome, 1963*	*The Martyrs of Uganda, 1886*
5	*Boniface, Archbishop of Mainz, missionary, 754*	*Boniface, Archbishop of Mainz, Missionary to Germany, and Martyr, 754*
7	*Seattle, Chief of the Duwamish Confederacy, 1866*	
9	*Columba, 597, Aidan, 651, Bede, 735, confessors*	*Columba, Abbot of Iona, 597*
10		*Ephrem of Edessa, Syria, Deacon, 373*
11	St. Barnabas, Apostle	**Saint Barnabas the Apostle**
12		*[Enmegahbowh, 1902]*
14	*Basil the Great, Bishop of Caesarea, 379*	*Basil the Great, Bishop of Caesarea, 379*
14	*Gregory of Nazianzus, Bishop of Constantinople*	
14	*Gregory, Bishop of Nyssa, c. 385*	
15		*Evelyn Underhill, 1941*
16		*Joseph Butler, Bishop of Durham, 1752*
18		*Bernard Mizeki, Catechist and Martyr in Rhodesia, 1896*
21	*Onesimos Nesib, translator, evangelist, 1931*	
22		*Alban, First Martyr of Britain, c. 304*
24	The Nativity of St. John the Baptist	**The Nativity of Saint John the Baptist**
25	*Presentation of the Augsburg Confession, 1530*	
25	*Philipp Melanchthon, renewer of the Church, 1560*	
28	*Irenaeus, Bishop of Lyons, c. 202*	*Irenaeus, Bishop of Lyons, c. 202*
29	St. Peter and St. Paul, Apostles	**Saint Peter and Saint Paul, Apostles**
30	*Johan Olof Wallin, Archbishop of Uppsala, 1839*	

JULY

1	*Catherine Winkworth, hymnwriter, 1878*	
1	*John Mason Neale, 1866, hymnwriter*	
4		**Independence Day**
6	*Jan Hus, martyr, 1415*	
11	*Benedict of Nursia, Abbot, c. 540*	*Benedict of Nursia, Abbot of Monte Cassino, c. 540*
12	*Nathan Söderblom, Archbishop of Uppsala, 1931*	
15	*Vladimir, first Christian ruler of Russia, 1015*	

SEPTEMBER

1		David Pendleton Oakerhater, Deacon and Missionary, 1931
2	Nikolai Frederik Severin Grundtvig, bishop, 1872	The Martyrs of New Guinea, 1942
4	Albert Schweitzer, missionary to Africa, 1965	
4		Paul Jones, 1941
9		Constance, Nun, and her Companions, 1878
10		Alexander Crummell, 1898
12		John Henry Hobart, Bishop of New York, 1830
13	John Chrysostom, Bishop of Constantinople, 407	Cyprian, Bishop and Martyr of Carthage, 258
14	Holy Cross Day	**Holy Cross Day**
16		Ninian, Bishop in Galloway, c. 430
17		Hildegard, 1179
18	Dag Hammarskjöld, peacemaker, 1961	Edward Bouverie Pusey, Priest, 1882
19		Theodore of Tarsus, Archbishop of Canterbury, 690
20		John Coleridge Patteson, Bishop of Melanesia, and his Companions, Martyrs, 1871
21	St. Matthew, Apostle and Evangelist	**Saint Matthew, Apostle and Evangelist**
25	Sergius of Radonezh, Abbot of Moscow 1392	Sergius, Abbot of Holy Trinity, Moscow, 1392
26		Lancelot Andrewes, Bishop of Winchester, 1626
29	St. Michael and All Angels	**Saint Michael and All Angels**
30	Jerome, translator and teacher, 420	Jerome, Priest, and Monk of Bethlehem, 420

OCTOBER

1		Remigius, Bishop of Rheims, c. 530
4	Francis of Assisi, renewer of the Church, 1226	Francis of Assisi, Friar, 1226
4	Theodor Fliedner, renewer of society, 1864	
6	William Tyndale, translator, martyr, 1536	William Tyndale, Priest, 1536
7	Henry Melchoir Muhlenberg, missionary, 1787	
9		Robert Grosseteste, Bishop of Lincoln, 1253
11		[Philip, Deacon and Evangelist]
14		Samuel Isaac Joseph Schereschewsky, Bishop of Shanghai, 1906

15		*Teresa of Avila, Nun, 1582*
16		*Hugh Latimer and Nicholas Ridley,*
		Bishops, 1555, and Thomas
		Cranmer, Archbishop of
		Canterbury,1556
17	*Ignatius, Bishop of Antioch, martyr,*	*Ignatius, Bishop of Antioch, and*
	c. 115	*Martyr, c. 115*
18	St. Luke, Evangelist	**Saint Luke the Evangelist**
19		*Henry Martyn, Priest, and Missionary*
		to India and Persia, 1812
23	*James of Jerusalem, martyr*	**Saint James of Jerusalem, Brother of**
		Our Lord Jesus Christ, and Martyr, c. 62
26	*Philipp Nicolai, 1608, hymnwriter*	*Alfred the Great, King of the*
		West Saxons, 899
26	*Johann Heermann, 1647, hymnwriter*	
26	*Paul Gerhardt, 1676, hymnwriter*	
28	St. Simon and St. Jude, Apostles	**Saint Simon and Saint Jude, Apostles**
29		*James Hannington, Bishop of*
		Eastern Equatorial Africa, and his
		Companions, Martyrs, 1885
31	Reformation Day	

NOVEMBER

1	All Saints' Day	**All Saints**
2		*Commemoration of All Faithful Departed*
3		*Richard Hooker, Priest, 1600*
7	*John Christian Frederick Heyer,*	*Willibrord, Archbishop of Utrecht,*
	missionary, 1873	*Missionary to Frisia, 739*
10		*Leo the Great, Bishop of Rome, 461*
11	*Martin, Bishop of Tours, 397*	*Martin, Bishop of Tours, 397*
11	*Søren Aabye Kierkegaard,*	
	teacher 1855	
12		*Charles Simeon, Priest, 1836*
14		*Consecration of Samuel Seabury, First*
		American Bishop, 1784
16		*Margaret, Queen of Scotland, 1093*
17	*Elizabeth of Thuringia, Princess*	*Hugh, Bishop of Lincoln, 1200*
	of Hungary, 1231	
18		*Hilda, Abbess of Whitby, 680*
19		*Elizabeth, Princess of Hungary, 1231*
20		*Edmund, King of East Anglia, 870*
23	*Clement, Bishop of Rome, c. 100*	*Clement, Bishop of Rome, c. 100*
25	*Isaac Watts, hymnwriter, 1748*	*James Otis Sargent Huntington, Priest*
		and Monk, 1935
28		*Kamehameha and Emma King and*
		Queen of Hawaii, 1862, 1885
30	St. Andrew, Apostle	**Saint Andrew the Apostle**

DECEMBER

1		*Nicholas Ferrar, Deacon, 1637*
2		*Channing Moore Williams, Missionary Bishop in China and Japan, 1910*
3	*Francis Xavier, missionary to Asia, 1552*	
4		*John of Damascus, Priest, c. 760*
5		*Clement of Alexandria, Priest, c. 210*
6	*Nicholas, Bishop of Myra, c. 342*	*Nicholas, Bishop of Myra, c. 342*
7	*Ambrose, Bishop of Milan, 397*	*Ambrose, Bishop of Milan, 397*
11	*Lars Olsen Skrefsrud, missionary to India, 1910*	
14	*John of the Cross, renewer of the Church, 1591*	
14	*Teresa of Avila, renewer of the Church, 1582*	
21	St. Thomas, Apostle	**Saint Thomas the Apostle**
25	**The Nativity of our Lord**	**The Nativity of our Lord Jesus Christ**
26	St. Stephen, Deacon and Martyr	**St. Stephen, Deacon and Martyr**
27	St. John, Apostle and Evangelist	**Saint John, Apostle and Evangelist**
28	The Holy Innocents, Martyrs	**The Holy Innocents**
29		*Thomas Becket, 1170*

GLOSSARY

SELECTED EVANGELICAL LUTHERAN CHURCH IN AMERICA TERMS

The definitions of Evangelical Lutheran Church in America terms presented here are drawn from the pamphlet "The Orderly Exchange of Pastors and Priests Under Called to Common Mission, Principles and Guidelines," issued jointly by the Episcopal Church and the Evangelical Lutheran Church in America, January 1, 2001. Used with permission.

Associate in Ministry. One of the three categories of rostered lay ministers in the ELCA. Associates in Ministry are called and commissioned for service in congregations, agencies, schools and institutions of the ELCA. Their primary areas of service are education, music and the arts, administration, service and general ministry.

Bishop. A bishop is an ordained minister of word and sacrament in the ELCA, given the responsibility to provide pastoral care and leadership in a synod and its congregations and to seek to strengthen the unity of the church. The bishop is the chief executive officer of the synod, elected to a term of six years and may be reelected.

Bishop's Assistant or Associate. A person who assists the synodical bishop in carrying out the responsibilities of the office. A bishop's assistant or associate may be an ordained minister, a rostered lay minister, or a lay person.

Bishop, Presiding. An ordained minister of word and sacrament who is a teacher of the faith of this church and provides leadership for the life and witness of this church. The presiding bishop is the chief executive officer of the churchwide organization, and is the chief ecumenical officer of the church. The presiding bishop is elected to a six-year term and may be reelected.

Book of Concord. The *Book of Concord is* the sixteenth-century statement of the Confessions of the Evangelical Lutheran Church (the most recent edition was published in 2000). Within it is the Augsburg Confession, which the ELCA accepts as a "true witness to the Gospel," as well as other confessional writings that the ELCA considers "further valid interpretations of the faith of the Church."

Church Council. The Church Council of the ELCA is its board of directors, serving as the interim legislative authority between meetings of the Churchwide Assembly. The Church Council meets at least two times each year, and is composed of the four churchwide officers (presiding bishop, vice-president, secretary and treasurer) and 33 other persons, elected to six-year terms by the Church-wide Assembly.

Churchwide Assembly. The Churchwide Assembly is the highest legislative authority of the churchwide organiza-tion. It reviews the work of the churchwide officers and churchwide units. It establishes churchwide policy and adopts the budget for the churchwide organization. It has the sole authority to amend the constitution and bylaws of the ELCA. The Churchwide Assembly meets biennially in regular session.

Churchwide Organization. The churchwide organization functions interdependently with the congregations and synods of the ELCA. It is responsible for developing churchwide policy, standards for leadership, including ordained and rostered lay ministries, and the coordination of the work of the ELCA both globally and throughout the territory of the ELCA.

Conference of Bishops. The Conference of Bishops is composed of the bishops of the 65 synods, the presiding bishop, and the secretary of the ELCA. The conference meets at least two times each year and is a forum in which goals, objectives, and strategies may be developed and shared concerning pastoral leadership, care and counsel for the synods. The Conference of Bishops reviews recommendations from the Division for Ministry pertaining to policies and programs related to the rosters of ordained ministers, and the three rosters of lay ministers (associates in ministry, deaconesses and diaconal ministers).

Confession of Faith. The ELCA Confession of Faith confesses the Triune God, Jesus Christ as Lord and Savior, the canonical scriptures of the Old and New Testaments as the written word of God, accepts the Apostles', Nicene and Athanasian Creeds as true declarations of the faith of this church, and accepts the Augsburg Confession and the other confessional writings in the Book of Concord as valid interpretations of the faith of this church.

Constitutions, Bylaws, and Continuing Resolutions. The basic commitments of the Evangelical Lutheran Church in America as well as its organizational outline, structural patterns, and rubrics of governance are expressed by its constitutions, bylaws, and continuing resolutions. These documents govern the life of the ELCA as congregations, synods, and churchwide organization.

Deaconess. One of the three categories of rostered lay ministers in the ELCA and an outgrowth of the European Deaconess movement of the nineteenth century. ELCA deaconesses are called and consecrated, and serve in congregations, agencies and institutions of the ELCA. They are members of the Deaconess Community of the ELCA, and participate in the life of that community.

Diaconal Minister. One of the three categories of rostered lay ministers in the ELCA, established in 1993. ELCA diaconal ministers are called and consecrated, and serve in congregations, agencies and institutions of the ELCA. Their focus for ministry is the extension of the church's ministry of witness and care into the world.

Evangelical. From the Greek word for "gospel" and its German derivative. Original designation for the early reformers that is still used in German-speaking areas for non-Roman and non-Orthodox Christians. Historically unrelated to twentieth-century evangelical movements in the United States.

Lutheran Book of Worship. The *Lutheran Book of Worship* (1978) is the primary worship resource for use within the Evangelical Lutheran Church in America and its liturgical texts and patterns of worship are considered the norm within the ELCA. It is supplemented by the worship resources, *With One Voice* (1995), *Libro De Liturgia Y Cantico* (1998), and *This Far by Faith* (1999).

Manual on the Liturgy. *Manual on the Liturgy,* published in 1979, is the primary interpretative resource based on the *Lutheran Book of Worship.* This manual provides a commentary and explanation of Lutheran liturgical practices.

Membership. The 1999 membership of the Evangelical Lutheran Church in America is 5.2 million baptized members in 10,862 congregations. There are 17,631 ordained ministers (11,335 active and serving under call), 1,074 associates in ministry (667 active and serving under call), 77 deaconesses (32 active and serving under call), and 36 diaconal ministers (34 active and serving under call).

Ministry. The ELCA affirms the universal priesthood of all its baptized members and commits itself to the equipping and supporting of all its members for their ministries in the world and in this church.

Occasional Services. *Occasional Services,* published in 1982, is a companion to the *Lutheran Book of Worship* and provides services for specific occasions and specific situations, as distinguished from services of worship of a more general character.

Ordained Ministry. The ELCA confesses that within the people of God and for the sake of the gospel ministry entrusted to all believers, God has instituted the office of ministry of word and sacrament. To carry out this ministry, the ELCA calls and ordains qualified persons.

Pastor. The normal term used to describe an ordained minister of word and sacrament. A parish pastor serves in a congregational setting. The term pastor may be used to describe an ordained minister serving in a non-congregational setting as well.

Principles of Organization. The Evangelical Lutheran Church in America understands itself as one church, recognizing that all power and authority in the church belongs to the Lord Jesus Christ. The congregations, synods, and churchwide organization of the ELCA are interdependent partners sharing responsibility in God's mission.

Representational Principle. Among the principles of organization, the Evangelical Lutheran Church in America has determined that at least 60 percent of the members of assemblies, councils, committees, boards and other organizations shall be laypersons; that, as nearly as possible, the lay members shall be 50 percent female and 50 percent male, and that, where possible, the representation of ordained ministers shall be both female and male. It is also determined that a minimum goal of 10 percent of the membership of its assemblies, councils, committees, boards, or other organizational units be persons of color and/or persons whose primary language is other than English.

Region. There are nine geographic regions within the Evangelical Lutheran Church in America, recognized as a partnership among groups of synods within the region and the churchwide organization.

Sacramental Practices. *The Use of the Means of Grace* (Augsburg Fortress, 1997) was adopted for "guidance and practice" by the Fifth Biennial Churchwide Assembly of the Evangelical Lutheran Church in America as a "statement on the practice of Word and Sacrament."

Synod. There are 65 synods (similar to Episcopal Church dioceses) in the ELCA. Each synod, in partnership with the churchwide organization, bears primary responsibility for the oversight of the life and mission of the ELCA in its territory.

Synod Assembly. The Synod Assembly is the highest legislative authority of the synod, with a regular meeting held at least biennially (with most synod assemblies meeting annually). All ordained ministers and all rostered lay ministers are voting members, as are representative lay members from every congregation within the synod.

Vision and Expectations. The document *"Vision and Expectations - Ordained Ministers in the Evangelical Lutheran Church in America"* was adopted by the ELCA

Church Council in 1990 as a statement of this church about the vision for ordained ministry in the life of the Evangelical Lutheran Church in America and the expectations of those who serve in that ministry. It is used primarily in the candidacy process.

SELECTED EPISCOPAL CHURCH TERMS

The definitions of Episcopal Church terms presented here are drawn from An Episcopal Dictionary of the Church: A User-Friendly Reference for Episcopalians *(New York: Church Publishing Incorporated, 2000), ed. Don S. Armentrout and Robert Boak Slocum. Used with permission.*

Anglicanism. This way of life is the system of doctrine, and approach to polity of Christians in communion with the see of Canterbury. The term derives from the word which, in a variety of forms, refers to the people of the British Isles, and especially the English. Anglicanism reflects the balance and compromise of the *via media* of the Elizabethan settlement between protestant and catholic principles. Anglicanism also reflects balance in its devotion to scripture, tradition, and reason as sources of authority. The *via media* of Anglicanism is expressed frequently in terms of a "golden mean" between extreme positions on either side of various issues. Anglicanism is both traditional and dynamic in the discovery of new expressions. It retains the ancient authorities of scripture and tradition. It also allows for development of new understandings of Christian faith and practice in continuity with the historical church. Until the twentieth century, Anglicanism was largely defined in terms of its English origins and preservation of the language and customs of English-speaking peoples. For example, the Episcopal Church and the various Anglican churches in the British colonies retained their English heritage through a common language, Prayer Book worship, and an episcopal polity. At the end of the nineteenth century, however, Anglicanism began to take on a new identity. The national churches which derived from the Church of England became more conscious of their own identity while remaining in communion with the see of Canterbury. They also retained a common Anglican theological and ecclesial identity. Anglicanism is now a worldwide family of churches which share a common theological heritage and polity.

Assistant Bishop. A bishop who assists the diocesan bishop by providing additional episcopal services. An assistant bishop is appointed by the diocesan bishop, with the approval of the Standing Committee of the diocese. The assistant bishop must already be exercising episcopal jurisdiction as a diocesan bishop, or serving as a suffragan bishop, or a qualified bishop who has previously resigned all previous responsibilities, or a qualified bishop of a church in communion with the Episcopal Church. The assistant bishop serves under the direction of the diocesan bishop, and may not serve beyond the termination of the appointing bishop's jurisdiction. In the nineteenth century, bishops coadjutor in the Episcopal Church were known as assistant bishops.

Authority, Sources of (in Anglicanism). The threefold sources of authority in Anglicanism are scripture, tradition, and reason. These three sources uphold and critique each other in a dynamic way. Scripture is the normative source for God's revelation and the source for all Christian teaching and reflection. Tradition passes down from generation to generation the church's ongoing experience of God's presence and activity. Reason is understood to include the human capacity to discern the truth in both rational and intuitive ways. It is not limited to logic as such. It takes into account and includes experience. Each of the three sources of authority must be perceived and interpreted in light of the other two.

The Anglican balance of authority has been characterized as a "three-legged stool" which falls if any one of the legs is not upright. It may be distinguished from a tendency in Roman Catholicism to overemphasize tradition relative to scripture and reason, and in certain Protestant churches to overemphasize scripture relative to tradition and reason. The Anglican balancing of the sources of authority has been criticized as clumsy or "muddy." It has been associated with the Anglican affinity for seeking the mean between extremes and living the *via media*. It has also been associated with the Anglican willingness to tolerate and comprehend opposing viewpoints instead of imposing tests of orthodoxy or resorting to heresy trials.

The balanced understanding of authority is based on the theology of Richard Hooker (c. 1554-1600). Urban T. Holmes III (1930-1981) provided a thorough and helpful discussion of the sources of authority in *What is Anglicanism?* (1982).

Bishop Coadjutor. Assistant bishop with the right of succession upon the resignation of the diocesan bishop. Before a bishop coadjutor is elected, the diocesan bishop must consent to such an election and state the duties which will be assigned to the bishop coadjutor when duly ordained and consecrated.

Bishop. One of the three orders of ordained ministers in the church, bishops are charged with the apostolic work of leading, supervising, and uniting the church. Bishops represent Christ and his church, and they are called to provide Christian vision and leadership for their dioceses. The BCP

(855) notes that the bishop is "to act in Christ's name for the reconciliation of the world and the building up of the church; and to ordain others to continue Christ's ministry." Bishops stand in the apostolic succession, maintaining continuity in the present with the ministry of the Apostles. Bishops serve as chief pastors of the church, exercising a ministry of oversight and supervision. Diocesan bishops hold jurisdiction in their dioceses, with particular responsibility for the doctrine, discipline, and worship of the church. Bishops serve as the focus for diocesan unity and for the unity of their dioceses with the wider church. Since the bishop's ministry is a ministry of oversight, the term "episcopal" (derived from the Greek *episcopos*, "overseer") is applied to matters pertaining to bishops. An "episcopal" church is a church governed by bishops, and "episcopal" services are led by bishops. Episcopal services in the BCP include the services for the ordination and consecration of bishops, ordination of priests, ordination of deacons, the celebration of a new ministry, and the consecration of a church or chapel. Bishops also preside at services of confirmation, reception, or reaffirmation. Bishops bless altars and fonts, and the blessing of chalices and patens and church bells are traditionally reserved for the bishop. In the Episcopal Church, diocesan and suffragan bishops are elected by diocesan convention. Bishops-elect are ordained and consecrated after consents have been received from a majority of the diocesan standing committees and from a majority of the bishops exercising jurisdiction in the Episcopal Church. If the episcopal election takes place within three months before General Convention, the consent of the House of Deputies is required instead of a majority of the standing committees. Three bishops are required to participate in the ordination and consecration of a bishop. Diocesan bishops may be succeeded by bishops-

coadjutor upon resignation of diocesan jurisdiction. Diocesan bishops may also be assisted by suffragan and assistant bishops, who have no right of succession upon the resignation of the diocesan bishop.

Book of Common Prayer, The (BCP). Official Book of worship of the Episcopal Church. The BCP provides liturgical forms, prayers, and instructions so that all members and orders of the Episcopal Church may appropriately share in common worship. Anglican liturgical piety has been rooted in the Prayer Book tradition since the publication of the first English Prayer Book in 1549. The first American BCP was ratified by the first General Convention of the Episcopal Church in 1789. It was based on the Proposed Book of 1786, and the 1662 English Book of Common Prayer, as well as the Scottish eucharistic rite of 1764. The BCP is ratified by General Convention, with alterations or additions requiring the approval of two successive General Conventions. The General Convention may also authorize services for trial use. The process of Prayer Book revision led to publication of editions of the BCP for the Episcopal Church in 1789, 1892, 1928, and 1979. The BCP notes that "The Holy Eucharist, the principal act of Christian worship on the Lord's Day and other major Feasts, and Daily Morning and Evening Prayer, as set forth in this Book, are the regular services appointed for public worship in this Church" (13). The BCP includes the calendar of the church year, and it provides forms for the daily office, the great litany, the collects, proper liturgies for special days, holy baptism, the holy eucharist, pastoral offices, and episcopal services. In addition to many forms for corporate worship, the BCP also provides forms for daily devotions for individuals and families (136-140). The BCP includes both contemporary language (Rite II) and traditional language

(Rite I) versions of the forms for morning and evening prayer, the collects, the eucharist, and the burial of the dead. The BCP also includes the Psalter, or Psalms of David; prayers and thanksgivings; An outline of the faith, or catechism; historical documents of the church (including the Articles of Religion); tables for finding the date of Easter and other holy days; and lectionaries for the holy eucharist and the daily office.

Book of Occasional Services, The (BOS). Book of optional services and texts prepared by the Standing Liturgical Commission in response to a directive from the General Convention of 1976 to replace *The Book of Offices* (third edition, 1960). The services and texts of the *BOS* are available for "occasional" pastoral and liturgical needs of congregations. The *BOS* includes special materials for the church year (such as forms for seasonal blessings, a Christmas festival of lessons and music, and a service for All Hallows' Eve); pastoral services (such as forms for welcoming new people to a congregation, the rites of the catechumenate, and a form for the blessing of a pregnant woman); and episcopal services (such as forms for the reaffirmation of ordination vows and the welcoming and seating of a bishop in the cathedral). The Preface to the *BOS* notes that "None of it is required, and no congregation is likely to make use of all of it."

Canon. The word is derived from the Greek *kanon,* a "measuring rod or rule." It has several different meanings in the church. 1) [Scripture] The canon of scripture is the list of inspired books recognized by the church to constitute the Holy Scriptures. 2) [Church Law] Canons are the written rules that provide a code of laws for the governance of the church. The canons of the Episcopal Church are enacted by the General Convention. Canons of the Episcopal

Church may only be enacted, amended, or repealed by concurrent resolution of the House of Deputies and the House of Bishops at General Convention. The canons of the Episcopal Church are organized by titles or sections concerning organization and administration, worship, ministry, ecclesiastical discipline, and general provisions. 3) [Ecclesiastical Title] A canon may be a member of the clergy on the staff of a cathedral or diocese. A canon on a cathedral staff assists the dean, and a canon on a diocesan staff assists the bishop. Members of the clergy and laity have at times been made honorary canons of a cathedral in recognition of significant service or achievement. Historically, canons were secular clergy who were connected to a cathedral or collegiate church, sharing the revenues and a common rule of life at the church. 4) [Liturgy] The canon designates the fixed portion of the great thanksgiving or the prayer of consecration at the holy eucharist, including the institution narrative.

Canonical Residence. Clergy serving under the jurisdiction of the ecclesiastical authority of a diocese (typically the diocesan bishop) are canonically resident in that diocese. Clergy may move from jurisdiction to jurisdiction by presenting Letters Dimissory, a testimonial by the ecclesiastical authority of the former diocese that the clergyperson has not "been justly liable to evil report, for error in religion or for viciousness of life, for the last three years." The transfer of canonical residence is dated from the acceptance of Letters Dimissory by the ecclesiastical authority.

Chasuble. The sleeveless outer vestment worn by the celebrant at the eucharist. The chasuble and cope are both derived from the outdoor cloak worn by all classes and both sexes in the Greco-Roman world. The chasuble may be oval or oblong, with an opening for the head. It typically reflects the liturgical color of the day. Chasubles vary widely in fabric and style. They may be plain cloth or decorated with orphreys or symbols.

Crozier, or Crosier. The pastoral staff of a bishop. It was originally a walking stick and later acquired the symbolism of a shepherd's crook. It is a sign of pastoral authority. It may also be carried by abbots and abbesses. In liturgy the diocesan bishop carries the crozier in the left hand, with the crook facing outward. Although the crozier was originally part of the insignia of all bishops, it is now used mainly by diocesans in their own jurisdictions. Its use dates from the seventh century.

Curate. The term typically refers to an assisting priest in a parish. It is from the Latin *curatus*, "entrusted with the care" of something. It was originally used to describe a priest entrusted with the care (or "cure") of souls in a particular area or parish.

Cure. The pastoral responsibility and charge of a member of the clergy. A cure is often a parish, but that pastoral responsibility may take other forms such as a specialized ministry or chaplaincy. In this regard, the member of the clergy has responsibility for the "cure of souls" of those entrusted to his or her pastoral care. The term "cure" is related in derivation to the word "care."

Deacon. Deacons are members of one of three distinct orders of ordained ministry (with bishops and presbyters). In the Episcopal Church a deacon exercises "a special ministry of servanthood" directly under the deacon's bishop, serving all people and especially those in need (BCP, 543). This definition reflects the practice of the early church, in which deacons were ordained "not to the priesthood but to the servanthood [*diakonia,* "ministry"] of the bishop"

(Hippolytus, *Apostolic Tradition*). In the ancient Greek-speaking world the term *diakonos* meant an intermediary who acted or spoke for a superior. Christian deacons were agents of the bishop, often with oversight of charity. Since ancient times the liturgical functions of deacons have suggested the activity of angels. As they proclaim the gospel, lead intercessions, wait at the eucharistic table, and direct the order of the assembly, deacons act as sacred messengers, agents, and attendants. The revival of the order of deacons in the twentieth century has emphasized social care and service. Many bishops in the Episcopal Church expect their deacons to promote care of the needy outside the church. In addition to those ordained deacon as a permanent vocation, there are also "transitional deacons" who are ordained deacon as a preliminary step toward ordination as a priest. This practice is required by the canons of the Episcopal Church, but its theology and usefulness has been questioned by those who favor direct ordination to the order for which one is chosen.

Diocese. The territorial jurisdiction of a diocesan bishop. The term also refers to the congregations and church members of the diocese. Before the church adopted the word it had a long secular usage. It was originally used in the Roman Empire for an administrative subdivision. A diocese was a division of a prefecture of the Roman Empire. In the reorganization of Diocletian and Constantine, the Roman Empire was divided into twelve dioceses. As the church expanded out from the cities, it adopted the use of the word "diocese," and ecclesiastical dioceses tended to correspond to civil units. For example, at first the Diocese of Georgia corresponded with the State of Georgia. Later, many statewide dioceses were divided into smaller dioceses for pastoral and practical reasons. For example, the State of New York includes six dioceses. In more recent years, some dioceses have been formed from portions of more than one state. The Diocese of the Rio Grande includes all of New Mexico and part of west Texas, and the Diocese of the Central Gulf Coast includes portions of southern Alabama and western Florida. In England, the diocese is the territory of the bishop and the parish is a subdivision of it. Every diocese in the Episcopal Church has a Standing Committee. When there is a bishop in charge of the diocese, the Standing Committee is the bishop's council of advice. When there is no bishop, bishop coadjutor or suffragan bishop, the Standing Committee is the ecclesiastical authority of the diocese. A diocese usually meets annually in a diocesan convention. Each diocese is entitled to representation in the House of Deputies by not more than four ordained persons, presbyters or deacons, canonically resident in the diocese, and not more than four lay persons, who are confirmed adult communicants of the Episcopal Church and in good standing in the diocese. Dioceses also elect clerical and lay deputies to the Provincial Synod. The Constitution and Canons of the Episcopal Church provide guidelines for the division of a diocese. Some persons insist that the diocese is the primary unit in the Episcopal Church.

Discipline. 1) In a general sense, the right ordering of Christian life and community. The Constitution, Canons, Prayer Book rubrics, and rules of the church are meant to govern the proper conduct, responsibilities, services, and actions of church life. At the time of ordination, all persons being ordained bishop, priest, or deacon state that "I do solemnly engage to conform to the Doctrine, Discipline, and Worship of the Episcopal Church" (Art. VIII of the Constitution of the Episcopal Church). The bishop may authorize a temporary inhibition of a priest or deacon who is charged with an offense or serious acts that would constitute grounds for a canonical Charge of an Offense. After allegations of the commission of an offense have been made to the ecclesiastical authority, or after charges of an offense have been filed, the accused member of the clergy may voluntarily submit to the discipline of the church prior to an ecclesiastical trial. The consent of the ecclesiastical authority is required. The canons also include provisions for renunciation of the ordained ministry by members of the clergy who may be charged with an offense. The canons make detailed provisions concerning ecclesiastical presentments, courts, trials, appeals, and remissions or modifications of judicial sentences. The three sentences that may be adjudged by an ecclesiastical trial court and imposed by the bishop are admonition, suspension, or deposition. The Prayer Book rites for holy eucharist include disciplinary rubrics authorizing the priest to bar from communion those who are living a notoriously evil life, those who have done wrong to their neighbors and are a scandal to others of the congregation, and those who hate other members of the congregation and refuse to forgive them. A priest who bars a person from communion must notify the bishop within fourteen days and explain the reasons for refusing communion (BCP, 409).

2) In a specific sense, ecclesiastical discipline refers to the canonical provisions for presentment and trial of a member of the clergy. Grounds for presentment and trial of a member of the clergy include crime; immorality; holding and teaching any doctrine contrary to the doctrine of the Episcopal Church; violation of the rubrics of the Prayer Book; violation of the Constitution or Canons of the General Convention; violation of the Constitution or Canons of the diocese of canonical residence; violation of the Constitution or Canons of a diocese in which one was located

temporarily; any act involving a violation of ordination vows (including, under certain circumstances, disregard or disobedience of a Pastoral Direction); habitual neglect of the exercise of the ministerial office without cause, or habitual neglect of public worship and holy communion, according to the order and use of the Episcopal Church; or conduct unbecoming a member of the clergy.

Efficacious Grace. This is grace that accomplishes its intended result in the human soul, especially in terms of a saving work or salvation. The English reformers affirmed the efficacious nature of the sacraments, urging that they are not mere "badges or tokens of Christian men's profession," but "they be certain sure witnesses, and effectual signs of grace" (Art. XXV, Articles of Religion, BCP, 872). The grace conveyed by the sacraments invariably affects the human soul, working to the soul's good. Richard Hooker stated in *Of the Laws of Ecclesiastical Polity* that the sacraments convey the "grace which worketh salvation," which he called a "saving efficacy."

Episcopal Church Center. The national headquarters for the Episcopal Church, located in New York City. It includes the executive offices of the Presiding Bishop. It is the place where the fiduciary responsibilities for the Domestic and Foreign Missionary Society are carried out; a focal point for the work of General Convention; a center for ecumenical and interfaith engagement; and a contact point for international and national agencies. The Episcopal Church Center is currently located at 815 Second Avenue, New York City.

Episcopal Church Flag and Seal. On Oct. 16, 1940, the House of Bishops and the House of Deputies adopted an official flag for the Episcopal Church. This was the 251st anniversary of the day the General Convention ratified the

Constitution and Canons and adopted the BCP. The flag was designed by William M. Baldwin (d. 1942), a member of the Cathedral of the Incarnation, Long Island, New York. The symbolism of the flag has been explained as follows: The white field represents the purity of the Christian religion. The red cross represents the sacrifice of Jesus and the blood of the martyrs. The red cross on a white field is the cross of Saint George, the patron saint of England, indicating our descent from the Church of England. The blue in the upper left-hand corner is the light blue of the sky, often used by artists for the clothing of the Blessed Virgin. It is called Madonna blue and represents the human nature of our Lord, which he received from his mother. The nine white crosslets on the blue field represent the nine original dioceses of the Episcopal Church in America in 1789: Massachusetts, Connecticut, New York, New Jersey, Pennsylvania, Maryland, Virginia, Delaware, and South Carolina. They are arranged in the form of a St. Andrew's Cross to commemorate the fact that Samuel Seabury, the first American bishop, was consecrated in Aberdeen, Scotland, on Nov. 14, 1784. The colors red, white, and blue represent the United States and stand for the American branch of the Anglican Communion. The same design is incorporated in the Episcopal Church seal, which was also adopted by the 1940 General Convention. The seal and flag serve as emblems of the Episcopal Church. The design is seen on signs, publications, decals, letterheads, pins, and many other places. Some congregations display the Episcopal Church flag and the American flag in the church or parish hall.

Episcopal Church, The. A conference of three clergy and twenty-four lay delegates met at Chestertown, Kent County, Maryland, on Nov. 9, 1780, and resolved that "the Church formerly known in the Province as the Church of England should now be called the Protestant Episcopal Church." On Aug. 13, 1783, the Maryland clergy met at Annapolis and adopted the name "Protestant Episcopal Church." At the second session of the 1789 General Convention, Sept. 29-Oct. 16, 1789, a Constitution of nine articles was adopted. William White was one of the chief architects of the new church. He was Presiding Bishop from July 28, 1789, to Oct. 3, 1789, and from Sept. 8, 1795, until his death on July 17, 1836. White had previously served as chaplain to the Continental and Constitutional Congresses and the United States Senate from 1777 until 1801. The new church was called the "Protestant Episcopal Church in the United States of America" (PECUSA). The word "Protestant" noted that this was a church in the reformation tradition, and the word "Episcopal" noted a characteristic of catholicity, the historic episcopate. The first American BCP was based on the Proposed Book of 1786 and the 1662 English BCP. It was ratified by the 1789 General Convention. Alterations or additions to the BCP require the approval of two successive General Conventions. BCP revisions were ratified in 1892, 1928, and 1979.

The church has grown from thirteen dioceses to more than one hundred dioceses. It is divided into nine geographical provinces. It is governed by a bicameral General Convention, which meets every three years, and by an Executive Council during interim years. The General Convention consists of the House of Bishops and the House of Deputies. The House of Bishops is composed of every bishop with jurisdiction, every bishop coadjutor, every suffragan bishop, every retired bishop, every bishop elected to an office created by General Convention, and every bishop who has resigned because of missionary strategy. All members of the House of Bishops have seat and voice in the House of Bishops. The House of Deputies is composed of up to four lay and four clerical deputies from each of the dioceses. The two top leaders of the church are the Presiding Bishop, who is also called Primate and Chief Pastor, and the president of the House of Deputies. Over the years there were numerous efforts to change the name of the church and to drop the word "Protestant." Among the names suggested were "The Reformed Catholic Church," "The American Catholic Church," "The American Church," and "The American Anglican Church." The 1967 General Convention voted to add a preamble to the Constitution, which states, "The Protestant Episcopal Church in the United States of America, otherwise known as The Episcopal Church (which name is hereby recognized as also designating the Church) ...." The title page of the 1979 BCP states that the Book of Common Prayer is "According to the use of The Episcopal Church." The Episcopal Church in the United States of America is sometimes called ECUSA. The Episcopal Church is a province of the Anglican Communion.

Episcopate, Episcopacy, Episcopos. Church governance under the leadership of bishops. The term is from the Greek for "overseer." The Prayer Book service for the ordination of a bishop states that a bishop "is called to be one with the apostles in proclaiming Christ's resurrection and interpreting the Gospel, and to testify to Christ's sovereignty as Lord of lords and King of kings." A bishop is called to guard the faith, unity, and discipline of the church, to celebrate and provide for the administration of the sacraments, to ordain priests and deacons and join in ordaining bishops, and to be a faithful pastor and whole-some example for the whole church. Bishops share in the leadership of the church throughout the world (BCP, 517). Episcopate or episcopacy may also indicate the body or college of bishops in a church or region, or the tenure or office of a bishop.

The terms may refer to the collective role of the order or office of bishops in the church. The "Historic Episco-pate, locally adapted in the methods of its administration to the varying needs of the nations and peoples called of God into the unity of His Church" is one of the four points of the Chicago-Lambeth Quadrilateral. The 1886 General Convention of the Episcopal Church in Chicago identified the historic episcopate as an inherent part of the sacred deposit of Christian faith and order committed by Christ and his apostles to the church until the end of the world. The Convention accounted the historic episcopate to be one of four essentials for the restoration of unity among the divided branches of Christendom (BCP, 877). The Lambeth Conference of 1888 included the historic episcopate as one of the four points that supply a basis on which approach may be made towards Home Reunion (BCP, 877-78).

Episcopate or episcopacy may also indicate the body or college of bishops in a church or region, or the tenure or office of a bishop.

Eucharist. The sacrament of Christ's body and blood, and the principal act of Christian worship. The term is from the Greek, "thanksgiving." Jesus instituted the eucharist "on the night when he was betrayed." At the Last Supper he shared the bread and cup of wine at a sacred meal with his disciples. He identified the bread with his body and the wine with his blood of the new covenant. Jesus command-ed his disciples to "do this" in remembrance of him (see 1

Cor 11:23-26; Mk 14:22-25; Mt 26:26-29; Lk 22:14-20). Christ's sacrifice is made present by the eucharist, and in it we are united to his one self-offering (BCP, 859). The Last Supper provides the basis for the fourfold eucharistic action of taking, blessing, breaking, and sharing. Christ's body and blood are really present in the sacrament of the eucharist and received by faith. Christ's presence is also known in the gathered eucharistic community.

In the BCP, the whole service is entitled the holy eucharist. The first part of the service is designated the word of God. It usually includes the entrance rite, the lessons and gradual psalm, the gospel, the sermon, the Nicene Creed, the prayers of the people, the confession of sin and absolution, and the peace. The second portion of the service is designated the holy communion. It includes the offertory, the consecration of the bread and wine in the great thanksgiving, the communion of the people, and the concluding prayers of thanksgiving and dismissal. A blessing may be given prior to the dismissal.

The eucharist is also called the Lord's supper, holy communion, the divine liturgy, the mass, and the great offertory (BCP, 859). *The Hymnal 1982* includes a section with a variety of hymns for the holy eucharist (300-347), including "Come, risen Lord, and deign to be our guest" (305-306), "Now, my tongue, the mystery telling" (329-331), and "I am the bread of life" (335).

Form (Sacramental). In sacramental theology, the words of prayer that express the meaning of the sacrament and the matter used in the sacrament. The words and the matter of the sacrament constitute a valid sacrament when used with appropriate intent by an appropriate minister. At the eucharist the form is the great thanksgiving that is said in the consecration of the bread and wine. The BCP notes that in an emergency any baptized person may administer baptism according to the following form, "I baptize you in the Name of the Father, and of the Son, and of the Holy Spirit." This form is joined to the ministration of water (BCP, 313). The sacramental form may be understood in terms of the minimum words required for the sacrament to be valid. It is not a particular verbal formula as such. For example, the BCP provides a variety of forms for the great thanksgiving at the eucharist.

General Convention. The national legislative body of the Episcopal Church. It consists of a House of Bishops, which includes all active and retired bishops, and a House of Deputies, which includes four lay persons and four clergy from each diocese, each area mission, and the Convocation of the American Churches in Europe. The Convention meets every three years. The Houses meet and act separately, and both must concur to adopt legislation. The General Convention alone has authority to amend the Prayer Book and the church's Constitution, to amend the canons (laws) of the church, and to determine the program and budget of the General Convention, including the missionary, educational, and social programs it authorizes. A majority of bishops may request the Presiding Bishop to call a Special General Convention. The General Convention elects twenty of the forty members of the Executive Council, which administers policy and program between the triennial meetings of the General Convention.

Historic Episcopate. The succession of bishops in the history of the church from the apostles until the present. During the colonial period there were several efforts to bring the historic episcopate to America, but none succeeded. Samuel Seabury went to England in 1783 to receive the historic episcopate. It proved impossible for Seabury to be ordained and consecrated a bishop in England because English law required all ordinands to swear an oath of loyalty to the English sovereign. Seabury was ordained and consecrated into the historic episcopate by nonjuring bishops of the Episcopal Church in Scotland on Nov. 14, 1784. On June 26, 1786, Parliament passed an act which granted the Archbishop of Canterbury the right to consecrate three bishops who would not be required to take the oath of loyalty to the sovereign. William White and Samuel Provoost were consecrated Bishops of Pennsylvania and New York, respectively, on Feb. 4, 1787, and James Madison was consecrated Bishop of Virginia on Sept. 19, 1790.

On Sept. 17, 1792, Thomas Claggett was consecrated Bishop of Maryland by Bishop Provoost, assisted by Bishops Seabury, White, and Madison. This combined the lines of succession of the historic episcopate in the Episcopal Church. The fourth point of the Chicago-Lambeth Quadrilateral states that one of the "inherent parts" of the sacred deposit of the Christian faith is "The Historic Episcopate, locally adapted in the methods of its administration to the varying needs of the nations and peoples called of God into the Unity of His Church" (BCP, 876-878).

Hymnal, The. The collection of hymns, tunes, and service music authorized for use in the Episcopal Church by General Convention. It is published by Church Publishing Incorporated, formerly Church Hymnal Corporation, a subsidiary of the Church Pension Fund. Hymnals have been authorized for the Episcopal Church by General Convention in 1789, 1826, 1871, 1892, 1916, 1940, and 1982. Prior to the 1982 revision of the *Hymnal,* the Standing Commission on Church Music adopted a statement of philosophy in 1981 for hymnal revision. This statement agreed that the *Hymnal* should be a companion for the new 1979 BCP, supporting its changes and areas of emphasis such as the expanded lectionary, the revised calendar, and the renewed emphasis on baptism as a public rite; the *Hymnal* should retain classic texts but also present a prophetic vision, speaking to the church of the future as well as the present; hymn texts should authentically and fully present the church's teaching, with the *Hymnal* serving as a practical book of theology for the people of God; the *Hymnal* should be comprehensive in its coverage of all major historic periods, reflecting and speaking to a variety of cultures and races; hymn texts should use inclusive language whenever possible; obscure language should be clarified for contemporary use; the *Hymnal* should be ecumenical in nature, although it is prepared for use in the Episcopal Church; the *Hymnal* should be a practical collection, with keyboard settings that can be used by a performer with average skills; the *Hymnal* should present various musical possibilities when tunes are used more than once; and the *Hymnal* should present a variety of musical styles that represent the best expressive artistic creativity of musicians.

Local Priest: "Canon 9 Clergy." Priests and deacons ordained to serve in a particular location which is "small, isolated, remote, or distinct in respect of ethnic composition, language, or culture." These locations cannot otherwise be provided sufficiently with the sacraments and pastoral ministrations of the Episcopal Church through ordained ministry. The term refers to the canon by which such "local priests and deacons" are ordained. The canonical requirements concerning standards of learning and other canonical requirements for ordination are relaxed or modified for those ordained under this canon. Canon 9 clergy are to be recognized as leaders in their congregation and firmly rooted in the local community. Such clergy are typically called from their own congregation, although a person from another community may be called if necessary. It is the normal expectation that persons ordained under this canon will not move from the congregation for which they were ordained.

Matter (Sacramental). The material or gesture constituting the outward and visible sign of a sacrament. A valid sacrament also requires the appropriate form, minister, and intent. In this sacramental context, form refers to the words of prayer that express the meaning of the sacrament and the matter used in the sacrament. In baptism, the matter is water; and in the eucharist, it is the bread and wine. In the sacramental rite of ordination, the matter is the imposition of hands. Contemporary theology has been willing to see ritual acts, such as the exchange of vows in marriage, or the confessing of sins in reconciliation, as the matter.

Notes of the Church. The Nicene Creed describes the church as one, holy, catholic, and apostolic (see BCP, 358-359). These four characteristics are the notes, or marks, of the church. The church is to be "notable" or distinguishable by its unity, holiness, catholicity, and apostolicity. The Prayer Book Catechism discusses the meaning of the notes of the church (see BCP, 854). The church is described as one because it is one body, under one head, Jesus Christ. The church is described as holy because the Holy Spirit dwells in it, consecrating the members of the church and guiding them to do God's work. The church is described as catholic because it proclaims the whole Christian faith to all people until the end of time. The church is described as apostolic because it continues the teaching and fellowship of the apostles, and because it is sent to carry out Christ's mission to all people.

Catholicity has also been understood in terms of the "Vincentian Canon" of Vincent of Lerins (d. before 450), who understood catholicity in terms of what has been believed everywhere, always, by all. In this regard, catholicity is understood in terms of universality, antiquity, and consent. Many protestants have not considered the apostolic succession of bishops, passed on with ordination by laying on of hands, to be a necessary condition for catholicity and apostolicity. Many Lutherans have understood apostolicity in terms of continuity with the witness of the apostles to the gospel, rather than a succession of bishops. Other churches, including the Anglican, Orthodox, Roman Catholic, and some Lutheran churches, have upheld the necessity of an apostolic succession of bishops ordained with the laying on of hands.

During the sixteenth century, the notes of the church were used polemically by Roman Catholic theologians who claimed their church to be the "true" church. The notes of the church were also appealed to by the Tractarians to uphold the catholicity of the Church of England. In more recent times, the notes of the church have been understood to be both the present characteristics and the future goal of the church. In the present, the church's unity, holiness, catholicity, and apostolicity are not yet fulfilled or perfect. But the notes of the church are already present and visible in an imperfect way. The notes of the church may become increasingly visible as the church grows in faithfulness to Christ, and manifests the authentic Christian faith more completely. The fulfillment and perfection of the notes of the church may be hoped for in terms of the eschatological coming of the kingdom of God.

Pastor, Pastoral Ministry. The word "pastor" derives from the work of tending sheep: a pastor is one who cares for sheep. The term came into the Christian understanding of the ordained ministry because of the frequent references in holy scripture to God as a shepherd of the people of Israel and Jesus as the good shepherd. A priest is a pastor for his or her congregation in the sense that he or she cares for the people, protects them and directs them, and feeds them with spiritual food in the holy eucharist. Similarly, a bishop is a chief pastor because she or he has oversight of all those pastors who care for the people committed to their care.

The work of pastoral care has always been deeply important in Anglicanism. It has been seen as the first work of the parish priest and of the bishop in a diocese. There have been times when pastoral care has been neglected on a wide scale. Those times have in turn provoked a demand among Christian people for a revival of pastoral care, as in the Wesleyan and evangelical revivals of the eighteenth century and the catholic revival of the nineteenth century. Each of those revivals resulted from a sense that the church and the ordained ministry of the church have the care of God's people as their first responsibility, even while the form of that care may vary in time and place.

In the church today pastoral care takes many different forms. For example, spiritual direction and pastoral counseling are both specialized forms of pastoral care that require specific training and responsibility. In the Episcopal Church there is great interest in enhancing the pastoral work of the bishops of the church for both the clergy and lay people of their dioceses. There is also great interest in developing the ministry of the laity for pastoral care.

Priest. Derived from the Greek *presbyteros,* "elder," or "old man," the term is used as a synonym for presbyter. Presbyters constituted a collegiate ruling body of institutions in Judaism. The Catechism notes that "the ministry of a priest or presbyter" is "to represent Christ and his Church, particularly as pastor to the people; to share with the bishop in the overseeing of the Church; to proclaim the gospel; to administer the sacraments; and to bless and declare pardon in the name of God" (BCP, 856). The term "priest" is more frequently used than "presbyter" in the Episcopal Church. The ordination service for this order of ministry is titled "The Ordination of a Priest" (BCP, 525). After the Reformation, the Anglican Church used the term "priest" for the second order of ministry. Some protestant churches began to use the term "presbyter" for the minister who preaches the word and administers the sacraments. The 1979 BCP uses both terms. Some members of the Episcopal Church have favored use of "presbyter" because of historic association of the term "priest" with eucharistic piety or with OT sacrifice.

Primate. The chief bishop in an Anglican Province is called a primate. In the United States, the Presiding Bishop serves as "Chief Pastor and Primate." The 1978 Lambeth Conference requested that primates' meetings should be established to enable regular consultation among the primates of the Anglican Communion. These meetings have taken place throughout the Anglican Communion. The primates' meeting provides opportunities for collegiality and enables the primates to provide support for the Archbishop of Canterbury.

Proper. Variable parts of the eucharistic liturgy and the Daily Office which are appointed for a particular day according to the season or occasion. These parts of the liturgy may be contrasted with the fixed portions and options of the liturgy which do not vary with the season or occasion. The proper for the eucharist includes the collect, the lessons, the selection from the Psalter, and the proper preface. The BCP collects for the church year are presented in both traditional and contemporary language versions (159-261). The Lectionary provides readings and psalms for the eucharist (BCP, 889-931). The daily office lectionary provides readings and psalms for morning and evening prayer (BCP, 936-1001). Propers for the Sundays in the Season after Pentecost are numbered one through twenty-nine. The BCP includes propers for holy days, such as "Saint Andrew" and "The Annunciation"; the common of saints, such as "Of a Martyr" and "Of a Monastic"; and various occasions, such as "Of the Holy Trinity" and "Of the Incarnation." The proper prefaces of the BCP include three prefaces of the Lord's Day, prefaces for seasons, and prefaces for other occasions, such as baptism and marriage (377-382). The BCP also has a section of proper liturgies for special days, such as Ash Wednesday and the Easter Vigil (264-295). The service for morning prayer includes proper opening sentences (37-41, 75-78) and antiphons (43-44, 80-82).

Province. 1) An internal division of an autonomous national (or multi-national) church of the Anglican Communion. The churches of England and Ireland, the Anglican Church of Canada, the Anglican Church of Australia, and the Episcopal Church are all divided into internal provinces. There are two each in England and Ireland, four in Canada, five in Australia, and nine in the Episcopal Church, including overseas jurisdictions. Article VII of the Episcopal Church Constitution provides for internal provinces. 2) An autonomous national church member of the Anglican Communion.

Psalm, Psalmody, Psalter. Psalm is the name given to the hymns of the OT. The psalms are found in the Psalter, a collection of songs, prayers, and other types of poetic compositions. The Book of Psalms has traditionally been attributed to David. The dates of the various hymns of the Psalter are usually impossible to determine, but they come from virtually every period of Israel's history. They were finally compiled for use in the Second Temple, which was completed c. 515 B.C. This hymnal of the Second Temple was divided into five parts (1-41; 42-72; 73-89; 90-106; 107-150), presumably following the fivefold division of the Pentateuch. The psalms were composed for both individual and community use. Psalms would have been used in various liturgical settings. The most common literary types of psalms were the hymn, the thanksgiving and the lament. Some can be related to specific festivals, such as Covenant Renewal (81) or Royal-Zion (132). Others call for reflection on the Torah, e.g., Pss. 1, 119. The psalms of the OT have been used through the centuries in both Jewish and Christian worship. This has given rise to psalmody, i.e., the art of singing the psalms. The complete Psalter is included in the BCP (585-848). The Prayer Book lectionaries appoint a selection from the complete Psalter for all services of the eucharist and the daily office.

Real Presence. The presence of Christ in the sacrament of the holy eucharist. The 1991 statement of the Anglican-Roman Catholic International Commission notes, "The elements are not mere signs; Christ's body and blood become really present and are really given. But they are really present and given in order that, receiving them, believers may be united in communion with Christ the Lord." A classic Anglican statement attributed to John Donne (or to Queen Elizabeth I) and included in *The Hymnal*

1982 (Hymn 322) is "He was the Word that spake it, he took the bread and brake it, and what that Word did make it, I do believe and take it." In Eucharistic Prayer A of Rite II, the celebrant prays that God the Father will sanctify the gifts of bread and wine "by your Holy Spirit to be for your people the Body and Blood of your Son, the holy food and drink of new and unending life in him" (BCP, 363). The Catechism notes that the inward and spiritual grace in the eucharist is "the Body and Blood of Christ given to his people and received by faith" (BCP, 859). Belief in the real presence does not imply a claim to know how Christ is present in the eucharistic elements. Belief in the real presence does not imply belief that the consecrated eucharistic elements cease to be bread and wine.

Reception (Christian Commitment). Baptized persons who have been members of another Christian fellowship and who wish to be affiliated with the Episcopal Church may make a public affirmation of their faith and commitment to the responsibilities of their baptism in the presence of a bishop. The bishop lays hands on each candidate for reception and says, "We recognize you as a member of the one holy catholic and apostolic Church, and we receive you into the fellowship of this Communion" (BCP, 418). Candidates for reception normally have made a mature commitment in another Christian fellowship. Some dioceses have reserved reception for those candidates who have previously received sacramental confirmation with laying on of hands by a bishop in apostolic succession.

Rector. The priest in charge of a parish. Typically, a rector is the priest in charge of a self-supporting parish, and a vicar is the priest in charge of a supported mission. The rector is the ecclesiastical authority of the parish. The term is derived from the Latin for "rule." The rector has authority and responsibility for worship and the spiritual jurisdiction of the parish, subject to the rubrics of the BCP, the constitution and canons of the church, and the pastoral direction of the bishop. The rector is responsible for selection of all assistant clergy, and they serve at the discretion of the rector. The church and parish buildings and furnishings are under the rector's control. The rector or a member of the vestry designated by the rector presides at all vestry meetings.

Rite I, Rite II. The 1979 BCP provides the services of morning and evening prayer, the holy eucharist, and the Burial Office in both traditional language and contemporary language rites. The traditional language rites are known as Rite I, and the contemporary language rites are known as Rite II. The BCP also presents the collects for the church year in both traditional and contemporary language. The Rite I liturgies reflect the language and piety of the Elizabethan era and the first BCP, although the structure of these liturgies also reflects the influence of modern liturgical scholarship. The Rite II liturgies reflect more fully the influence of the liturgical movement and contemporary theology. Rite II liturgies tend to reflect greater sensitivity for inclusive language issues. The proper liturgies for special days (such as Ash Wednesday and Palm Sunday), pastoral offices (such as the Celebration and Blessing of a Marriage), and episcopal services (such as ordinations) are printed in contemporary language in the BCP. When these services are celebrated in the context of a Rite I eucharist, the contemporary idiom may be conformed to traditional language (BCP, 14). *The Hymnal* 1982 and *The Hymnal* 1982 *Accompaniment Edition, Vol.* I, provide service music settings that are designated for Rite I and Rite II services of morning and evening prayer and the eucharist.

Sacramental Rites. The sacramental rites of the Episcopal Church include confirmation, ordination, holy matrimony, reconciliation of a penitent, and unction (BCP, 860-861). These rites are distinguished from the sacraments of baptism and eucharist, which were given by Christ and are understood to be necessary for the Christian life of all persons. The Roman Catholic Church recognizes seven sacraments, including baptism, eucharist, and the five other sacramental rites. Peter Lombard (c. 1095-1160) identified these seven rites as sacraments of the church. This position was affirmed by the Council of Florence (1439) and the Council of Trent (1545-1563). The Orthodox Church also accepts seven sacraments. Martin Luther (1483-1546) was willing to identify reconciliation of a penitent as a sacrament, in addition to baptism and eucharist. In 1521 Henry VIII was awarded the title "Defender of the Faith" by Pope Leo X in recognition of Henry's treatise *Assertio Septem Sacramentorum* (Assertion of the Seven Sacraments) which defended the doctrine of the seven sacraments against Luther. After the English Reformation, marriage or the reconciliation of a penitent are presented as sacraments by some Elizabethan homilies and formularies. Article XXV of the Articles of Religion acknowledged baptism and the Lord's supper as the two sacraments ordained by Christ in the gospel. Article XXV states that the five other sacramental rites "have not like nature of Sacraments with baptism, and the Lord's supper, for that they have not any visible sign or ceremony ordained of God" (BCP, 872). The five sacramental rites are not understood to be necessary for all Christians.

Standing Committee. The ecclesiastical authority of the diocese in the absence of a bishop. The standing committee is elected by the diocesan convention. Half of its members are clerical, half lay. It serves as the bishop's council of advice. The standing committee is requested to give consent for all bishops elected in the Episcopal Church. It recommends persons for ordination. It gives the bishop advice and consent on the purchase, sale, or encumbrance of any property held by a congregation or the diocese. It gives the bishop advice and consent as to any judicial sentence given to a clergy person or concurs in allowing a clergy person to cease functioning as a member of the clergy. It investigates and reports to the bishop on the charge that a deacon or priest has abandoned the Episcopal Church. It also receives the bishop's resignation.

Supplemental Liturgical Materials (SLM). A booklet prepared by the Standing Liturgical Commission and published by Church Hymnal Corporation in 1991 to supplement the existing Rite II liturgies of the BCP. It includes materials for morning and evening prayer, complete eucharistic prayers, and forms for the eucharistic prayer for use with the order for celebrating the holy eucharist (BCP, 400-401). These texts reflect awareness of the power of words and images in worship to shape our understanding of and relationship with God.

Validity (Sacramental). A sacrament is recognized by the church to be genuine and true when certain minimum requirements are met. These requirements concern proper form, matter, minister, and intent. The form means the words of prayer that are used in the sacramental rite, and the matter concerns the material or gesture constituting the outward and visible sign of a sacrament. The matter in baptism is water; bread and wine are the matter in the eucharist.

The minister must be properly qualified and intend to do what the church intends in celebrating the sacrament. The minister at the eucharist is the celebrant, who must be a bishop or priest. The minimum form for a valid sacrament does not require the entire BCP liturgy. For example, an emergency baptism may be administered according to the form, "I baptize you in the Name of the Father, and of the Son, and of the Holy Spirit" (BCP, 313). In the situation of an emergency baptism, any baptized person can be a qualified minister of the sacrament. This minister would need to baptize with water, and intend to do what the church does in baptism. The concept of sacramental validity dates from the third century, when the Church of Rome held that schismatics and heretics could administer valid baptism. This contradicted the position of Cyprian, Bishop of Carthage, that the church's sacraments could not be administered by anyone outside the church. Augustine of Hippo subsequently insisted in his controversy with Donatism that the personal unworthiness of the minister does not impair the validity of sacraments celebrated by the minister (see Art. XXVI, Articles of Religion, BCP, 873).

Vestry. In England the annual election of churchwardens took place in Easter week. The parishioners gathered at the church to hear the outgoing wardens render their accounts and elect their successors. The parishioners assembled in the vestry, the room off the chancel where the clergy vested. The assembled parishioners came to be known as the vestry. These were open vestries in that all adult male parishioners could participate. It was like a modern annual congregational meeting. In Virginia the parishes were very large and it was difficult to get all the male parishioners together. So they would meet only once and elect twelve of their number to serve for life. This was known as a closed vestry. The transition to a closed vestry was completed by 1633 or 1634, when a Vestry Act was passed. It provided that "there be a vestrie held in each parish." The current vestry evolved from this colonial pattern.

The vestry is the legal representative of the parish with regard to all matters pertaining to its corporate property. The number of vestry members and the term of office varies from parish to parish. Vestry members are usually elected at the annual parish meeting. The presiding officer of the vestry is the rector. There are usually two wardens. The senior warden leads the parish between rectors and is a support person for the rector. The junior warden often has the responsibility for church property and buildings. A treasurer and a secretary or clerk may be chosen. These officers may or may not be vestry members. The basic responsibilities of the vestry are to help define and articulate the mission of the congregation, to support the church's mission by word and deed, to select the rector, to ensure effective organization and planning, and to manage resources and finances.

Vicar. In the Episcopal Church, the title generally applies to the priest in charge of a mission congregation. The diocesan bishop is the rector, and the priest representing the bishop is the vicar. The term is derived from the Latin *vicarius*, "substitute." Historically, as early as the twelfth century in England, clergy known as vicars were appointed to act as substitutes or vicarious representatives of the bishop to serve congregations. The use of terms such as vicar, priest in charge, and rector is not consistent in the dioceses of the Episcopal Church.

Wardens of a Parish. Officers of a parish. Two wardens are typically selected to serve with members of the vestry. The wardens are generally ranked "senior" and "junior." The mode of selection and duties of the wardens are determined by state law, diocesan canon, or parish bylaws. The senior warden is usually the primary elected lay leader of the congregation, and serves as a principal liaison between the parish and the rector. The junior warden is often given responsibility for the upkeep of the parish buildings and grounds. The senior warden typically presides at vestry meetings in the absence of the rector, and the junior warden presides at vestry meetings if both the rector and the senior warden are absent. In case of clerical vacancy, the senior warden may be the ecclesiastical authority of the parish for certain purposes. In the BCP service for the celebration of a new ministry (559), the wardens begin the institution at the beginning of the service by addressing the bishop. They express the congregation's intent to welcome the new minister and state that the new minister has been selected in a prayerful and lawful manner. If the new minister is the rector or vicar of the congregation, a warden may present the keys of the church to the new minister during the induction ceremony. In some parishes, the senior warden is known as the "priest's warden," and the junior warden is known as the "people's warden." Historically, in the Church of England, one warden was named by the priest and the other chosen by the congregation.

BIBLIOGRAPHY

Called to Common Mission: A Lutheran Proposal for a Revision of "Concordat of Agreement." An Agreement of Full Communion with the Episcopal Church as amended and adopted by the Churchwide Assembly of the Evangelical Lutheran Church in America, August 19, 1999. Chicago: Office of the Secretary and the Department for Ecumenical Affairs, Evangelical Lutheran Church in America, 1999.

Lutheran-Episcopal Dialogue: A Progress Report. Cincinnati: Forward Movement, 1972.

Lutheran-Episcopal Dialogue: Report and Recommendations. Cincinnati: Forward Movement, 1981.

Norgren, William A., and William G. Rusch, eds. *Implications of the Gospel: Lutheran-Episcopal Dialogue. Series III.* Cincinnati: Forward Movement; Minneapolis: Augsburg; 1988.

"Toward Full Communion" and "Concordat of Agreement." Lutheran-Episcopal Dialogue. Series III. Cincinnati: Forward Movement; Minneapolis: Augsburg; 1991.

NOTE: The above four volumes are the official reports of the Episcopal-Lutheran dialogues.

"The Orderly Exchange of Pastors and Priests Under Called to Common Mission, Principles and Guidelines." Episcopal Church and Evangelical Lutheran Church in America, January 1, 2001.

Anglican-Lutheran Dialogue: The Report of the European Commission, 1982. The Helsinki Report. London: S.P.C.K., 1983.

Anglican-Lutheran International Conversations: *The Report of the Conversations 1970-1972 authorized by the Lambeth Conference and the Lutheran World Federation.* London: SPCK, 1973.

Anglican-Lutheran Relations, Report of the Anglican-Lutheran Joint Working Group, 1983. The Cold Ash Report. London and Geneva: Anglican Consultative Council and Lutheran World Federation, 1983.

Armentrout, Don S. "Chronology and Bibliography of the Lutheran-Episcopal Dialogues." *Sewanee Theological Review* 40:2 (Easter, 1997): 228-231.

Armentrout, Don S. "Lutheran-Episcopal Conversations in the Nineteenth Century." *Historical Magazine of the Protestant Episcopal Church* 43 (1974): 167-187.

Armentrout, Don S., and Robert Boak Slocum. *An Episcopal Dictionary of the Church: A User-Friendly Reference for Episcopalians* (New York: Church Publishing Incorporated, 2000).

Austin, Victor L. "Implicit Ecclesiologies of the Proposed Lutheran-Episcopal 'Concordat of Agreement.'" *Mid-Stream* 36:2 (April, 1997): 173-184.

Bauerschmidt, John. "The Episcopal-Lutheran Concordat." *The Anglican Catholic* 6 (Spring, 1997): 3-5.

Birmelé, André. "The Unity of the Church: The Different Approaches of the Lutheran-Anglican and Lutheran-Reformed Dialogues." In *Community—Unity—Communion, Essays in Honour of Mary Tanner*, ed. Colin Podmore. London: Church House Publishing, 1998: 252-261.

Booty, John. "Anglican Identity: What Is This Book of Common Prayer?" *Sewanee Theological Review* 40:2 (Easter, 1997): 137-145.

Borgegård, Gunnel and Christine Hall. "The Ministry of the Deacon, 1. Anglican-Lutheran Perspectives." Uppsala, Sweden: Nordic Ecumenical Council, 1999.

Bouman, Walter R. "In Defense of the Lutheran Episcopal Agreement." *Trinity Seminary Review* 17 (Fall, 1995): 65-79.

Braaten, Carl E. "Episcopacy and the E.L.C.A." *dialog* 39:3 (Fall, 2000): 214-221.

Lutheran-Episcopal Dialogue: A Progress Report. Cincinnati: Forward Movement, 1972.

Countryman, L. William. "The Gospel and the Institutions of the Church with Particular Reference to the Historic Episcopate." *Anglican Theological Review* 66 (1984): 402-415.

Countryman, L. William. "The Lutheran-Episcopal Concordat: Why I Voted Yes." *dialog* 32 (1993): 142-143.

Duke, James O. "A Comparison of 'A Common Calling' and the 'Concordat of Agreement' in Light of Faith and Order and COCU." *Ecumenical Trends* 23 (1994): 99-102.

Edwards, O. C., Jr. "'The Concordat of Agreement' and 'A Common Calling' in the Context of Faith and Order and COCU." *Ecumenical Trends* 23 (1994): 113-114, 122-128.

Edwards, O. C., Jr. "The Word of God in Anglican (as Opposed to Lutheran) Theology." *dialog* 13 (1974): 217-223.

Evans, Gillian R. "Episcope and Episcopacy: The Niagara Report." *One in Christ* 25 (1989): 281-286.

Fackre, Gabriel, and Michael Root. *Affirmations and Admonitions: Lutheran Decisions and Dialogues with Reformed Episcopal and Roman Catholic Churches.* Grand Rapids: William B. Eerdmans Publishing Company, 1998.

Franklin, R. William. "The Concordat and Catholicism." *The Living Church* (October 6, 1996): 8-9.

Fuller, Reginald. "Lutheran-Episcopal Unity: The Proposed Concordat." *Sewanee Theological Review* 40:2 (Easter, 1997): 158-164.

Gaither, Linda L. "Ecclesiology and Episcopacy in the Contemporary Context." *Sewanee Theological Review* 40:2 (Easter, 1997): 192-212.

Gassmann, Günther. "Anglican-Lutheran Convergence and the Anticipation of Full Communion." *Journal of Ecumenical Studies* 34:1 (Winter, 1997): 1-12.

Goeser, Robert, Norman Nagel, and William Weiblin. "Lutheran-Episcopal Dialogue." In *Lutherans in Ecumenical Dialogue: A Reappraisal*, ed. Joseph A. Burgess (Minneapolis: Augsburg, 1990): 46-53.

Goeser, Robert. "The Historic Episcopate and the Lutheran Confessions." *Lutheran Quarterly* 1 (1987): 214-232.

Gregg, William O. "'By Solemn Prayer and Laying-on of Episcopal Hands': Ordination and Implementing Full Communion." *Sewanee Theological Review* 40:2 (Easter, 1997): 213-227.

Griffin, Eric R. "Anglican-Lutheran Dialogue on Episcope: 'The Niagara Report.'" *Consensus* (Canada) 21 (1995): 25-37.

Griffiss, James E. "The Theology of the Historic Episcopate in Anglicanism." *dialog* 29 (1990): 92-100.

Griffiss, James E., and Daniel F. Martensen, eds. *A Commentary on "Concordat of Agreement."* Cincinnati: Forward Movement; Minneapolis; Augsburg, 1994.

Gritsch, Eric W. "Lutheran Identity: What Is This Augsburg Confession?" *Sewanee Theological Review* 40:2 (Easter, 1997): 146-157.

Howe, John and Colin Craston. *Anglicanism and the Universal Church: Highways and Hedges, 1958-1984, with an Overview 1984-1990.* Toronto: Anglican Book Centre, 1990.

Hultgren, Arland J. "Lutheranism and the Historic Episcopate: Are They Compatible?" *dialog* 37:2 (Spring, 1998): 134-141.

Klein, Leonard. "The Concordat—Not Now." *Lutheran Forum* 25, 2 (May, 1991): 7-8.

Koenig, Richard E. "On the Way to Full Communion? The ELCA's Moment to Decide." *Christian Century* (September 11-18, 1996): 858-863.

Kremkau, Klaus. "The Meissen Declaration: Some Observations from the Gallery." In *Community—Unity—Communion*: 189-200.

Lutheran Understanding of the Episcopal Office. Geneva: Lutheran World Federation, 1985.

The Report of the Lutheran-Episcopal Dialogue, Second Series, 1976-1980. Cincinnati: Forward Movement, 1981.

Madson, Meg H. "The Episcopal 'No Spin Zone.'" *dialog* 39:4 (Winter, 2000): 293-295.

Marshall, Bruce D. "The Lutheran-Episcopal Concordat: What Does It Say and Why Does It Matter?" *Pro Ecclesia* 3 (1994): 419-435.

Marshall, Bruce D. "What Is To Be Done? 'The Concordat of Agreement' and 'A Common Calling' in Light of Faith and Order and COCU." *Ecumenical Trends* 23 (1994): 97, 106-110.

Martensen, Daniel F., ed. *Concordat of Agreement: Supporting Essays.* Cincinnati: Forward Movement; Minneapolis: Augsburg; 1995.

Martensen, Daniel F., ed. *Concordat of Agreement: Supporting Essays.* Minneapolis and Cincinnati: Augsburg and Forward Movement, 1995.

Meyer, Harding. "Apostolic Continuity, Ministry and Apostolic Succession from a Reformation Perspective." *Louvain Studies* 21 (1996): 169-182.

Meyer, Harding. "The Doctrine of Justification in the Lutheran Dialogue with Other Churches." *One in Christ* 17 (1981): 86-116.

Neill, Stephen. "An Anglican in a Lutheran Atmosphere." *Lutheran World* 12 (1965): 238-247.

Nestingen, James A., and Gerhard O. Forde. "Beware of Greeks Bearing Gifts." *dialog* 39:4 (Winter, 2000): 291-292.

Norgren, William A, compiler. *What Can We Share? A Lutheran-Episcopal Resource and Study Guide.* Cincinnati: Forward Movement, 1985.

Norgren, William A. and William G. Rusch. *"Toward Full Communion" and "Concordat of Agreement," Lutheran-Episcopal Dialogue, Series III.* Minneapolis and Cincinnati: Augsburg and Forward Movement, 1991.

Norgren, William A. and William G. Rusch. *Implications of the Gospel, Lutheran-Episcopal Dialogue, Series III.* 1988.

Pannenberg, Wolfhart. "Lutherans and Episcopacy." In *Community—Unity—Communion*: 183-188.

Petersen, William H., and Robert Goeser. *Traditions Transplanted, The Story of Anglican and Lutheran Churches in America*. Cincinnati: Forward Movement, 1981.

Peterson, C. Richard. "WordAlone: Extreme, Unfocused, or What?" *dialog* 39:4 (Winter, 2000): 298-303.

Pfatteicher, Philip H. "Orthodoxy: Right Praise and Right Doctrine." *Sewanee Theological Review* 40:2 (Easter, 1997): 174-191.

Radner, Ephraim, and R. R. Reno, eds. *Inhabiting Unity: Theological Perspectives on the Proposed Lutheran-Episcopal Concordat*. Grand Rapids: William B. Eerdmans Publishing Company, 1995.

Reumann, John. "Bridging a Historic Impasse? A Lutheran's Analysis of the US Lutheran-Episcopal Dialogue, Series III." *Ecumenical Trends* 25 (1996): 161-168.

Rogerson, Barry. "The Diaconate: Taking the Ecumenical Opportunity." In *Community—Unity—Communion*: 204-215.

Root, Michael, "An Anglican-Lutheran Ecumenical Bibliography." Institute for Ecumenical Research, 1997. Unpublished. **Editors' Note**—Root's bibliography has provided references for many of the works listed in this bibliography.

Root, Michael. "'Reconciled Diversity' and the Visible Unity of the Church." In *Community—Unity—Communion*: 237-251.

Root, Michael. "An Examination of the 'Concordat of Agreement' in Relation to International Agreements." *Ecumenical Trends* 23 (1994): 103-106.

Root, Michael. "The Implications of *The Implications of the Gospel*." *dialog* 28 (1989): 143-145.

Root, Michael. "*The Niagara Report*: A Possible Lutheran-Anglican Future?" *dialog* 28 (1989): 300-302.

Root, Michael. "The Proposal for Lutheran-Episcopal Fellowship: Unity and the Gospel." *Lutheran Forum* 25, 2 (May, 1991): 22-25.

Rusch, William G. "'Recognition' as an Ecumenical Concept in the Lutheran-Episcopal Dialogue." *Mid-Stream* 30 (1991): 316-322.

Schlenker, Richard J. "A Roman Catholic Comment on the Lutheran-Episcopal Concordat." *Journal of Ecumenical Studies* 31:1-2 (Winter-Spring, 1994): 111-121.

Schneider, Edward D. "The Lutheran-Episcopal Concordat: Why I Voted No." *dialog* 32 (1993): 143-146.

Seastrand, Paul J. "Episcopal Office and the Augsburg Confession: Five Approaches in Contemporary American Lutheranism." *Currents in Theology and Mission* 28:5 (October, 2001): 465-472.

Snook, Lee E. "Called to Common Mission: An Unsatisfactory Compromise," *Word & World* 19 (Spring, 1999): 181, 184-186.

Standing Commission on Ecumenical Relations of the Episcopal Church, USA. "Report to the General Convention, 1991." *Ecumenical Bulletin* 104 (March, 1991): 15-23.

Sykes, Stephen. "Whither Lutheranism? An Anglican Perspective." *Word & World* 11 (1991): 297-300.

Tanner, Mary. "Mission: Strategies and Prospects in the Context of the Anglican-Lutheran Porvoo Agreement." *Ecumenical Trends* 25 (1996): 169-174.

The Diaconate as Ecumenical Opportunity: The Hanover Report of the Anglican-Lutheran International Commission. London and Geneva: Anglican Consultative Council and Lutheran World Federation, 1996.

The Meissen Agreement: Texts, Occasional Paper 2. London: Council for Christian Unity, 1992. An agreement in 1988 on eucharistic sharing and closer relationships involving the Church of England and the Lutheran, United, and Reformed Churches in the Federal Republic of Germany and the German Democratic Republic.

The Niagara Report, Report of the Anglican-Lutheran Consultation on Episcope, Niagara Falls, September, 1987. London: Church House Publishing, 1988.

Veal, David L. "ELCA Has Broken the Covenant." *The Living Church* (November 11, 2001): 27-28.

Veal, David L. *An Essential Unity; A Contemporary Look at Lutheran and Episcopal Liturgies.* Harrisburg, PA: Morehouse Publishing, 1997.

Wainwright, Geoffrey. "Is Episcopal Succession a Matter of Dogma for Anglicans? The Evidence of Some Recent Dialogues." In *Community—Unity—Communion*: 164-179.

Wantland, William C. "The Anglican-Lutheran Dialogue." *The Living Church* (January 24, 1982): 8-9.

Watson, J. Francis. "How to Revise the Concordat." *dialog* 37 (Summer, 1998): 229-230.

Weinhauer, William G. and Robert L. Wietelmann, eds. *The Report of the Lutheran Episcopal Dialogue: Second Series, 1976-1980.* Cincinnati: Forward Movement Publications, 1981.

Weinhauer, William. "Nineteen Years of Lutheran-Episcopal Dialogue." In *Joy in the Struggle, Personal Memoirs of Ecumenical Dialogue*, ed. Edward W. Jones. Cincinnati: Forward Movement, 1992: 123-143.

Westhelle, Vitor. "Augsburg Confession VII and the Historic Episcopate." *dialog* 39:3 (Fall, 2000): 222-228.

Williamson, Raymond K., ed. *Stages on the Way*. Melbourne: The Joint Board of Christian Education, 1994.

Wright, J. Robert, ed. *A Communion of Communions: One Eucharistic Fellowship*. The Detroit Report and Papers of the Triennial Ecumenical Study of the Episcopal Church, 1976-1979. New York: Seabury Press, 1979. 94-104.

Wright, J. Robert. "An Episcopalian View of the Historic Episcopate." *dialog* 38:1 (Winter, 1999): 53-62.

Wright, J. Robert. "Cold Water for Common Mission." *The Anglican* (October, 2001): 3-4.

Wright, J. Robert. "Denver & Common Mission." *The Anglican* (October, 2000): 3-4.

Wright, J. Robert. "Called to Common Mission: Our Best Opportunity." *Word & World* 19 (Spring, 1999): 180, 182-183.

Wright, J. Robert. "In Support of the Concordat: A Response to Its Opponents." *Sewanee Theological Review* 40:2 (Easter, 1997): 165-173.

Wright, J. Robert. "Martin Luther: An Anglican Ecumenical Appreciation." *Anglican and Episcopal History* 56 (1987): 319-329.

Wright, J. Robert. "Reflections on Lutheran/Episcopal Interim Eucharistic Sharing." *Ecumenical Trends* (1984): 147-150.

Wright, J. Robert. "To Walk in Love & Charity: Further Reflections on Common Mission." *The Anglican* (January, 2002): 3-4.

CONTRIBUTORS

J. Neil Alexander is the Bishop of the Episcopal Diocese of Atlanta. Before his election to the episcopate, he was the Norma and Olan Mills Professor of Divinity in the School of Theology of the University of the South. He has also served on the faculties of The General Theological Seminary, Drew University, Yale University, and Waterloo Lutheran Seminary. His publications include *Time and Community: In Honor of Thomas J. Talley*; *Waiting for the Coming: The Liturgical Meaning of Advent, Christmas, Epiphany*; and *With Ever Joyful Hearts: Essays on Liturgy and Music Honoring Marion J. Hatchett*. Before becoming an Episcopalian, he was a parish pastor in the Lutheran Church in America, and a Lutheran Seminary Professor in the Evangelical Lutheran Church In Canada.

Don S. Armentrout (Lutheran) has taught church history at the School of Theology, the University of the South, since 1967. He is professor of church history and historical theology and associate dean of academic affairs at the School of Theology. He is the co-editor of *An Episcopal Dictionary of the Church* and *Documents of Witness, A History of the Episcopal Church, 1782-1985*; and editor of *A DuBose Reader*.

Robert Busch (Lutheran) is chair of the Worship Committee at Saint Peter's Lutheran Church in New York City and has served on the Executive Committee and Strategic Planning Task Force. His publications include a liturgy for Holy Week, "We Call This Friday Good" in *Reformed Worship*.

Mark Dyer (Episcopalian) has served as professor of theology and spiritual formation at Virginia Theological Seminary since 1996. He was consecrated Bishop Coadjutor of Bethlehem (Pennsylvania) on November 6, 1982, and became the seventh Bishop of Bethlehem on December 3, 1983. He served in that position until December 31, 1995. He was a Roman Catholic priest from 1965 until he was received into the Episcopal Church as a priest on June 1, 1971.

Jon S. Enslin (ELCA) is Interim Director and Assistant to the Presiding Bishop, Department of Ecumenical Affairs, Evangelical Lutheran Church in America. He served for ten years as Bishop of the South-Central Synod of Wisconsin, ELCA. As a bishop he also served on the Ecumenical Affairs Liaison Committee. He represents the ELCA on the National Council of Churches of Christ, where he serves as a Vice President.

Reginald H. Fuller (Episcopalian) was Molly Laird Downs Professor of New Testament at the Virginia Theological Seminary, 1972-1985. He also served as Baldwin Professor of Sacred Literature at Union Theological Seminary, New York, 1966-1972, professor of New Testament languages and literature, Seabury-Western Theological Seminary, 1955-1966, and professor of theology, St. David's College, Lampeter, Wales, 1950-1955. He participated in the national Lutheran-Episcopal dialogues (I-II), and the international Anglican-Lutheran dialogue. He is the author of *Foundations of New Testament Christology* and *Preaching the Lectionary*.

Martin E. Marty (Lutheran) is professor emeritus of the Divinity School at the University of Chicago, where he taught for 35 years. The Martin Marty Center was founded at the University of Chicago to promote "public religion."

A pastor of the Evangelical Lutheran Church in America, he was chair of the revision committee that produced "Called to Common Mission," the document approved by Episcopalians and Lutherans as the basis for a relationship of full communion. He is a speaker, consultant, and author of more than 50 books, including the three-volume *Modern American Religion* and *The One and the Many: America's Search for the Common Good*. Marty is past president of the American Academy of Religion, the American Society of Church History, and the American Catholic Historical Association.

Robert Boak Slocum (Episcopalian) is a lecturer in the Department of Theology at Marquette University in Milwaukee, Wisconsin. He has served parishes in the Dioceses of Milwaukee and Louisiana. He is the author of *The Theology of William Porcher DuBose, Life, Movement and Being*; editor of *Engaging the Spirit, Essays on the Life and Theology of the Holy Spirit*; and co-editor of *An Episcopal Dictionary of the Church*. He has been a visiting professor at Nashotah House, and an instructor at Carthage College. He is the Review Articles Editor of the *Anglican Theological Review*.

George H. Tavard (Roman Catholic) is professor emeritus of theology, Methodist Theological School in Ohio. He was "peritus" at Vatican Council II and has been involved in the ecumenical dialogues of the Roman Catholic Church with Anglicans, Lutherans, and Methodists. His publications include *The Church, Community of Salvation, An Ecumenical Ecclesiology*, and *The Thousand Faces of the Virgin Mary*.

J. Robert Wright (Episcopalian) is the St. Mark's Church-in-the-Bowerie Professor of Ecclesiastical History at the General Theological Seminary, where he has taught since 1968. He was also an instructor in church history at the Episcopal Divinity School from 1966 to 1968. He has served Episcopal/Anglican parishes both in England and in America. He has been a member of or consultant to the Anglican-Roman Catholic Consultation (USA), and he serves as theological consultant to the ecumenical office of the Episcopal Church. He is the Historiographer of the Episcopal Church. He has been a visiting professor at Nashotah House, Philadelphia Divinity School, Claremont School of Theology in California, Union Theological Seminary in New York City, Trinity College in Toronto, and St. George's College in Jerusalem. He is editor of *On Being a Bishop: papers on Episcopacy from the Moscow Consultation* 1992 and *They Still Speak: Readings for the Lesser Feasts.*